debris

Shadowline™

image®

www.S———————.om

debris

First Printing: FEBRUARY 2013

ISBN: 978-1-60706-720-7

Published by Image Comics, Inc. Office of publication: 2001 Center Street, Sixth Floor, Berkeley, California 94704. Copyright © 2013 KURTIS WIEBE and RILEY ROSSMO. Originally published in single magazine form as DEBRIS #1-4. All rights reserved. DEBRIS™ (including all prominent characters featured herein), its logo and all character likenesses are trademarks of KURTIS WIEBE and RILEY ROSSMO, unless otherwise noted. Image Comics® and its logos are registered trademarks of Image Comics, Inc. Shadowline and its logos are ™ and © 2013 Jim Valentino. No part of this publication may be reproduced or transmitted, in any form or by any means (except for short excerpts for review purposes) without the express written permission of Mr. Wiebe or Mr. Rossmo. All names, characters, events and locales in this publication are entirely fictional. Any resemblance to actual persons (living or dead), events or places, without satiric intent, is coincidental. For information regarding the CPSIA on this printed material call: 203-595-3636 and provide reference # RICH – 470030. PRINTED IN USA.
International Rights / Foreign Licensing -- foreignlicensing@imagecomics.com

STORY

KURTIS WIEBE

ART

RILEY ROSSMO

COLORS
ART FINISHES CHAPTERS THREE and FOUR

OWEN GIENI

LETTERS

ED BRISSON

EDITS

LAURA TAVISHATI

PUBLISHER/BOOK DESIGN

JIM VALENTINO

IMAGE COMICS, INC.
Robert Kirkman - chief operating officer
Erik Larsen - chief financial officer
Todd McFarlane - president
Marc Silvestri - chief executive officer
Jim Valentino - vice-president
Eric Stephenson - publisher
Todd Martinez - sales & licensing coordinator
Jennifer de Guzman - pr & marketing director
Branwyn Bigglestone - accounts manager
Emily Miller - accounting assistant
Jamie Parreno - marketing assistant
Jenna Savage - administrative assistant
Sarah deLaine - events coordinator
Kevin Yuen - digital rights coordinator
Jonathan Chan - production manager
Drew Gill - art director
Monica Garcia - production artist
Vincent Kukua - production artist
Jana Cook - production artist
www.imagecomics.com

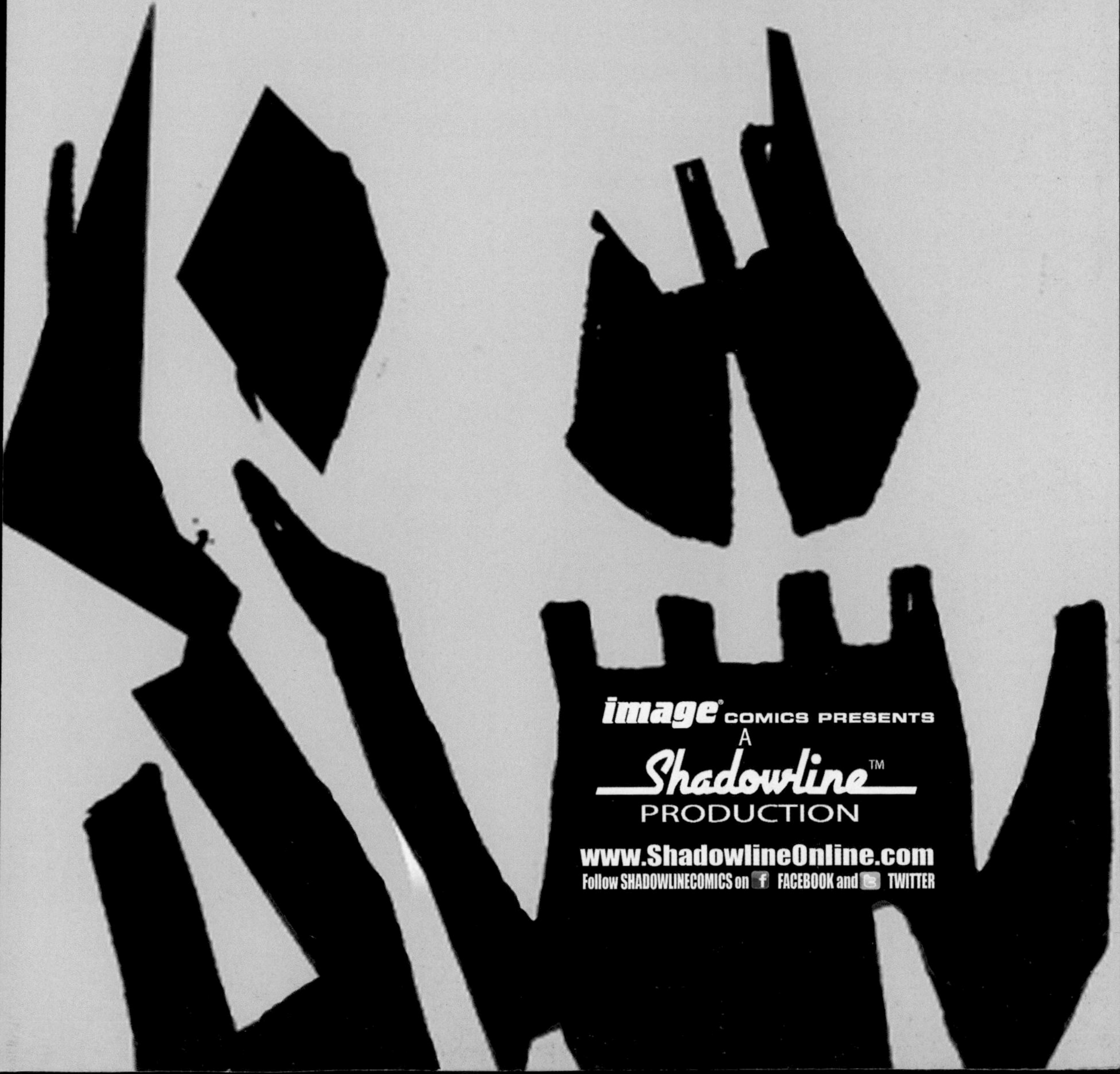

image® COMICS PRESENTS
A
Shadowline™
PRODUCTION
www.ShadowlineOnline.com
Follow SHADOWLINECOMICS on FACEBOOK and TWITTER

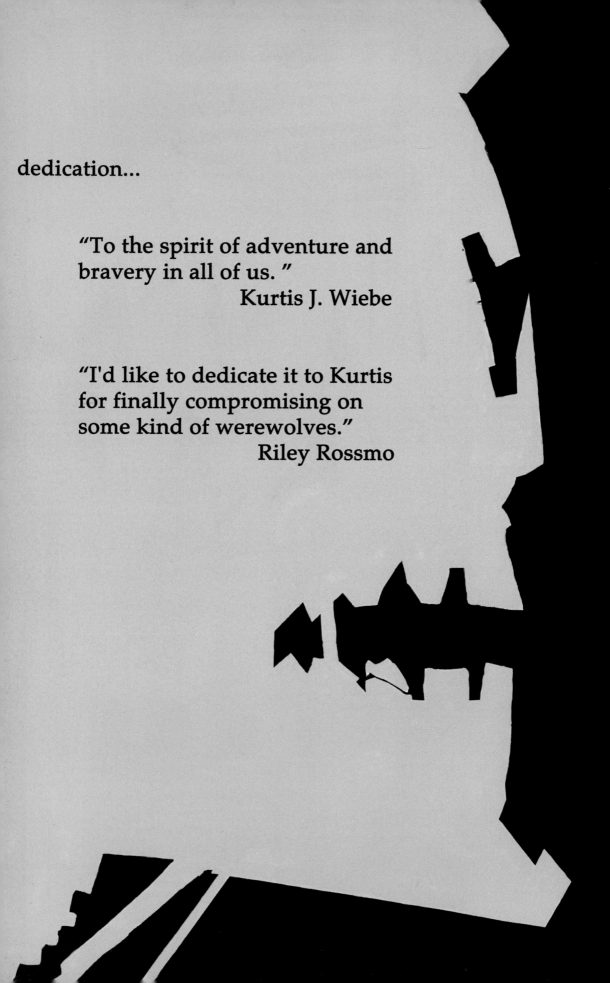

dedication...

"To the spirit of adventure and bravery in all of us. "
Kurtis J. Wiebe

"I'd like to dedicate it to Kurtis for finally compromising on some kind of werewolves."
Riley Rossmo

ONE

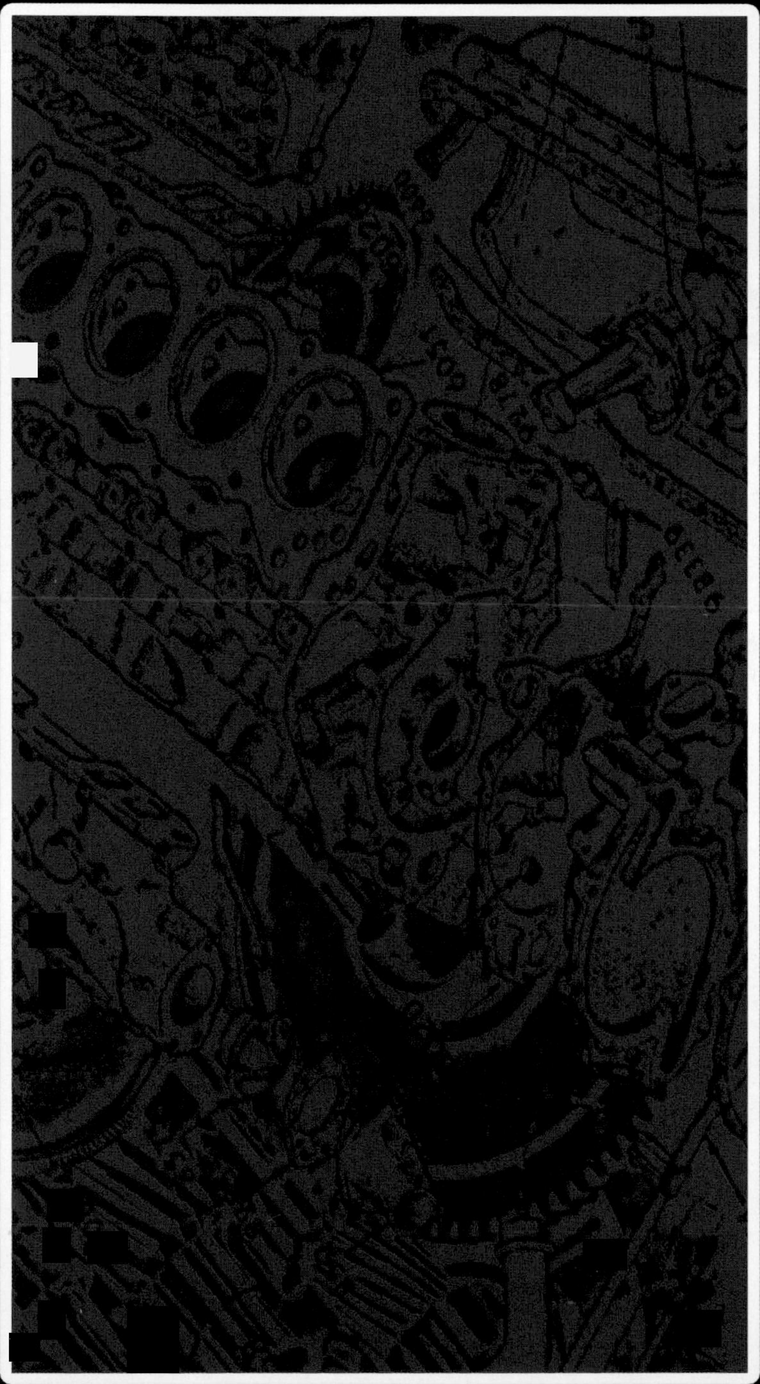

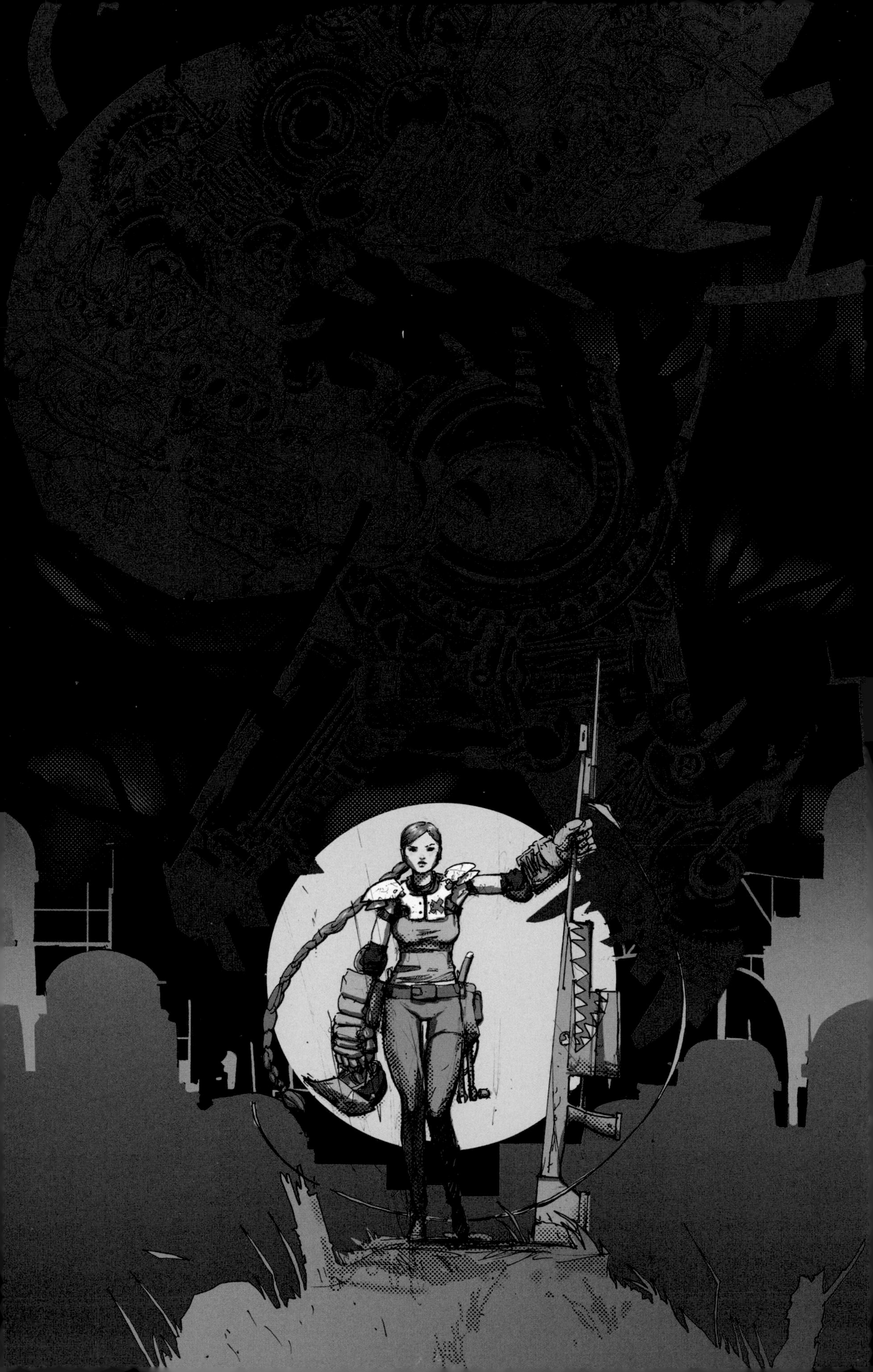

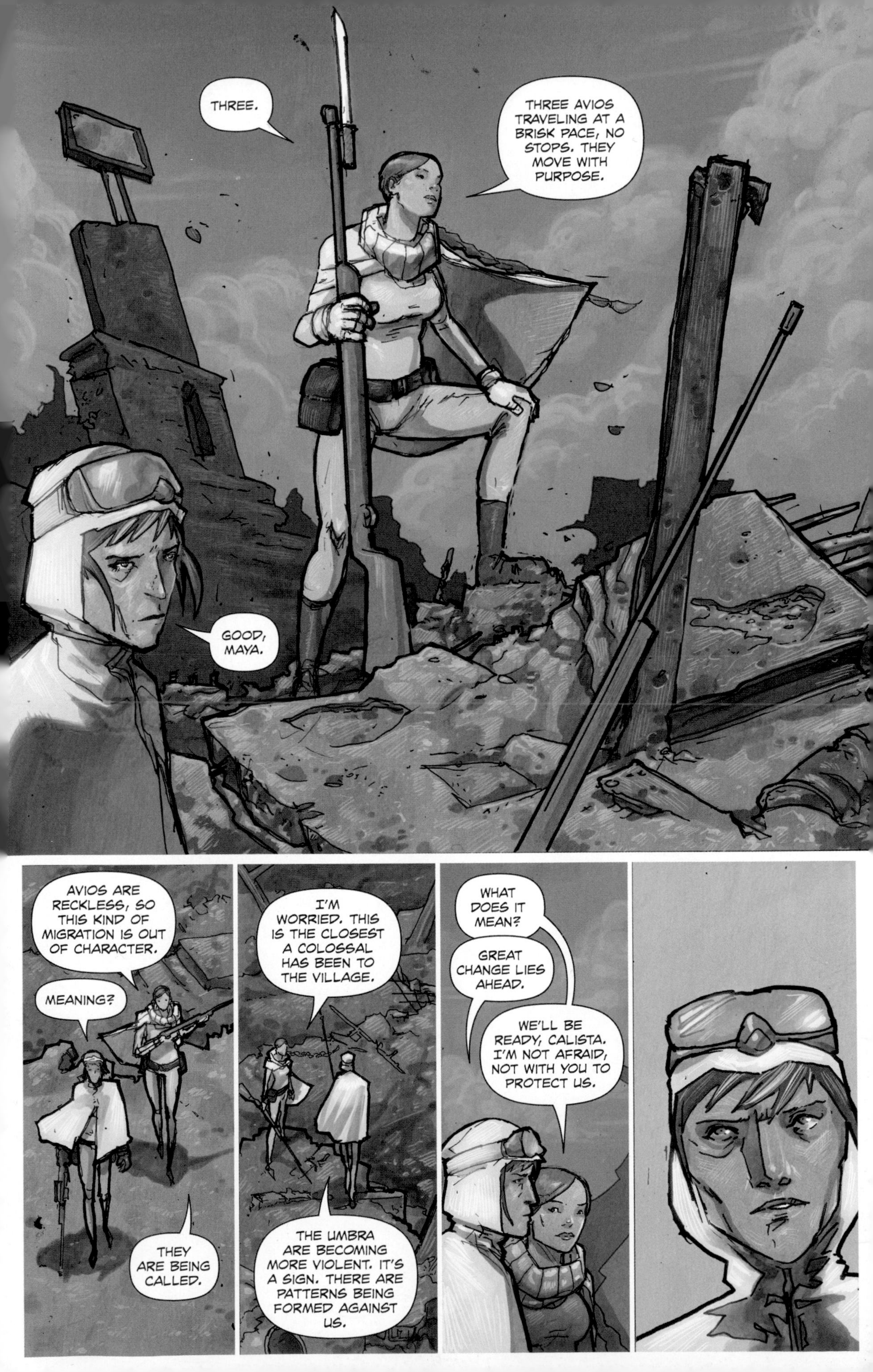
THREE.
THREE AVIOS TRAVELING AT A BRISK PACE, NO STOPS. THEY MOVE WITH PURPOSE.
GOOD, MAYA.
AVIOS ARE RECKLESS, SO THIS KIND OF MIGRATION IS OUT OF CHARACTER.
MEANING?
THEY ARE BEING CALLED.
I'M WORRIED. THIS IS THE CLOSEST A COLOSSAL HAS BEEN TO THE VILLAGE.
THE UMBRA ARE BECOMING MORE VIOLENT. IT'S A SIGN. THERE ARE PATTERNS BEING FORMED AGAINST US.
WHAT DOES IT MEAN?
GREAT CHANGE LIES AHEAD.
WE'LL BE READY, CALISTA. I'M NOT AFRAID, NOT WITH YOU TO PROTECT US.

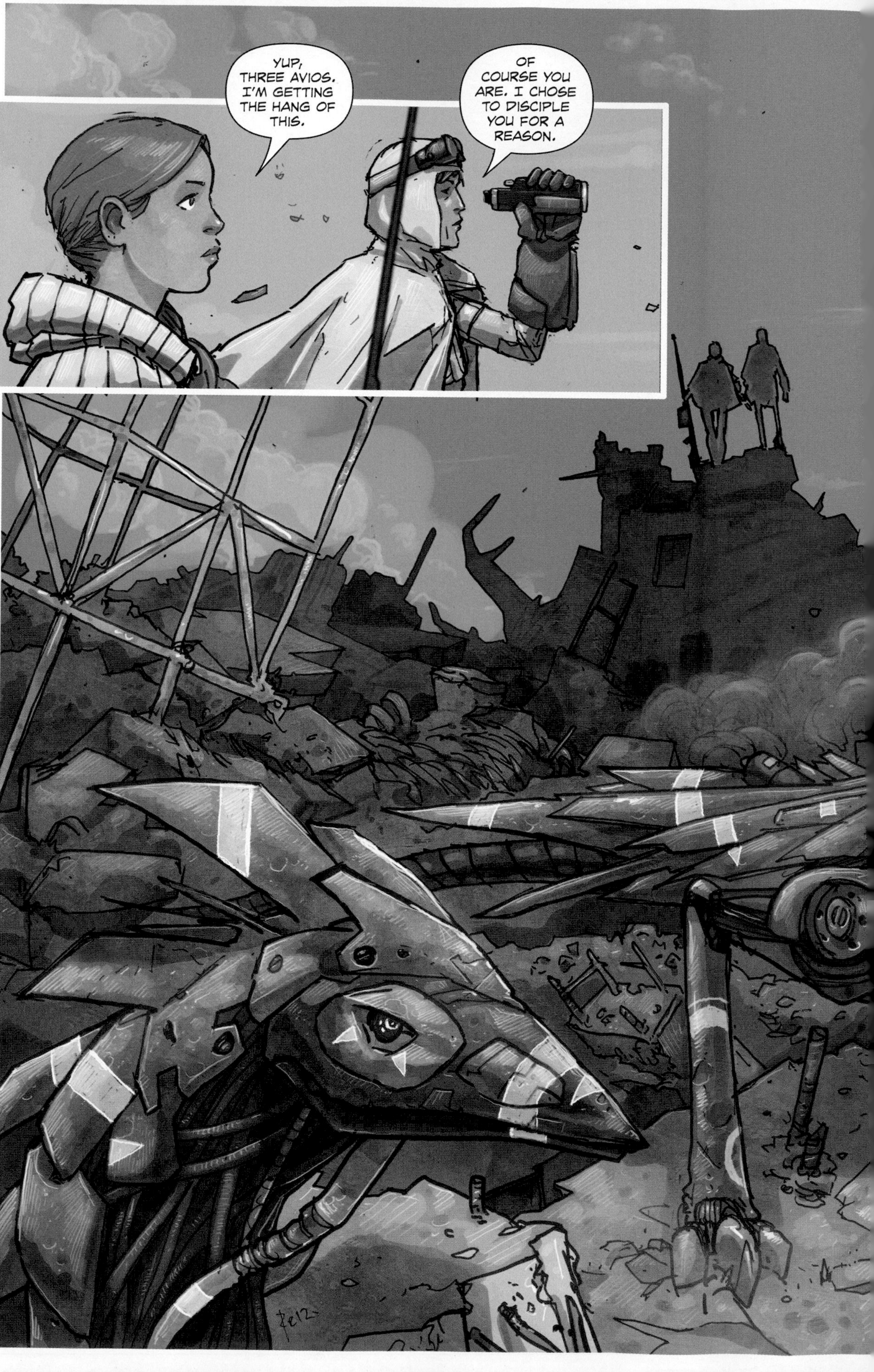
YUP, THREE AVIOS. I'M GETTING THE HANG OF THIS.
OF COURSE YOU ARE. I CHOSE TO DISCIPLE YOU FOR A REASON.

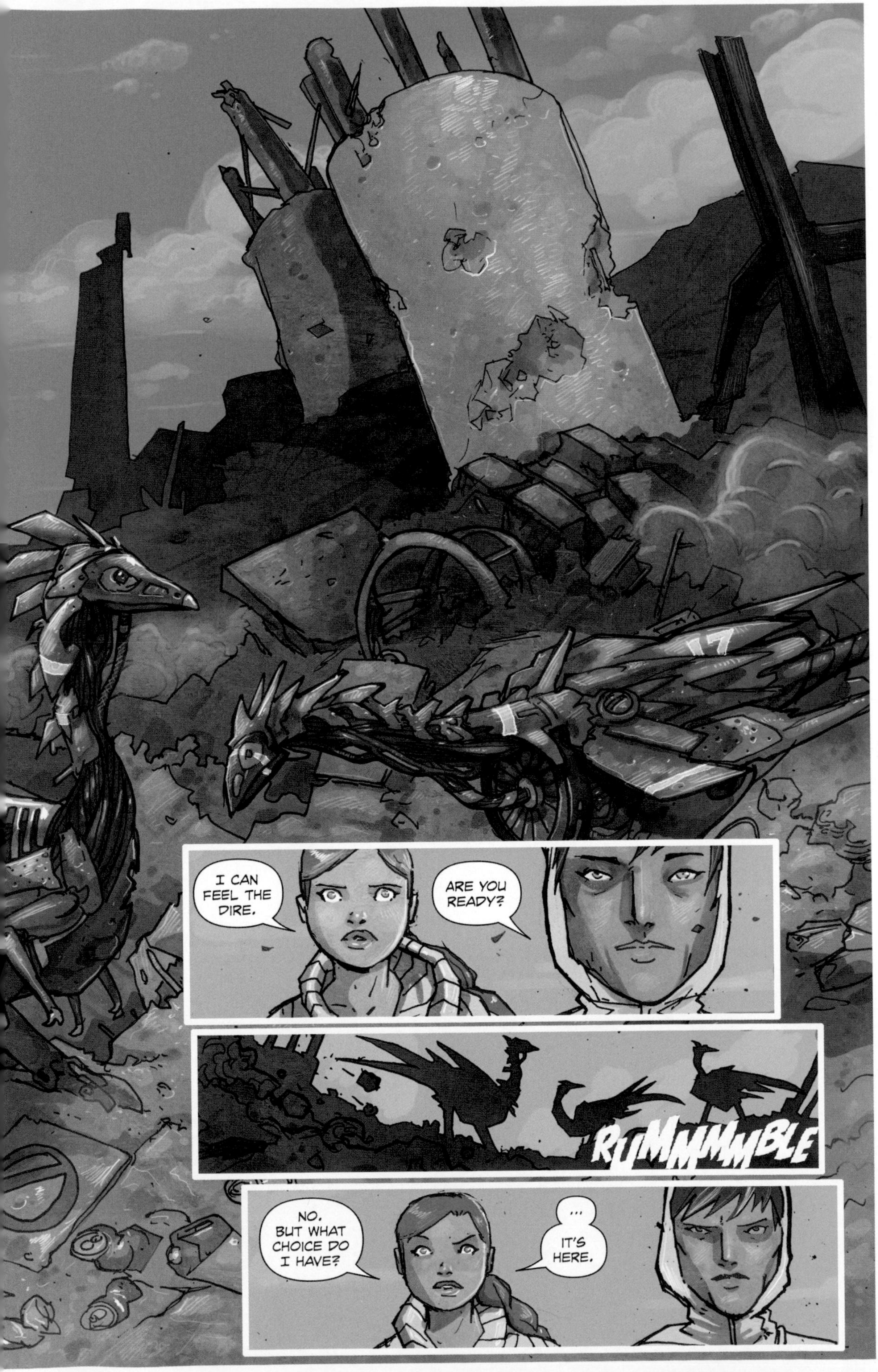
I CAN FEEL THE DIRE.
ARE YOU READY?
RUMMMMBLE
NO. BUT WHAT CHOICE DO I HAVE?
...
IT'S HERE.

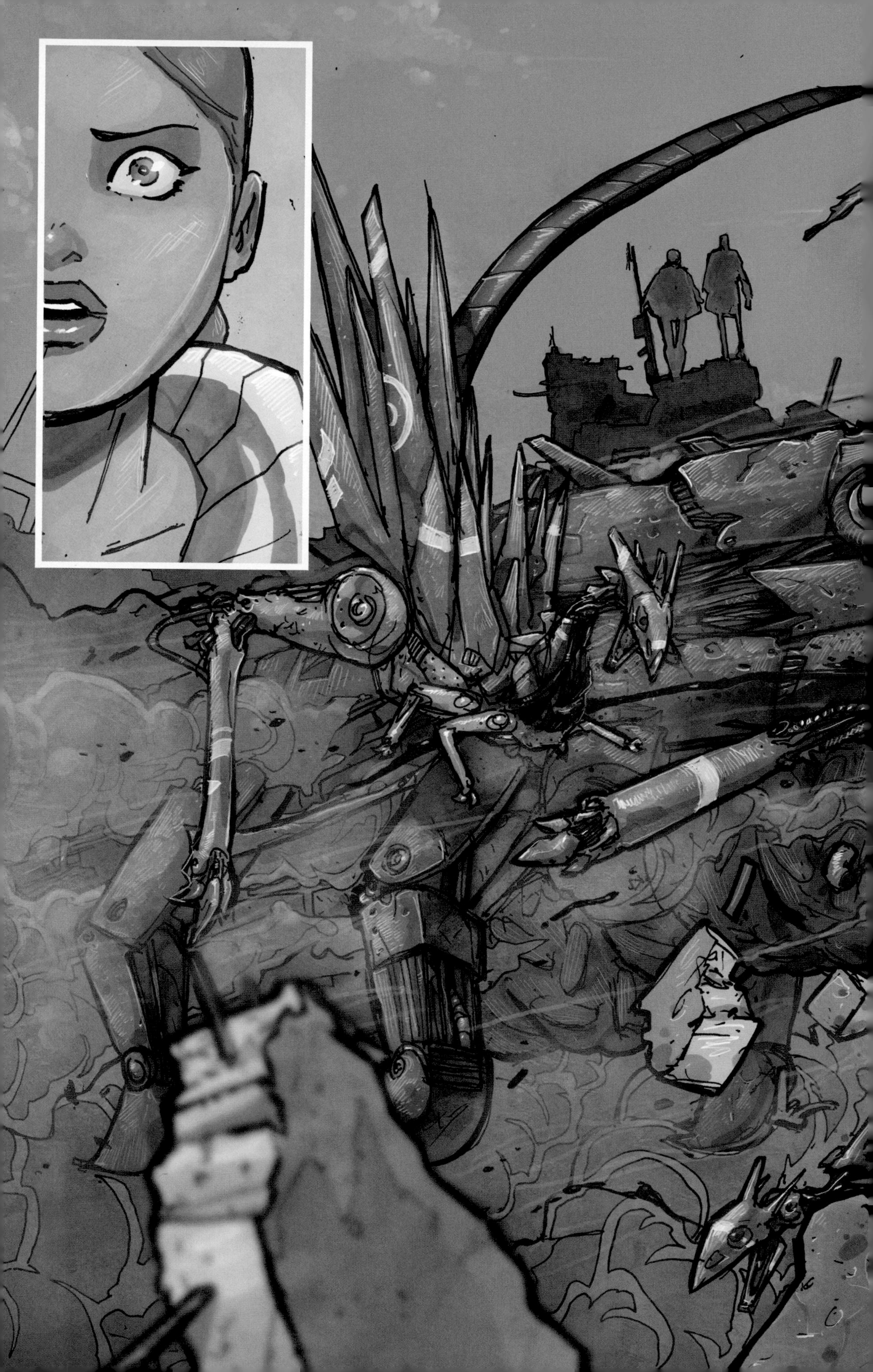

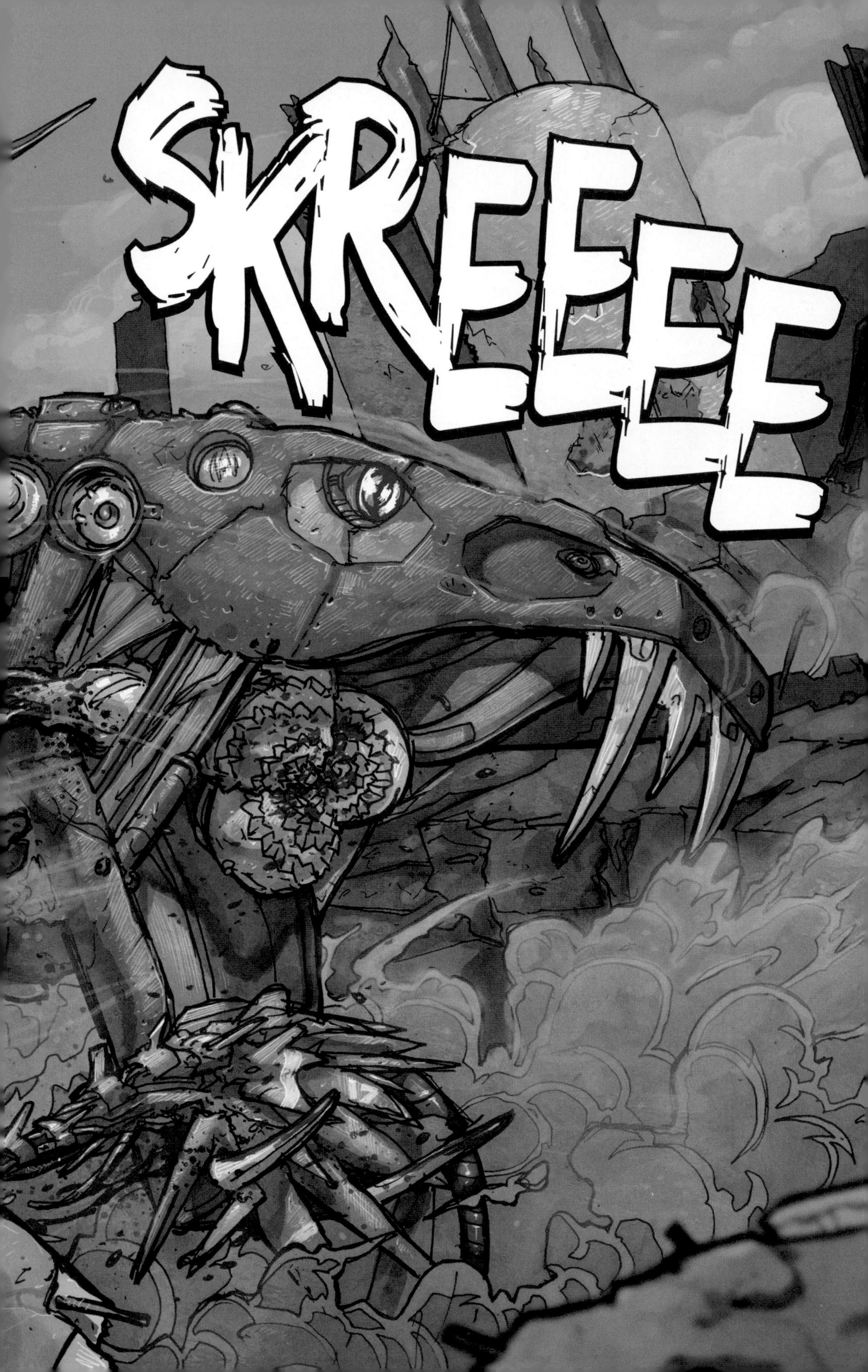
SKREEEEE

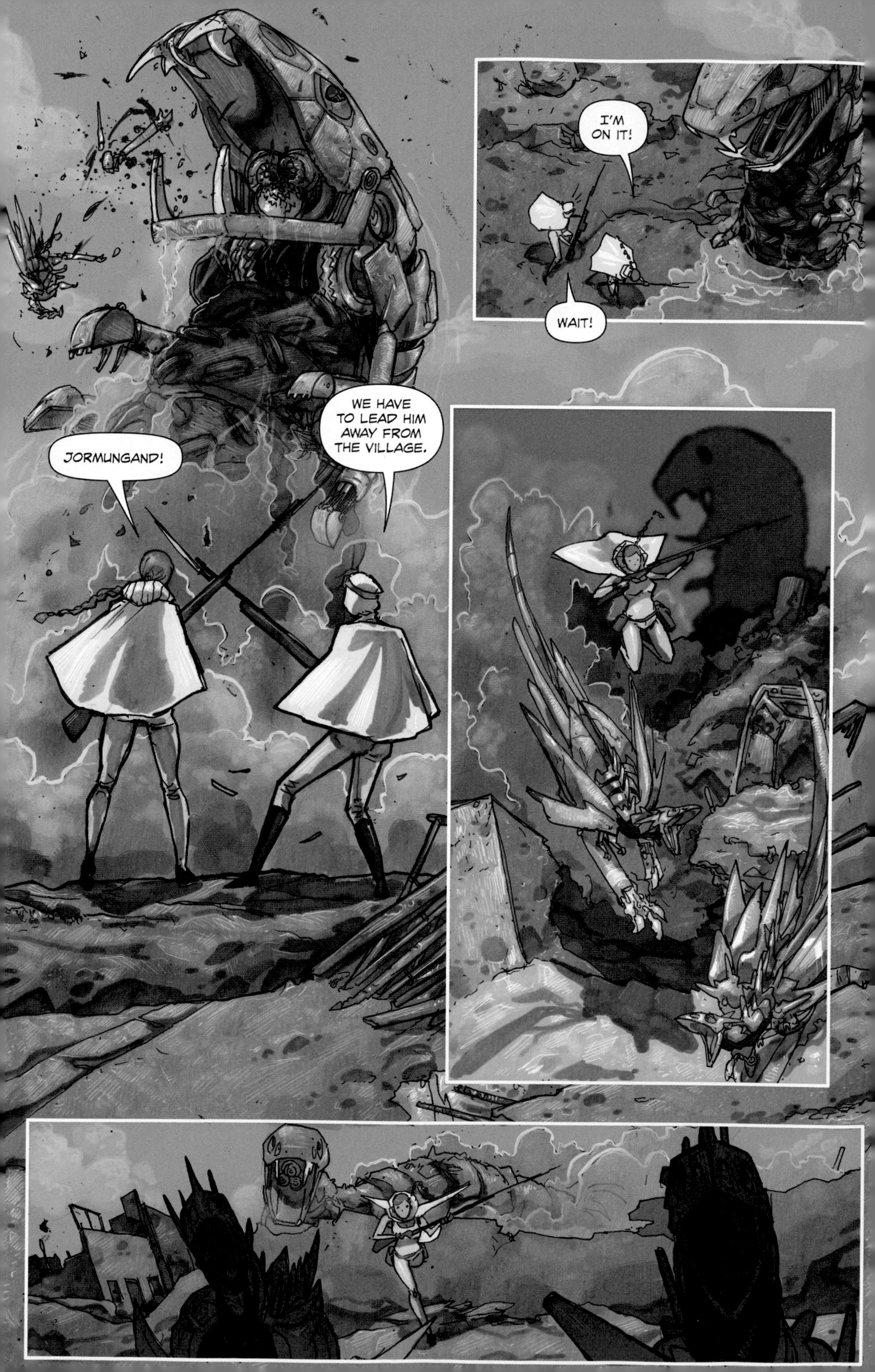
I'M ON IT!
WAIT!
JORMUNGAND!
WE HAVE TO LEAD HIM AWAY FROM THE VILLAGE.

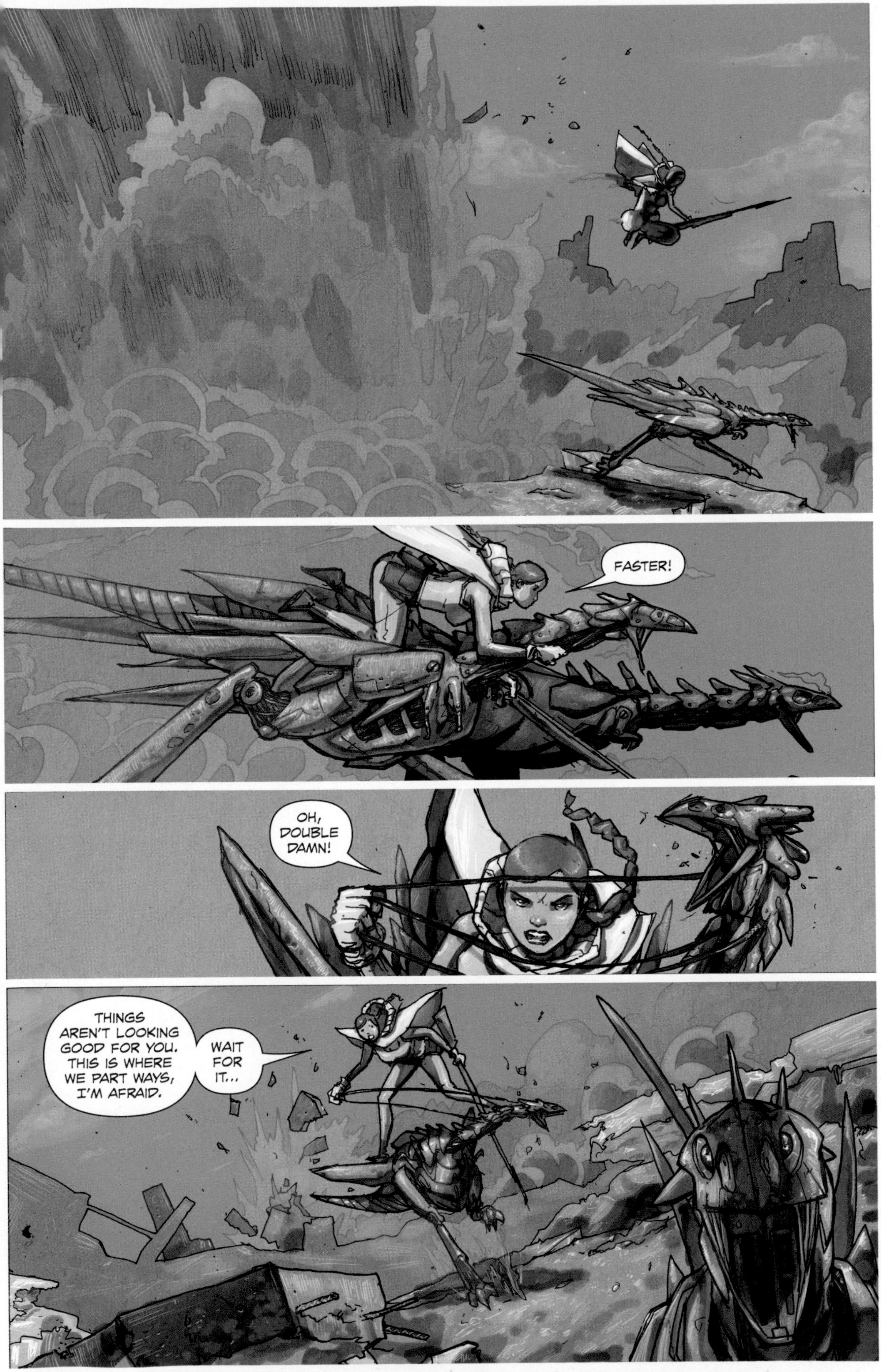
FASTER!
OH, DOUBLE DAMN!
THINGS AREN'T LOOKING GOOD FOR YOU. THIS IS WHERE WE PART WAYS, I'M AFRAID.
WAIT FOR IT...

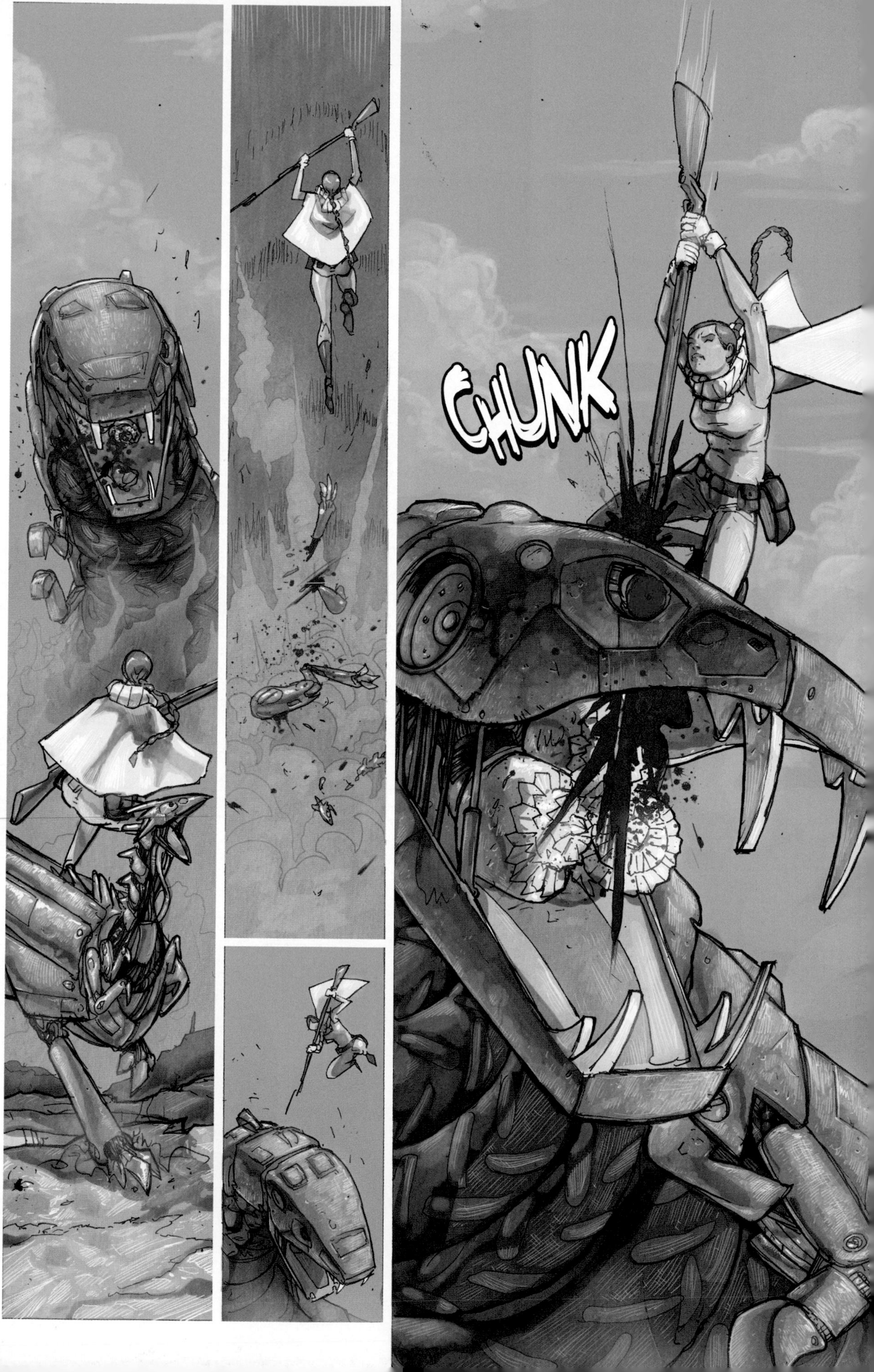
CHUNK

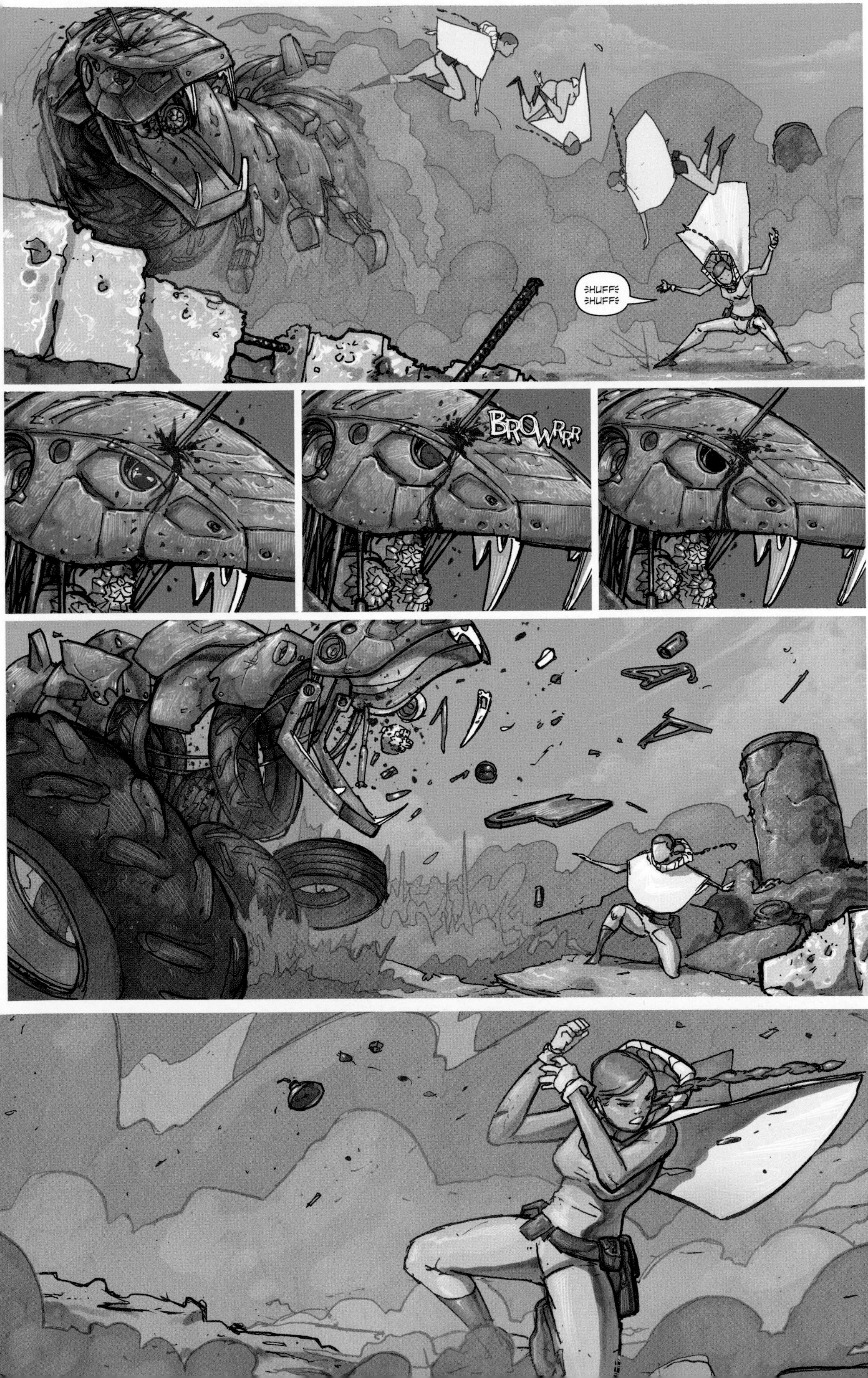
HUFF HUFF
BROWRRR

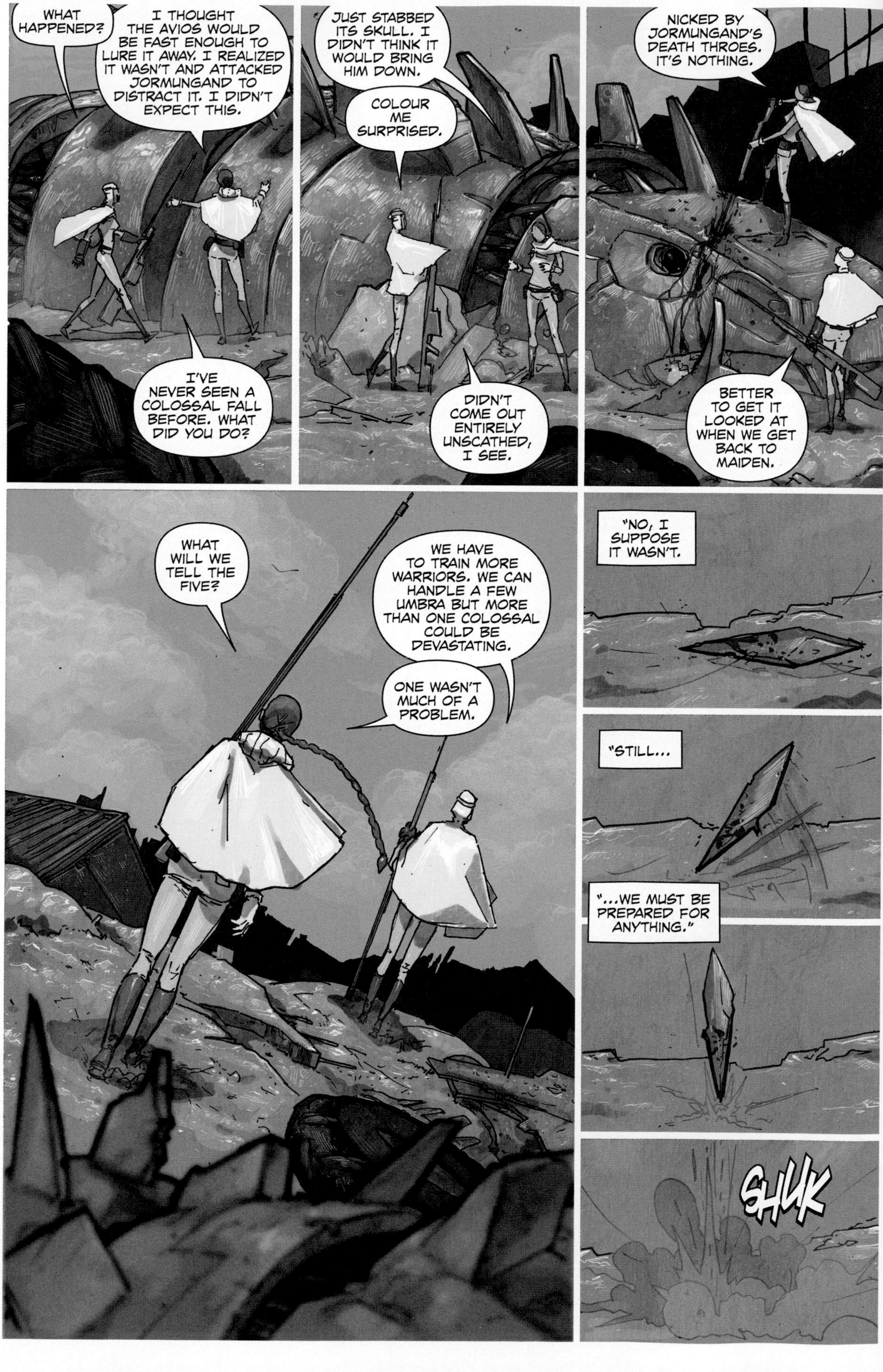
WHAT HAPPENED?
I THOUGHT THE AVIOS WOULD BE FAST ENOUGH TO LURE IT AWAY. I REALIZED IT WASN'T AND ATTACKED JORMUNGAND TO DISTRACT IT. I DIDN'T EXPECT THIS.
I'VE NEVER SEEN A COLOSSAL FALL BEFORE. WHAT DID YOU DO?
JUST STABBED ITS SKULL. I DIDN'T THINK IT WOULD BRING HIM DOWN.
COLOUR ME SURPRISED.
DIDN'T COME OUT ENTIRELY UNSCATHED, I SEE.
NICKED BY JORMUNGAND'S DEATH THROES. IT'S NOTHING.
BETTER TO GET IT LOOKED AT WHEN WE GET BACK TO MAIDEN.
WHAT WILL WE TELL THE FIVE?
WE HAVE TO TRAIN MORE WARRIORS. WE CAN HANDLE A FEW UMBRA BUT MORE THAN ONE COLOSSAL COULD BE DEVASTATING.
ONE WASN'T MUCH OF A PROBLEM.
"NO, I SUPPOSE IT WASN'T.
"STILL...
"...WE MUST BE PREPARED FOR ANYTHING."
SHUK

AS PROTECTOR, I AM TASKED WITH MANY RESPONSIBILITIES. YOU HAVE GIVEN ME MUCH FREEDOM THAT I MIGHT KEEP MAIDEN SAFE.

MY ACOLYTE MAYA AND I HAVE DISCOVERED THAT THE COLOSSALS ARE CLOSING ON OUR VILLAGE WITH EACH PASSING DAY. OUR TOWN FACES EXPOSURE; DISCOVERY IS IMMINENT.

WHAT WOULD YOU HAVE US DO?

"I ASK THAT WE TAKE MEMBERS OF THE WORKFORCE AND TRAIN THEM AS WARRIORS."

"WHAT OF THE VATS? TO TAKE NUMBERS FROM THE PROCESS ENDANGERS OUR SUPPLY OF WATER AND THE FOOD WE GROW FROM IT."

"I UNDERSTAND, COUNCILOR. YOU MUST REMEMBER THAT IF A GROUP OF COLOSSALS ATTACK MAIDEN, A SOURCE OF WATER AND FOOD WILL NOT MATTER."

"THE DEVICE CAN NEVER STOP TURNING. WE WILL BE FORCED TO PUT OUR YOUNGER CIVILIANS TO WORK."

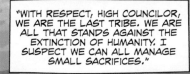

"WITH RESPECT, HIGH COUNCILOR, WE ARE THE LAST TRIBE. WE ARE ALL THAT STANDS AGAINST THE EXTINCTION OF HUMANITY. I SUSPECT WE CAN ALL MANAGE SMALL SACRIFICES."

YOU SPEAK SENSE, PROTECTOR. WE GIVE YOU THE RIGHT TO RECRUIT TWENTY NEW WARRIORS TO TRAINING.

COUNCILOR REDMOND, SEE TO REPLENISHING THE DEVICE WORKERS. ALL CIVILIANS AGED FIFTEEN ARE NOW ELIGIBLE FOR WORK DETAIL.

UNDERSTOOD, COUNCILOR NIZOA.

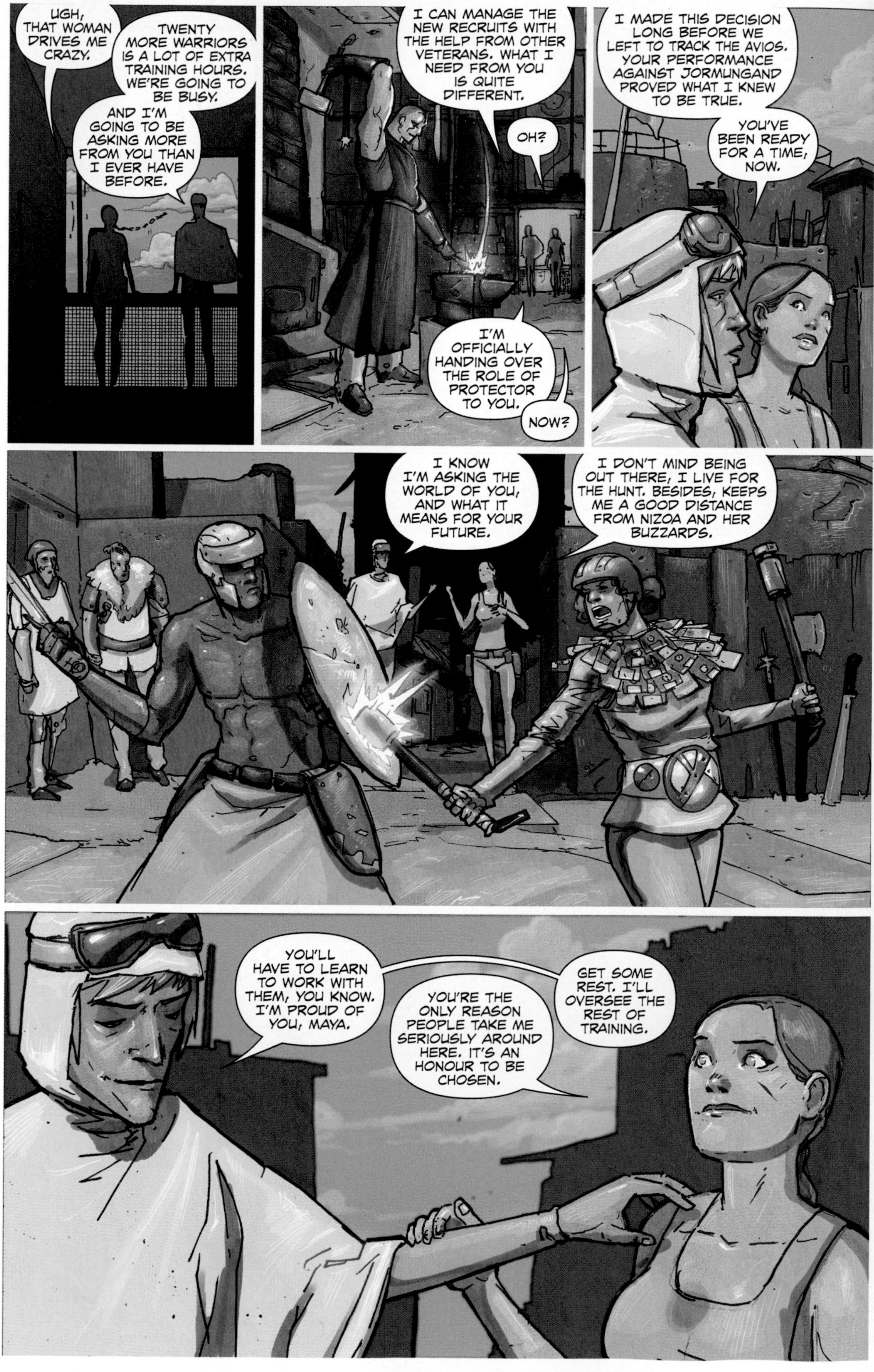
UGH, THAT WOMAN DRIVES ME CRAZY.
TWENTY MORE WARRIORS IS A LOT OF EXTRA TRAINING HOURS. WE'RE GOING TO BE BUSY.
AND I'M GOING TO BE ASKING MORE FROM YOU THAN I EVER HAVE BEFORE.
I CAN MANAGE THE NEW RECRUITS WITH THE HELP FROM OTHER VETERANS. WHAT I NEED FROM YOU IS QUITE DIFFERENT.
OH?
I'M OFFICIALLY HANDING OVER THE ROLE OF PROTECTOR TO YOU.
NOW?
I MADE THIS DECISION LONG BEFORE WE LEFT TO TRACK THE AVIOS. YOUR PERFORMANCE AGAINST JORMUNGAND PROVED WHAT I KNEW TO BE TRUE.
YOU'VE BEEN READY FOR A TIME, NOW.
I KNOW I'M ASKING THE WORLD OF YOU, AND WHAT IT MEANS FOR YOUR FUTURE.
I DON'T MIND BEING OUT THERE, I LIVE FOR THE HUNT. BESIDES, KEEPS ME A GOOD DISTANCE FROM NIZOA AND HER BUZZARDS.
YOU'LL HAVE TO LEARN TO WORK WITH THEM, YOU KNOW. I'M PROUD OF YOU, MAYA.
YOU'RE THE ONLY REASON PEOPLE TAKE ME SERIOUSLY AROUND HERE. IT'S AN HONOUR TO BE CHOSEN.
GET SOME REST. I'LL OVERSEE THE REST OF TRAINING.

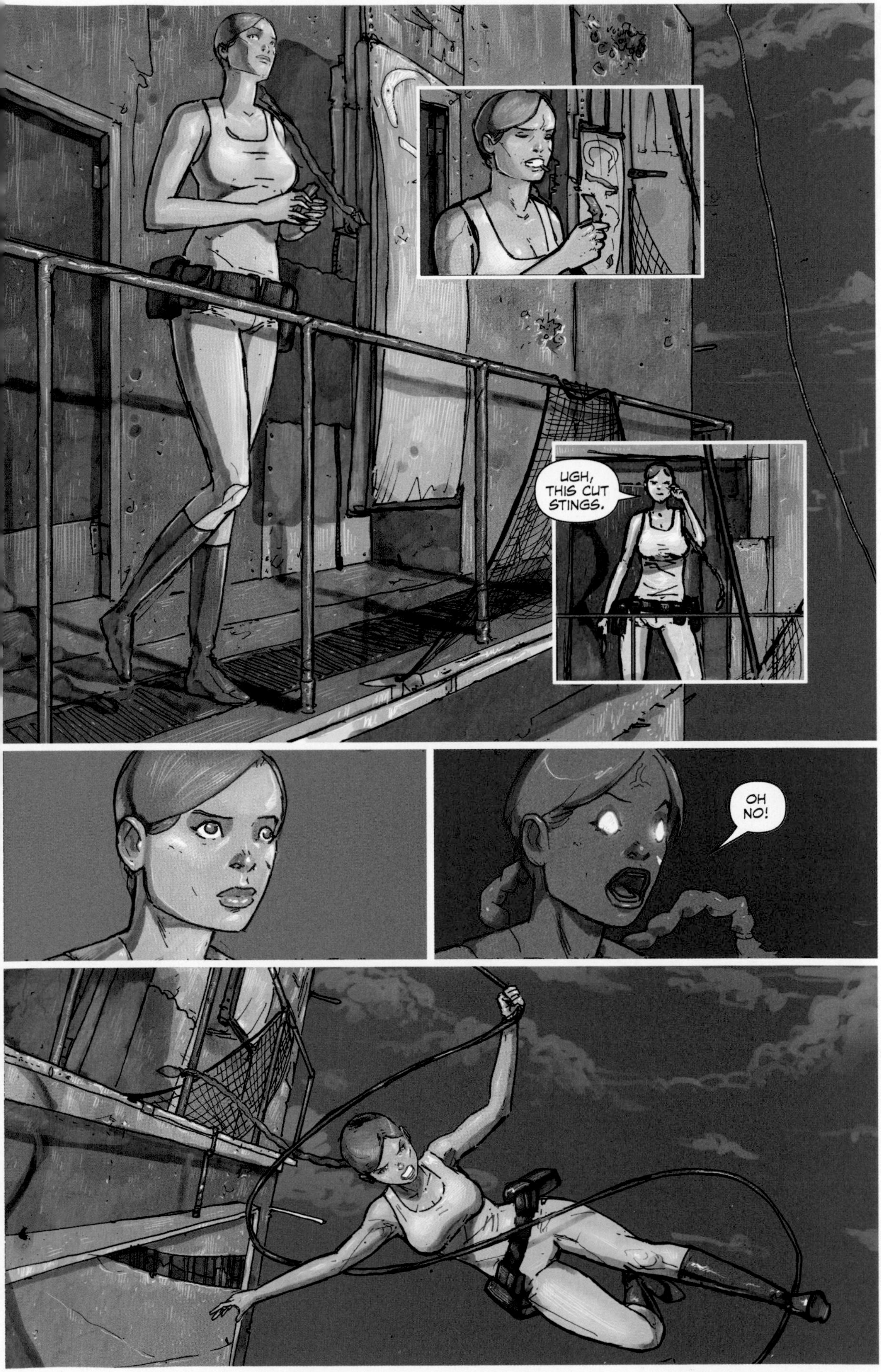
UGH, THIS CUT STINGS.
OH NO!

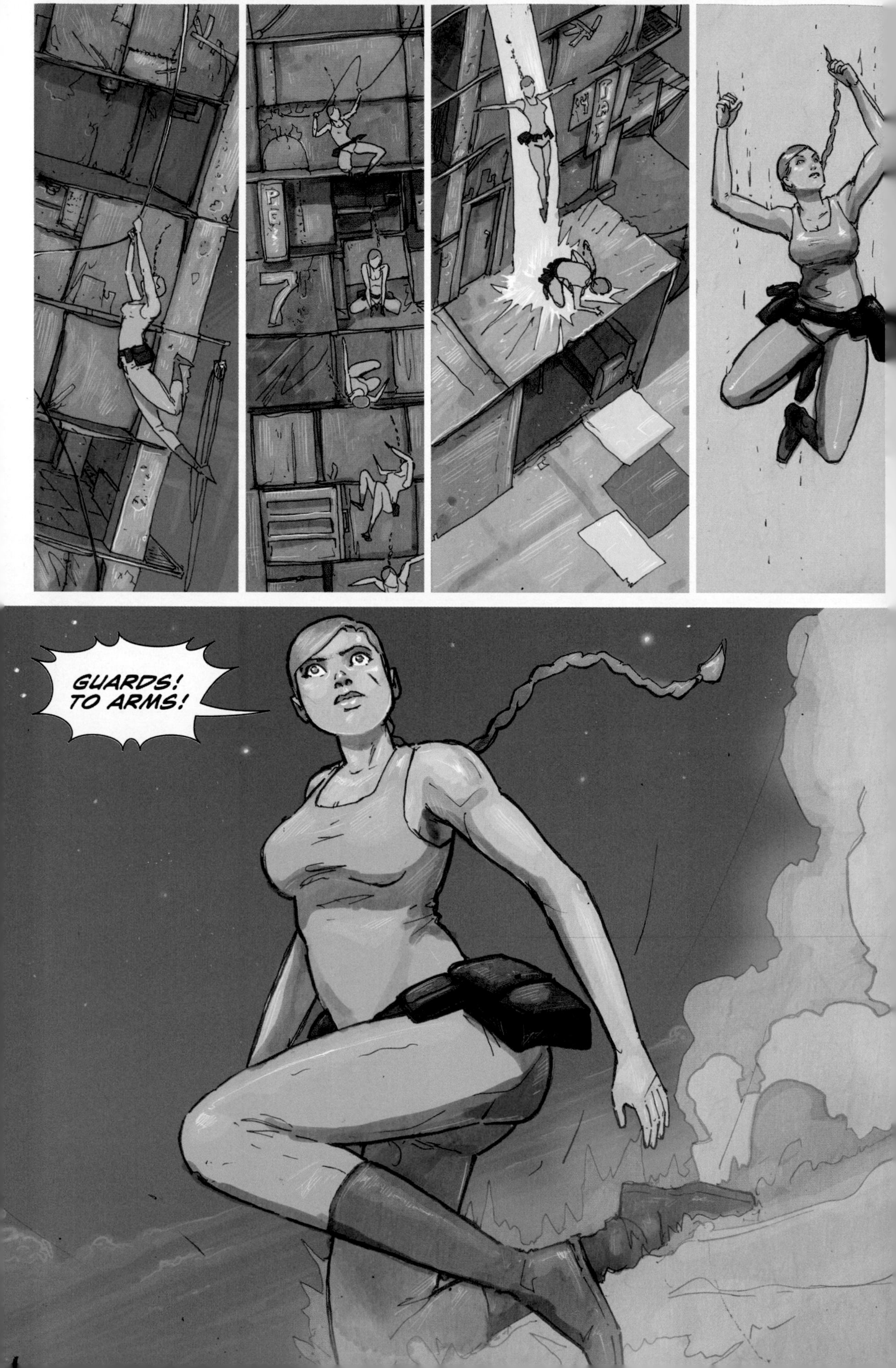
GUARDS! TO ARMS!

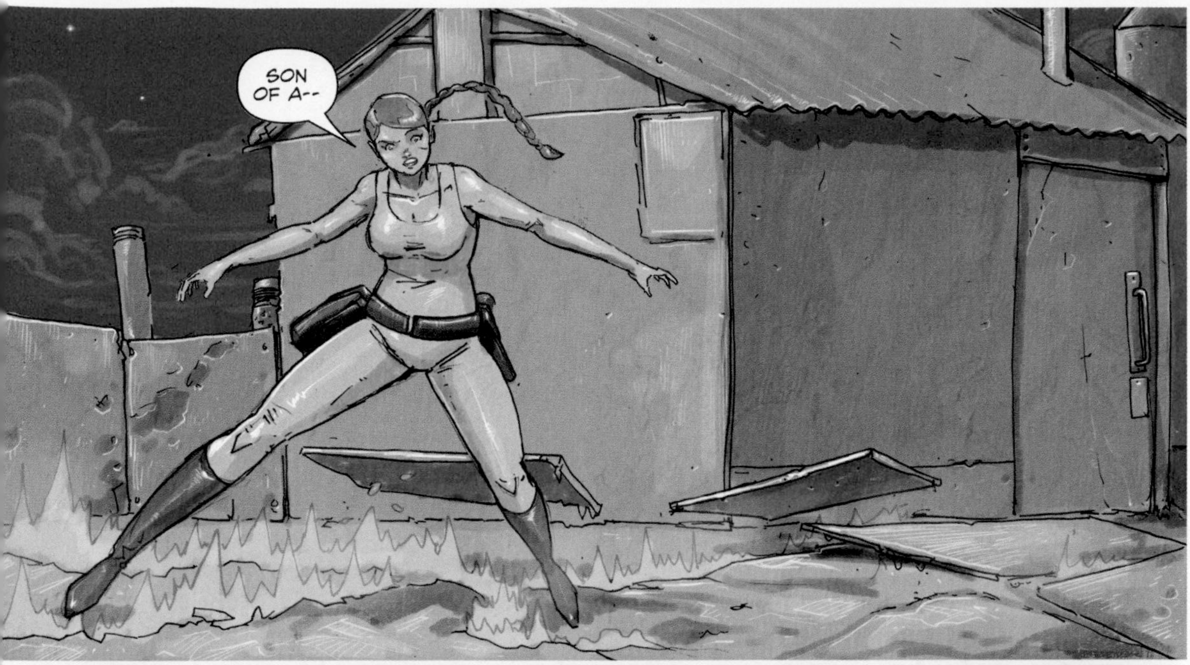
SON OF A--

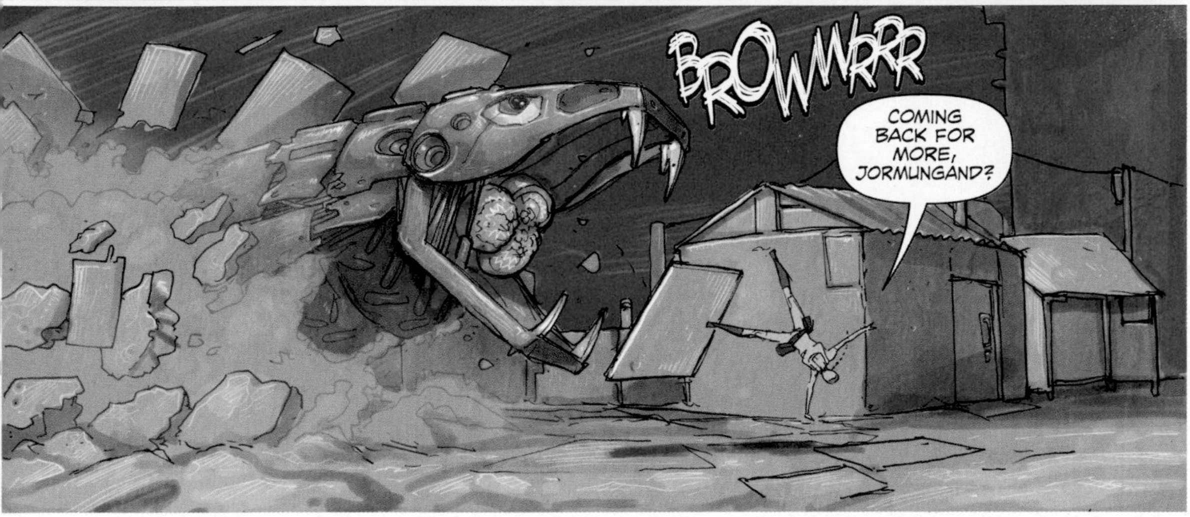
BROWWRRR
COMING BACK FOR MORE, JORMUNGAND?

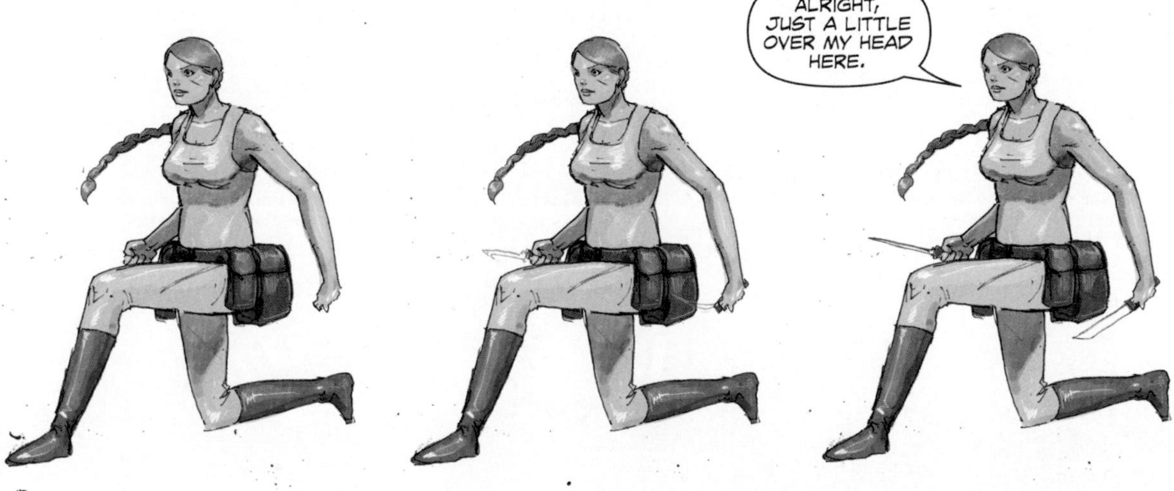
ALRIGHT, JUST A LITTLE OVER MY HEAD HERE.

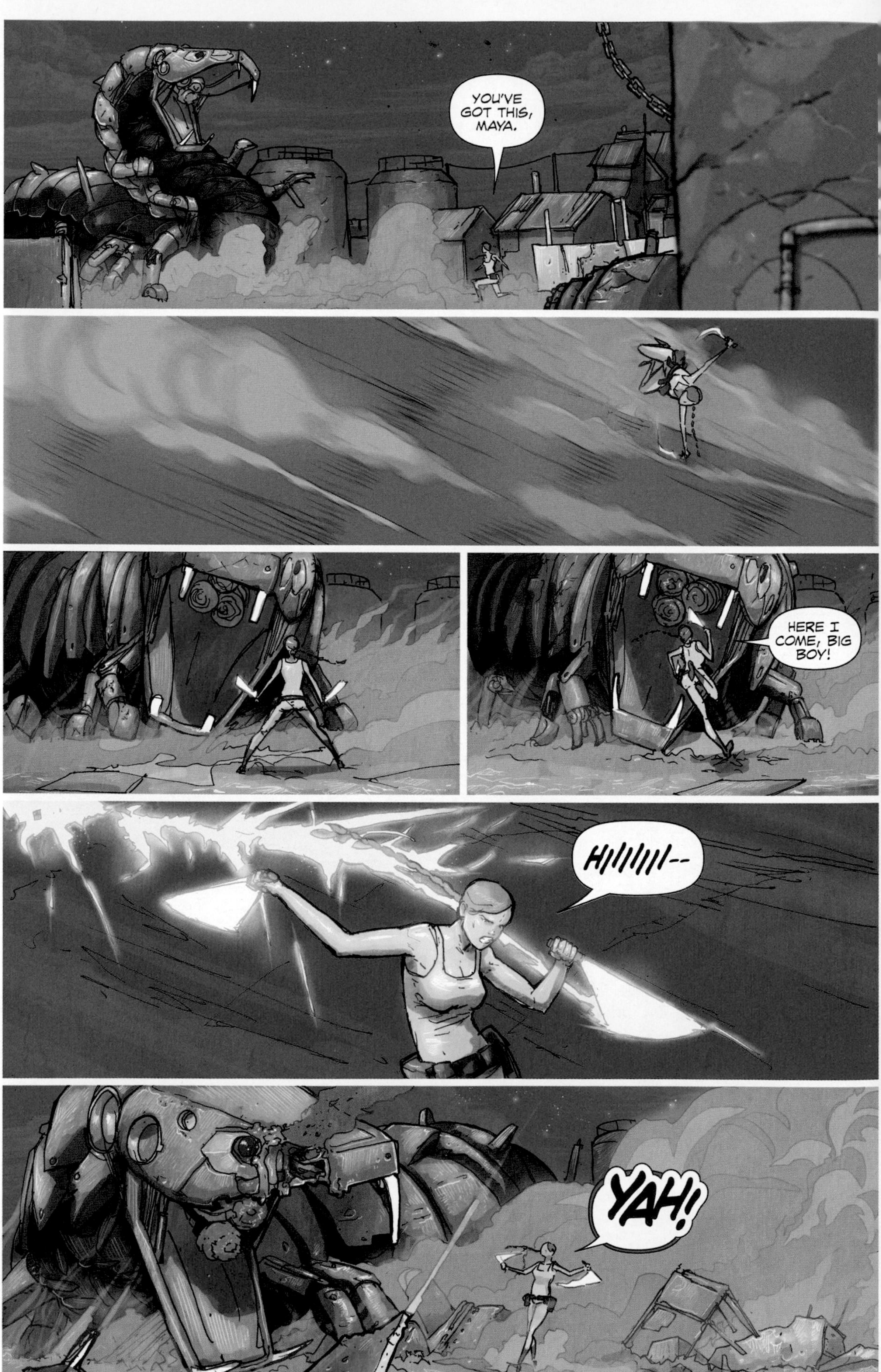
YOU'VE GOT THIS, MAYA.
HERE I COME, BIG BOY!
HIIIIIII--
YAH!

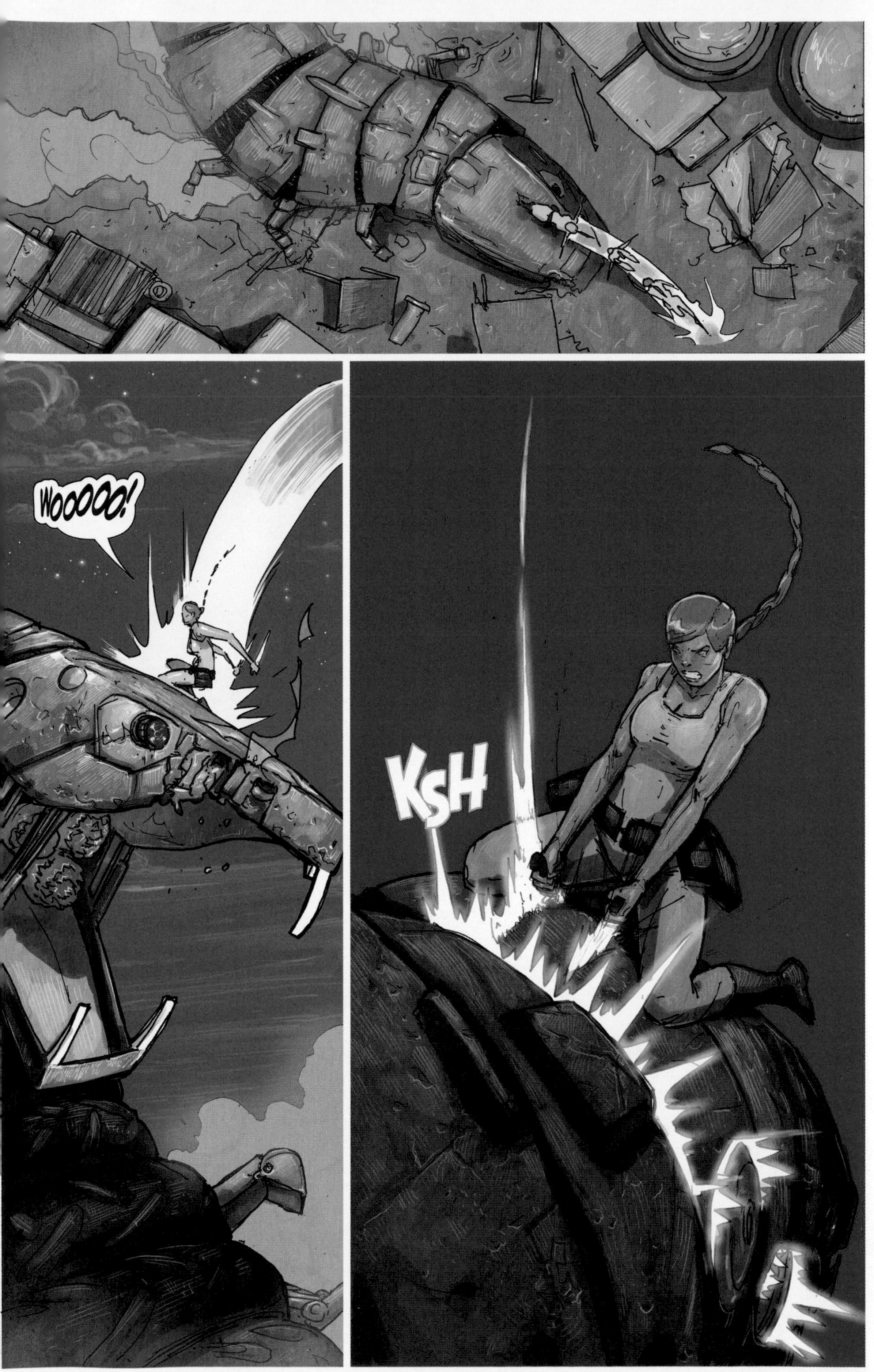
WOOOOO!
KSH

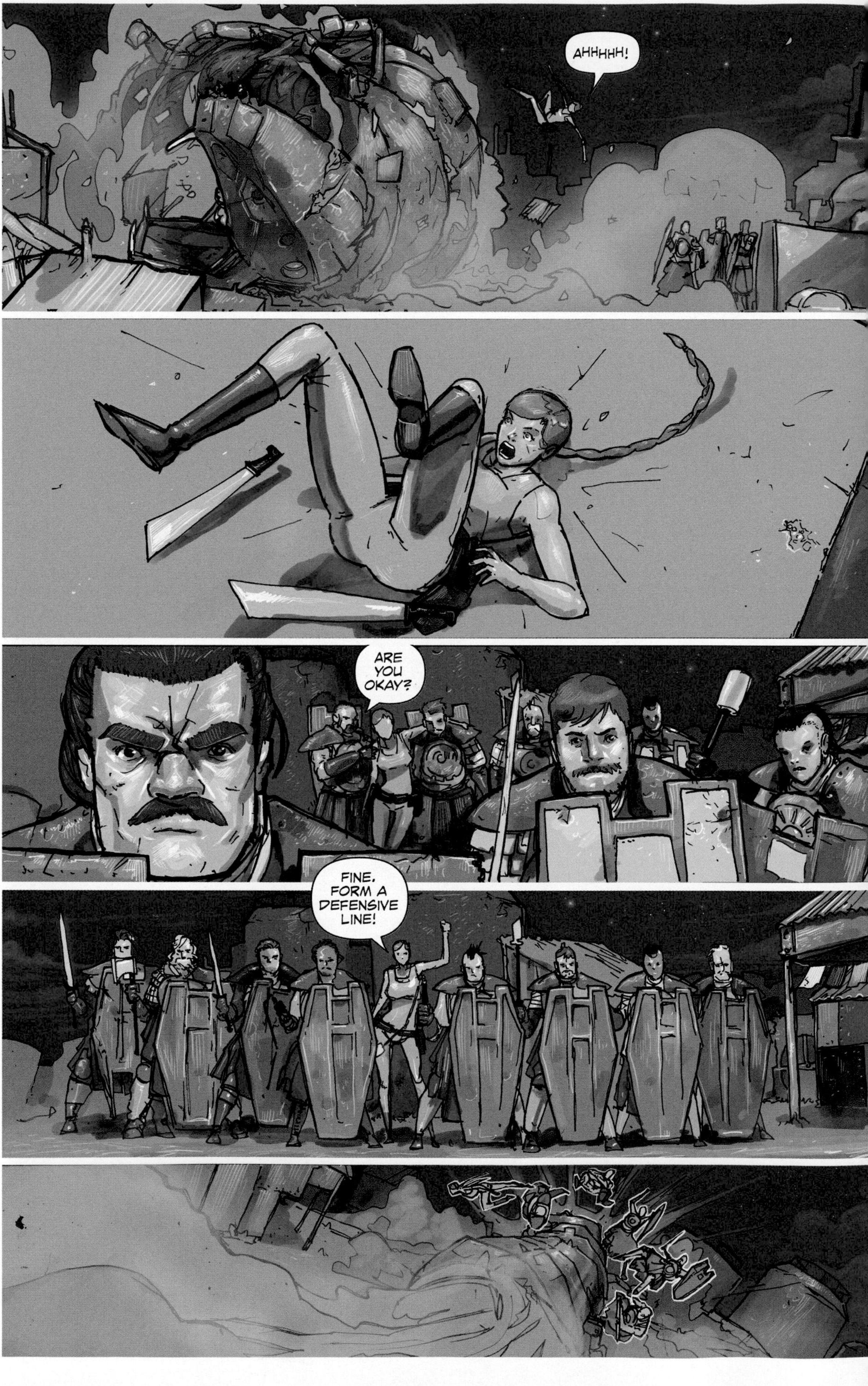
AHHHHH!
ARE YOU OKAY?
FINE. FORM A DEFENSIVE LINE!

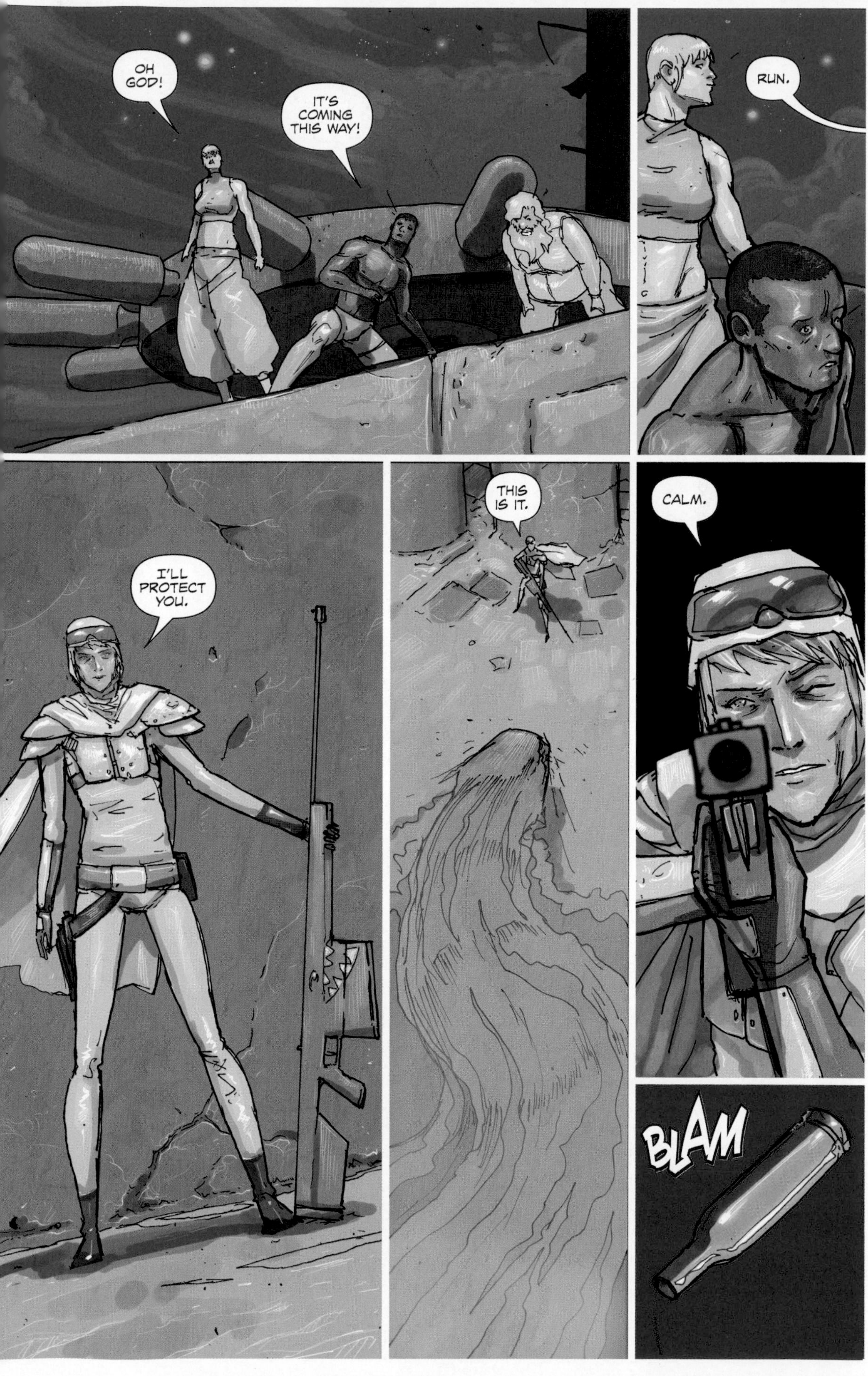
OH GOD!
IT'S COMING THIS WAY!
RUN.
I'LL PROTECT YOU.
THIS IS IT.
CALM.
BLAM

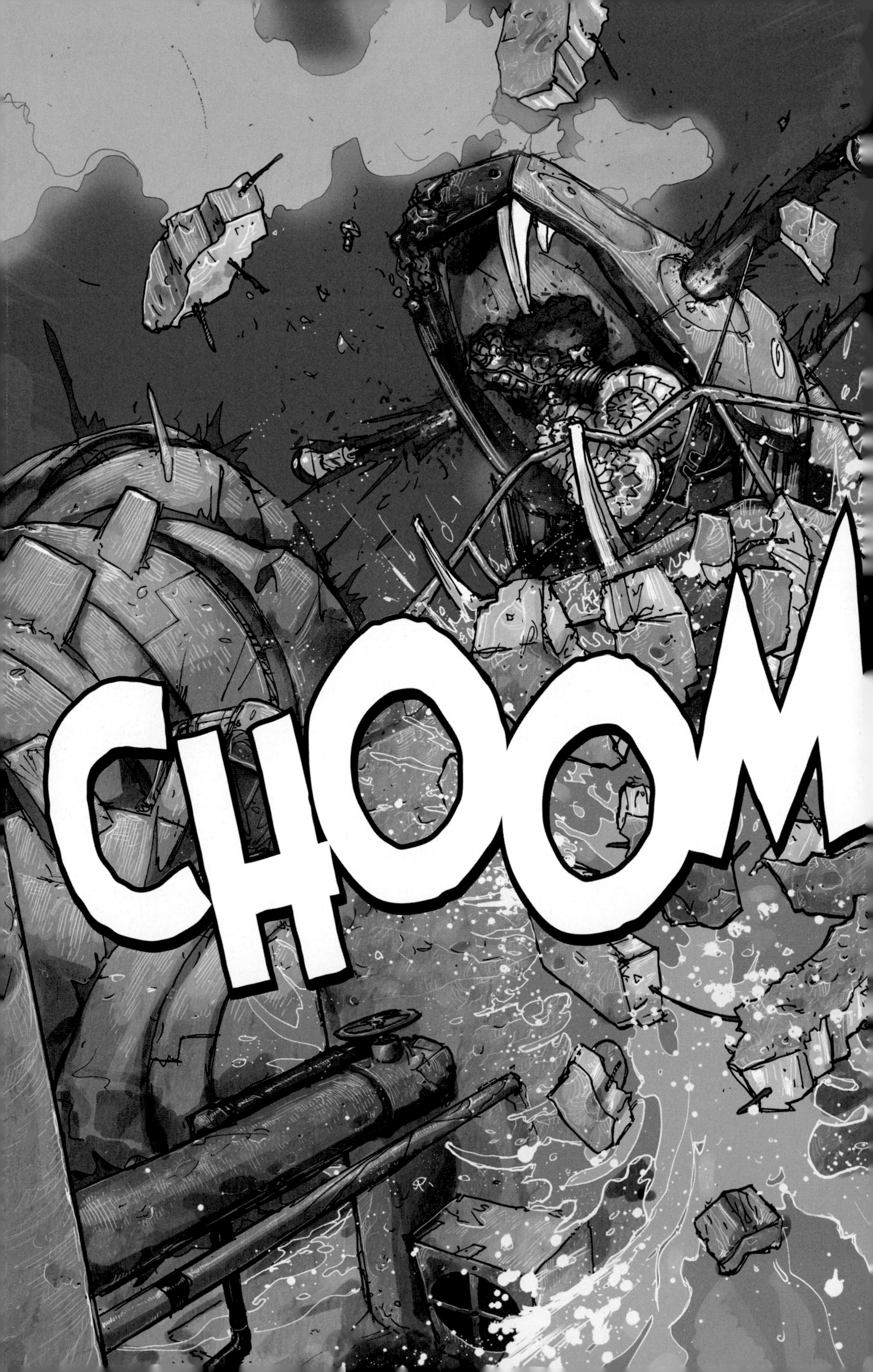
CHOOM

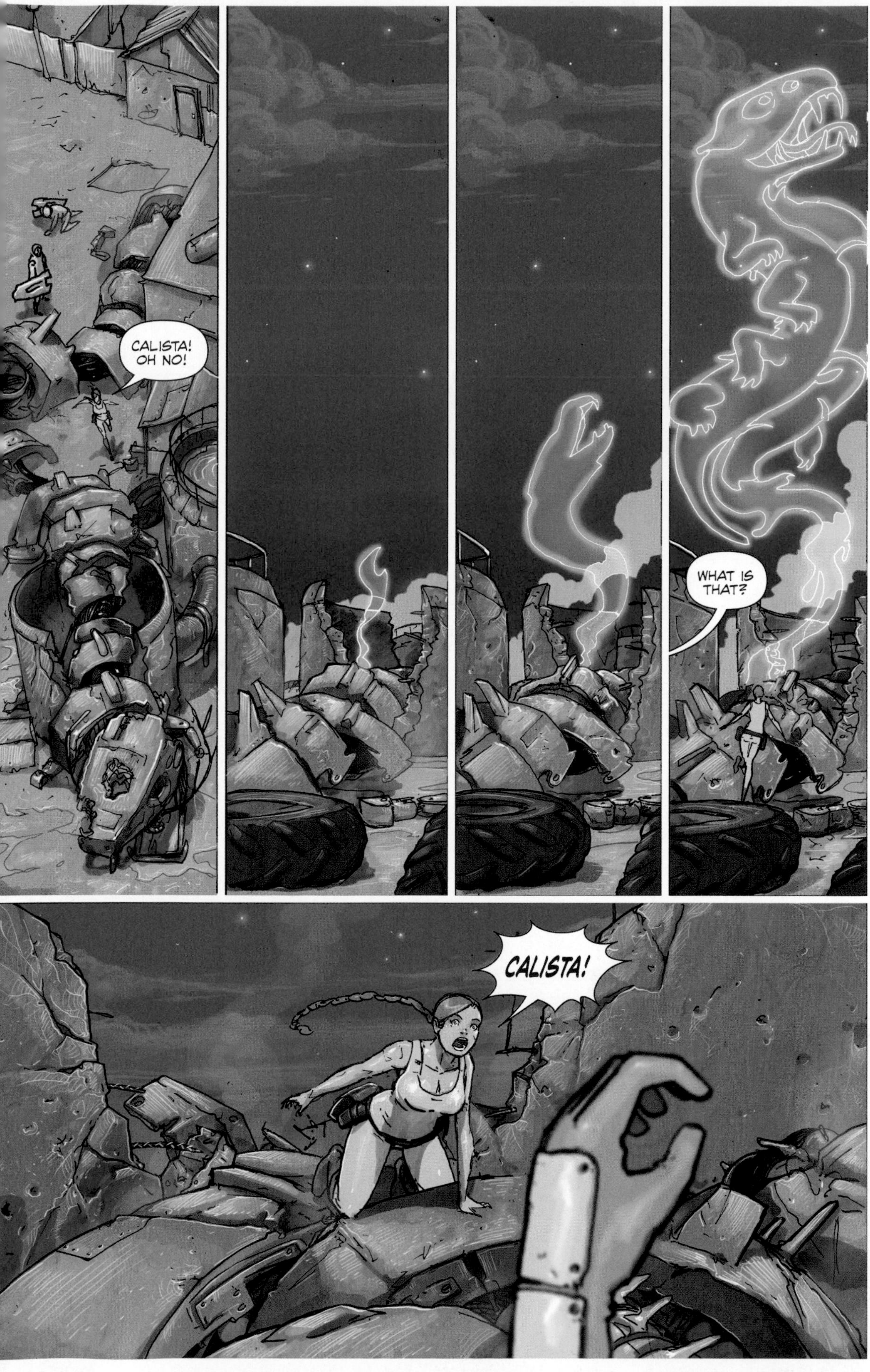
CALISTA! OH NO!
WHAT IS THAT?
CALISTA!

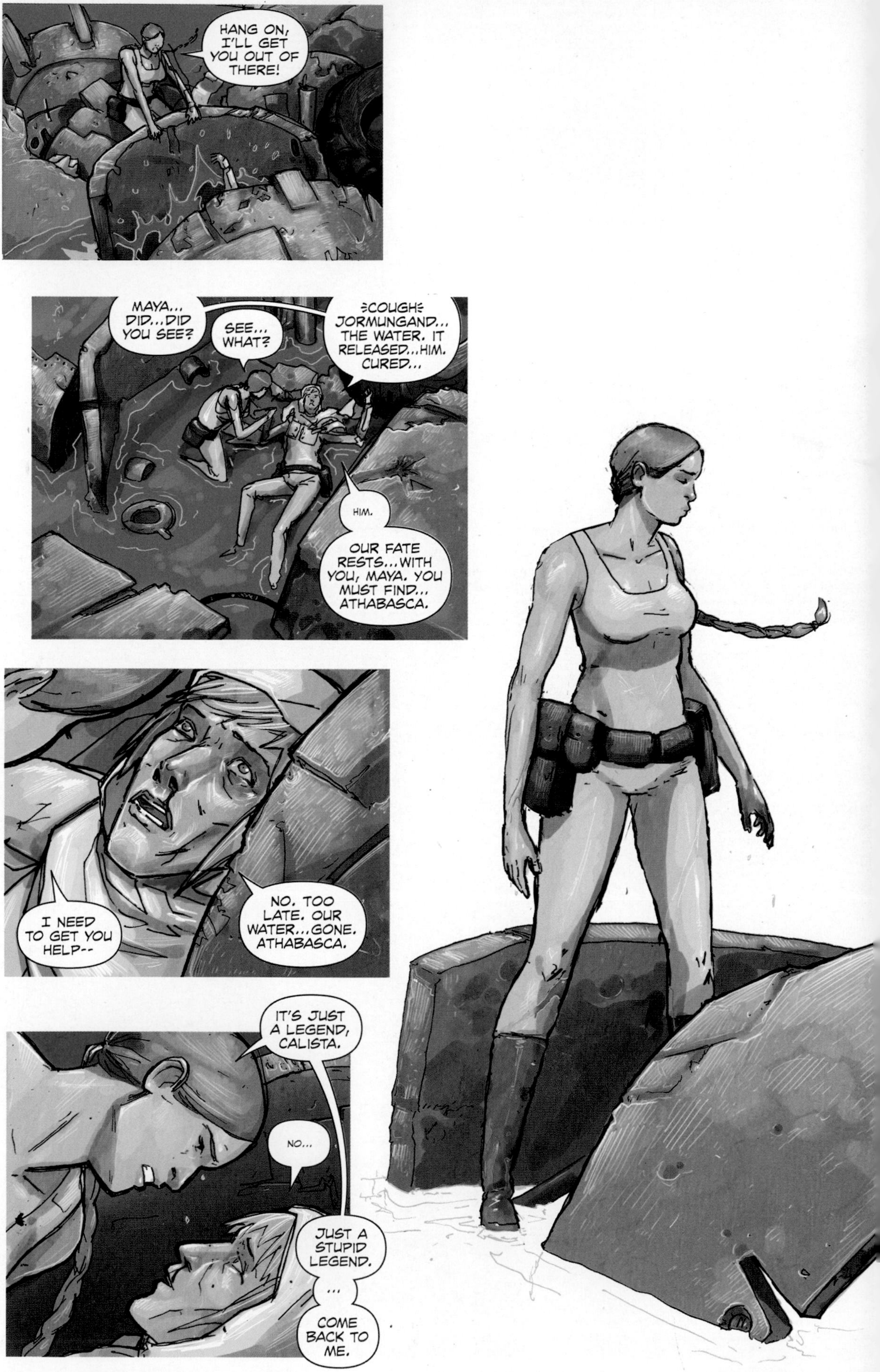
HANG ON, I'LL GET YOU OUT OF THERE!
MAYA... DID...DID YOU SEE?
SEE... WHAT?
≈COUGH≈ JORMUNGAND... THE WATER. IT RELEASED...HIM. CURED...
HIM.
OUR FATE RESTS...WITH YOU, MAYA. YOU MUST FIND... ATHABASCA.
I NEED TO GET YOU HELP--
NO. TOO LATE. OUR WATER...GONE. ATHABASCA.
IT'S JUST A LEGEND, CALISTA.
NO...
JUST A STUPID LEGEND.
...
COME BACK TO ME.

"NO ONE HAS GONE BEYOND THE LINE, MAYA. I CANNOT ALLOW IT. YOU MUST STAY HERE AND TAKE CALISTA'S PLACE."

"WE NEED WATER."

"WE CAN REBUILD THE DEVICE EASIER THAN WE COULD DISCOVER A FICTIONAL PLACE. YOU KNOW THIS."

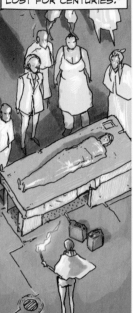

"NONE OF US UNDERSTOOD HOW THE DEVICE WORKED, COUNCILOR. THAT KNOWLEDGE HAS BEEN LOST FOR CENTURIES."

"YOU WILL NOT BE SWAYED?"

"WOULD YOU BE?"

"CALISTA WAS RIGHT. YES, YOU ARE READY..."

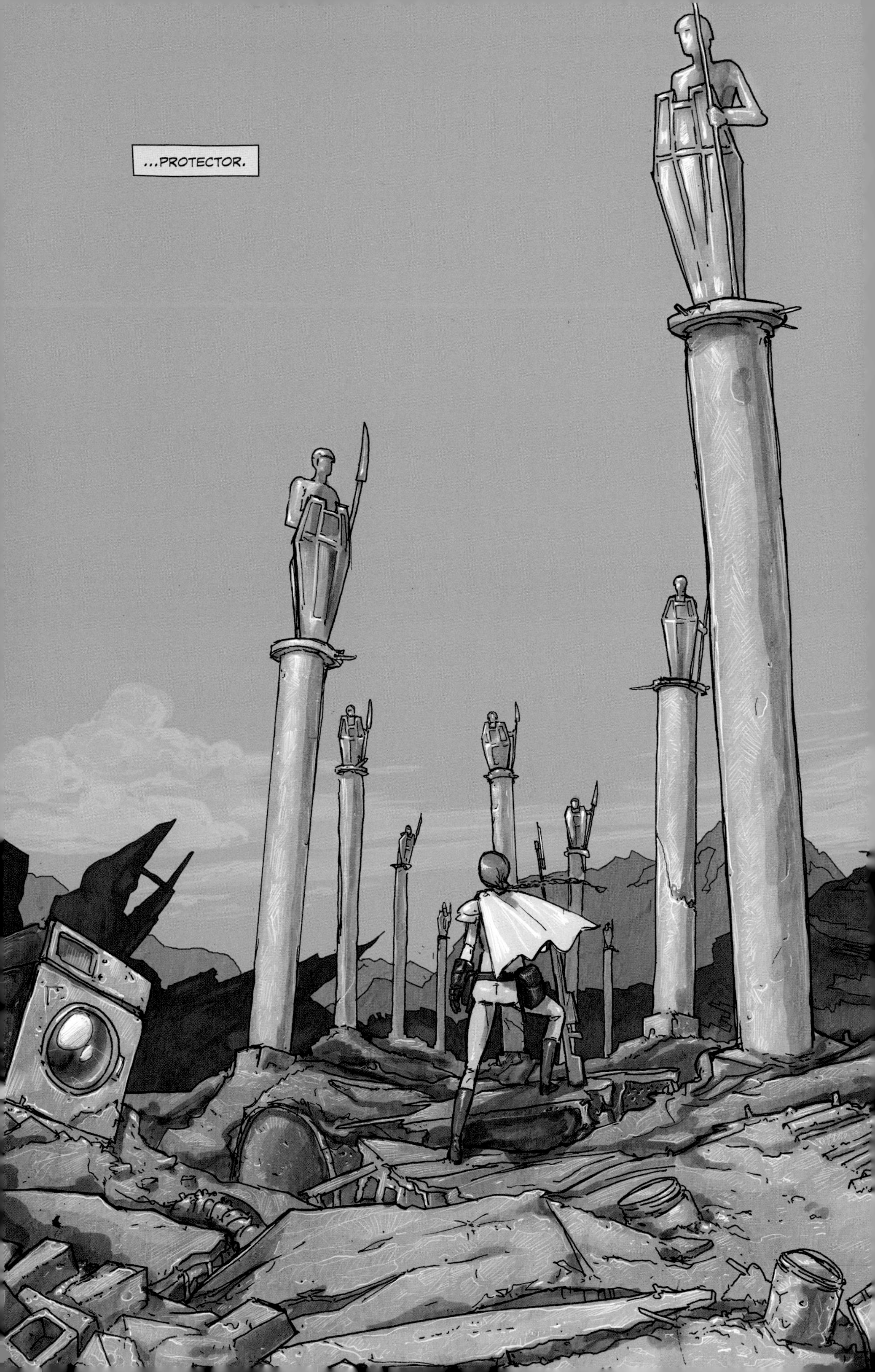
...PROTECTOR.

TWO

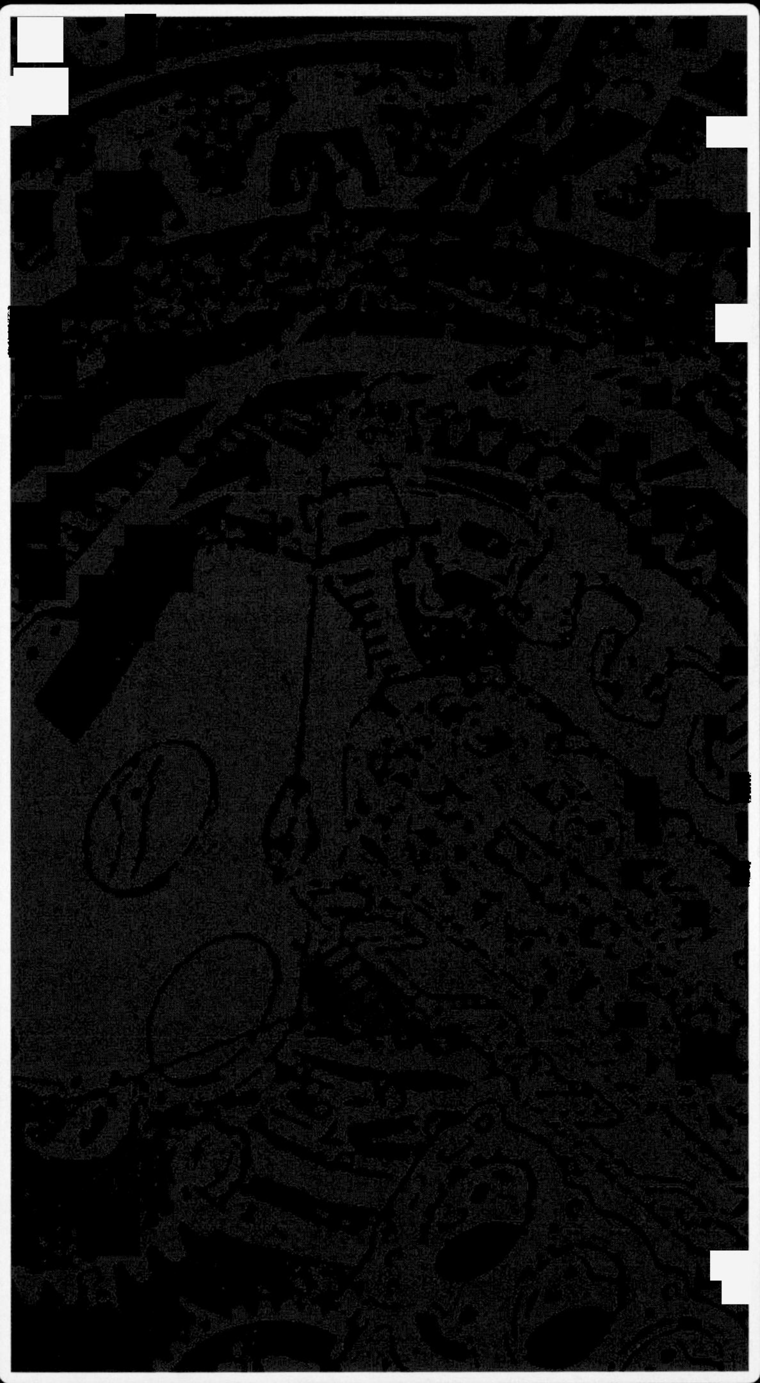

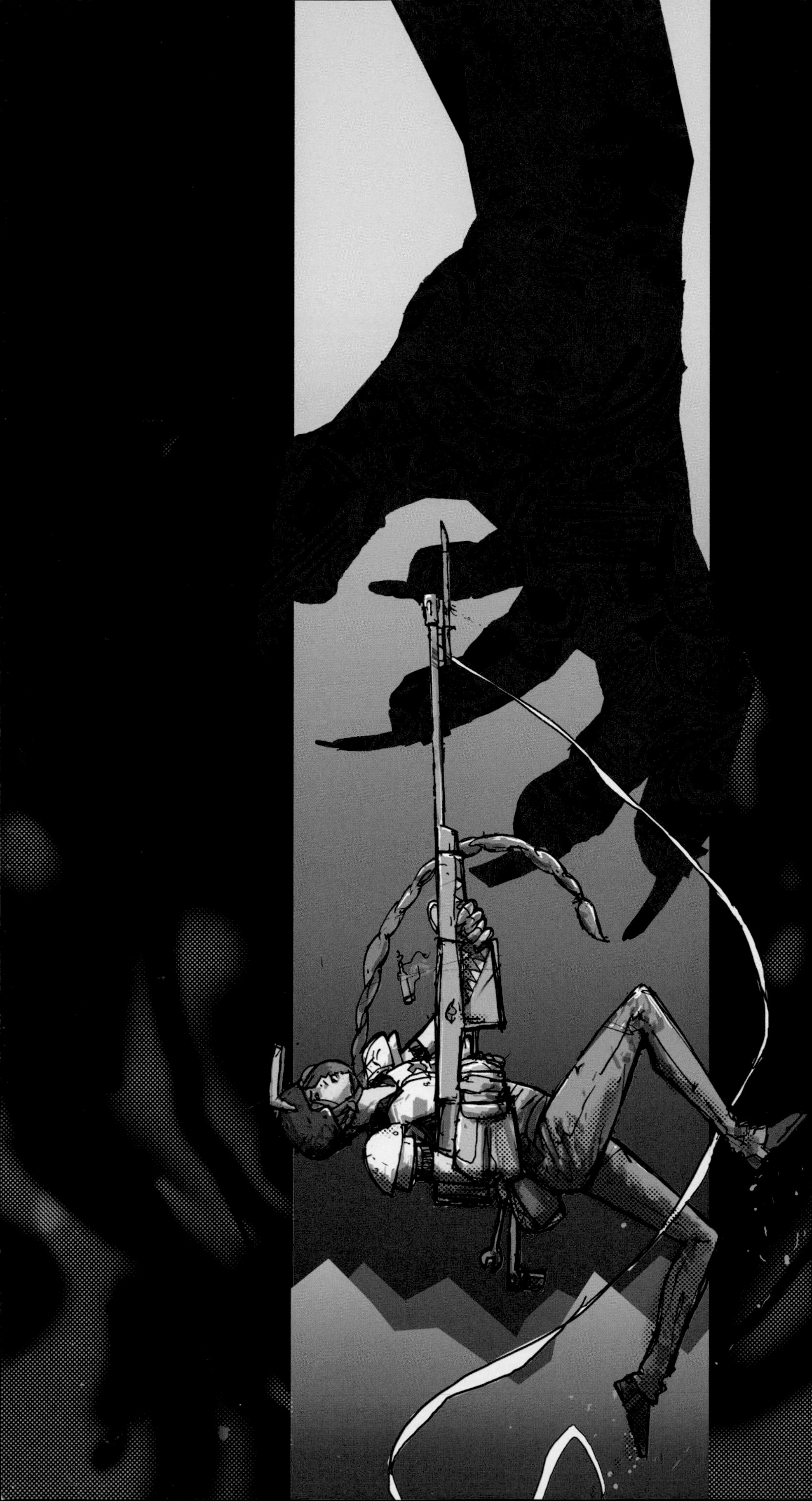

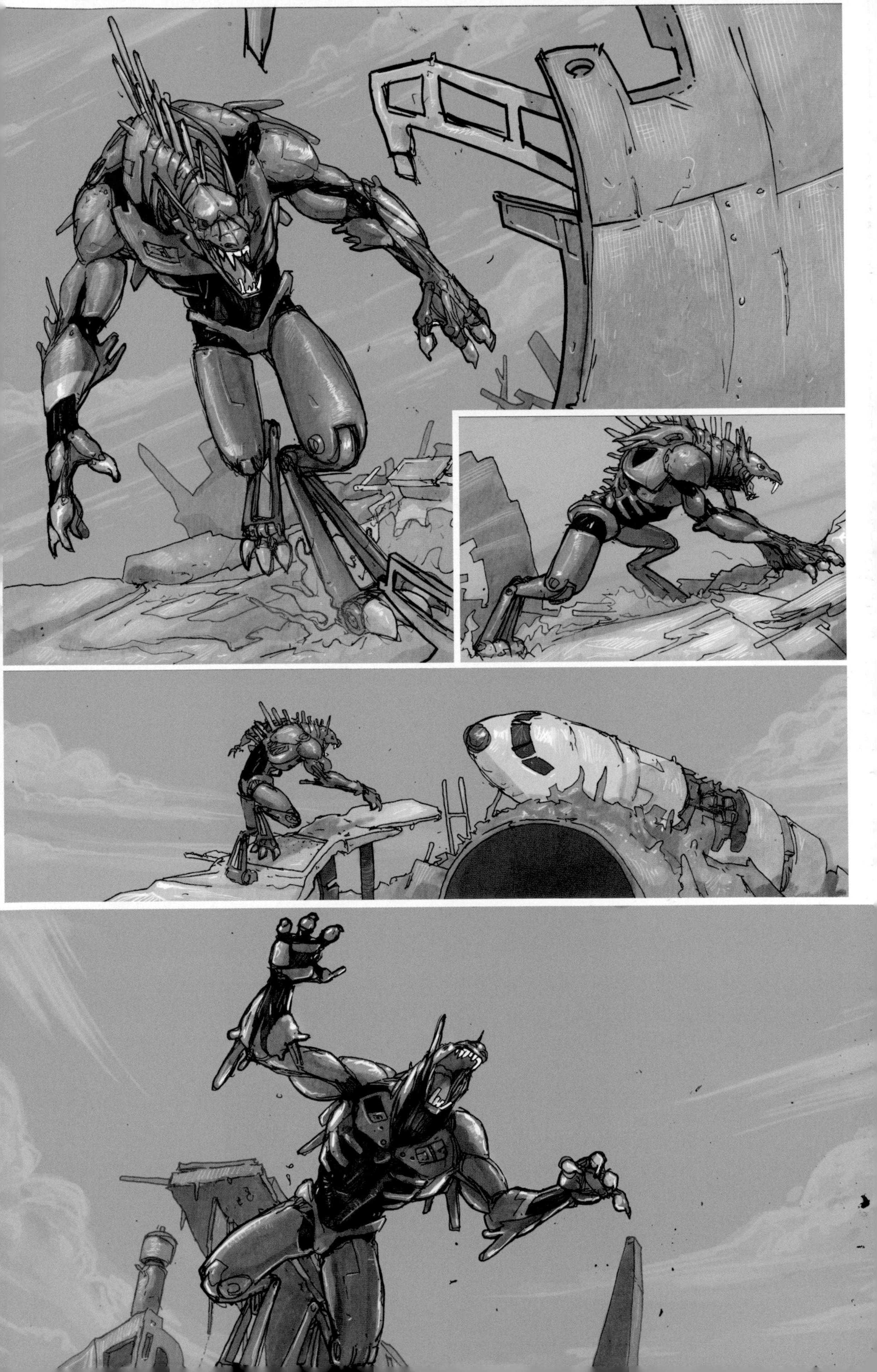

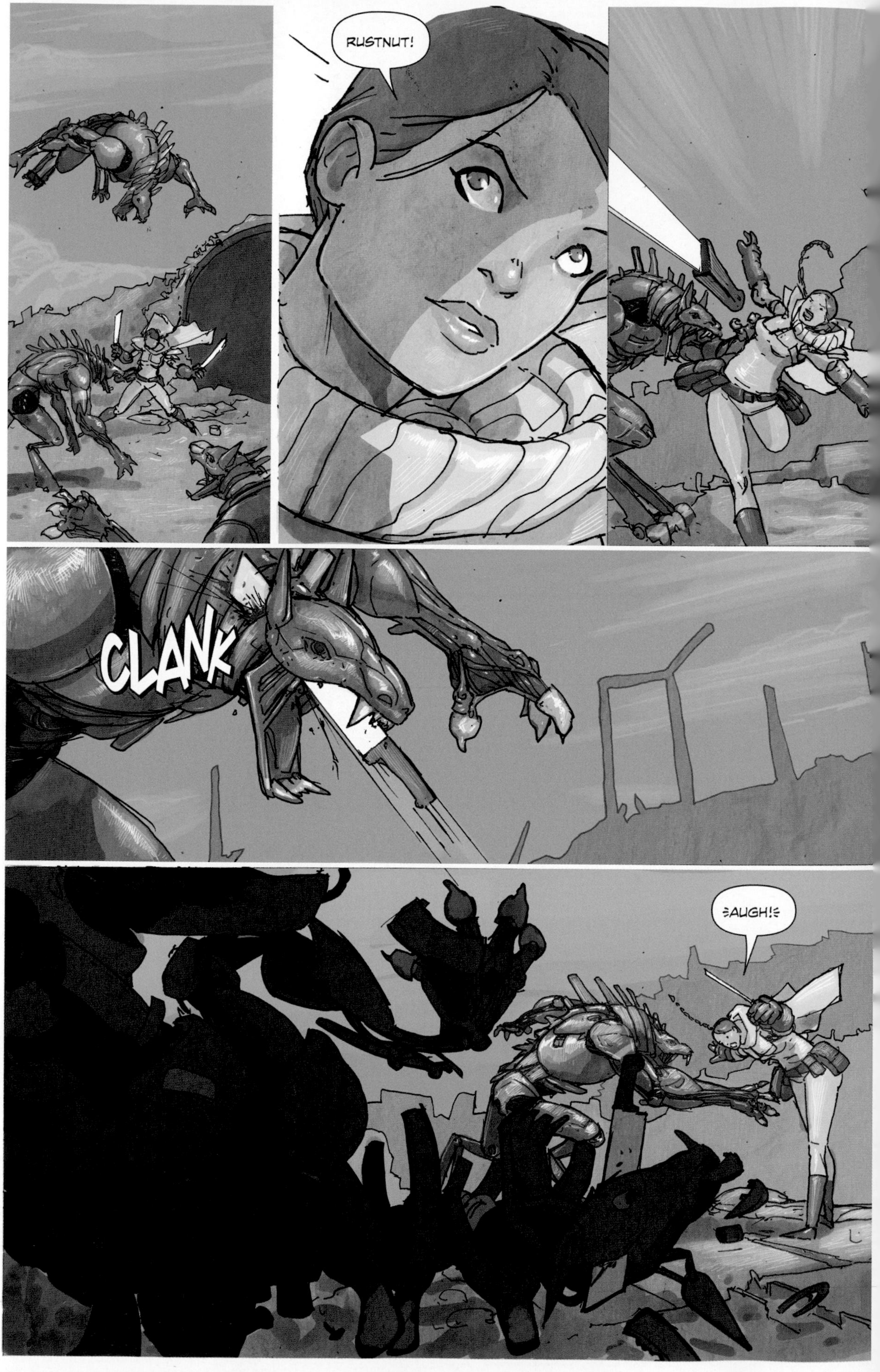
RUSTNUT!
CLANK
AUGH!

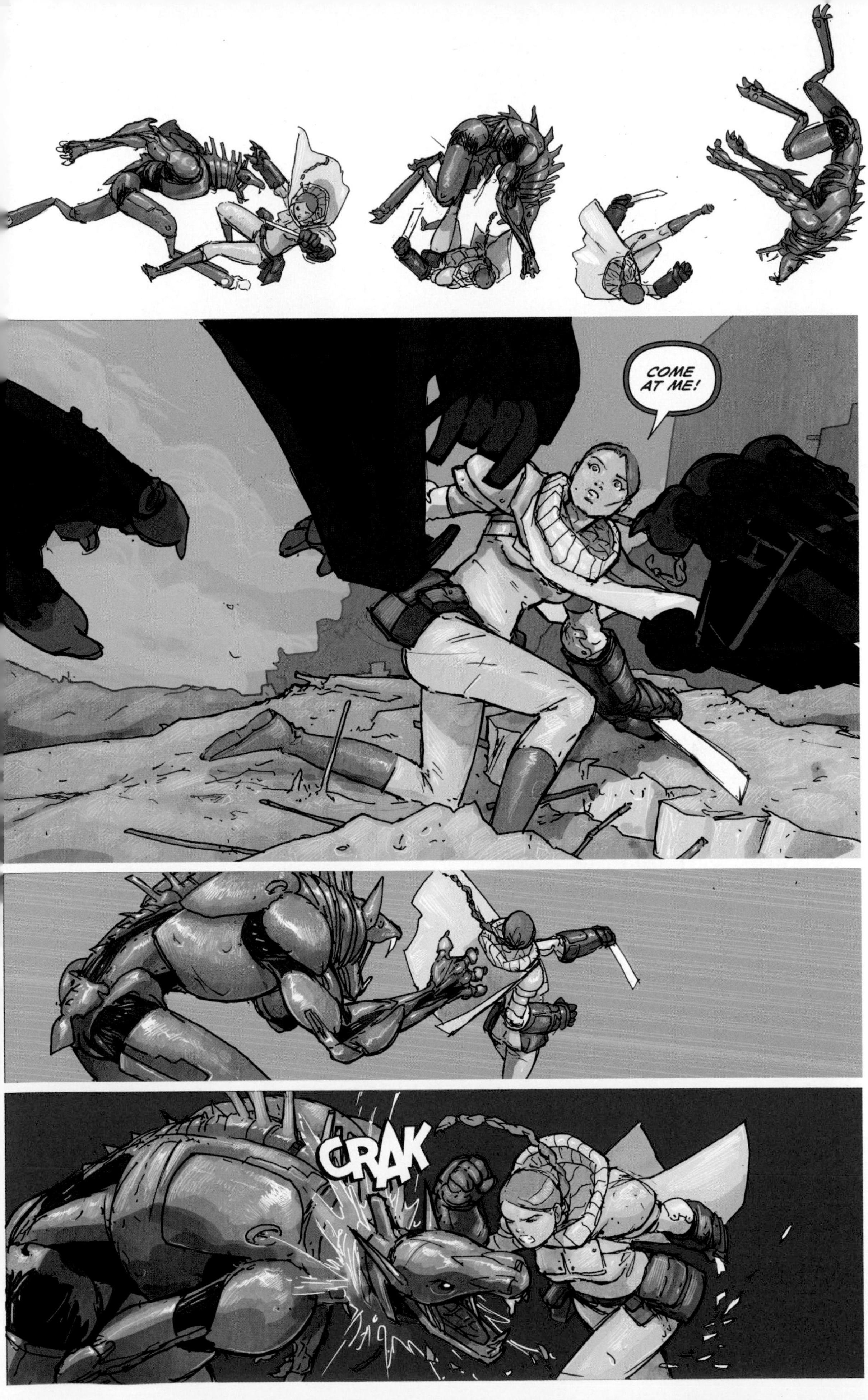
COME AT ME!
CRAK

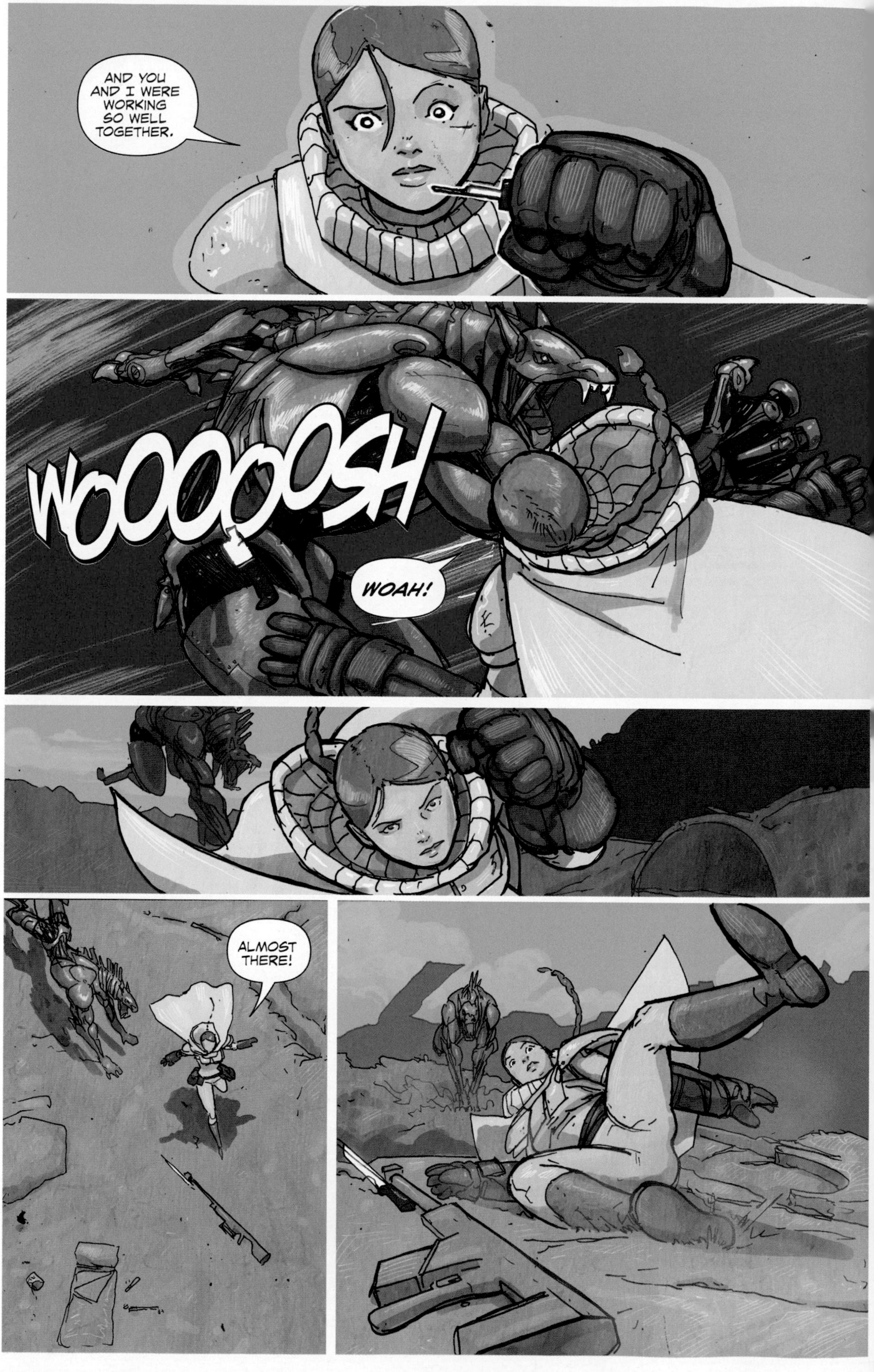
AND YOU AND I WERE WORKING SO WELL TOGETHER.
WOOOOOSH
WOAH!
ALMOST THERE!

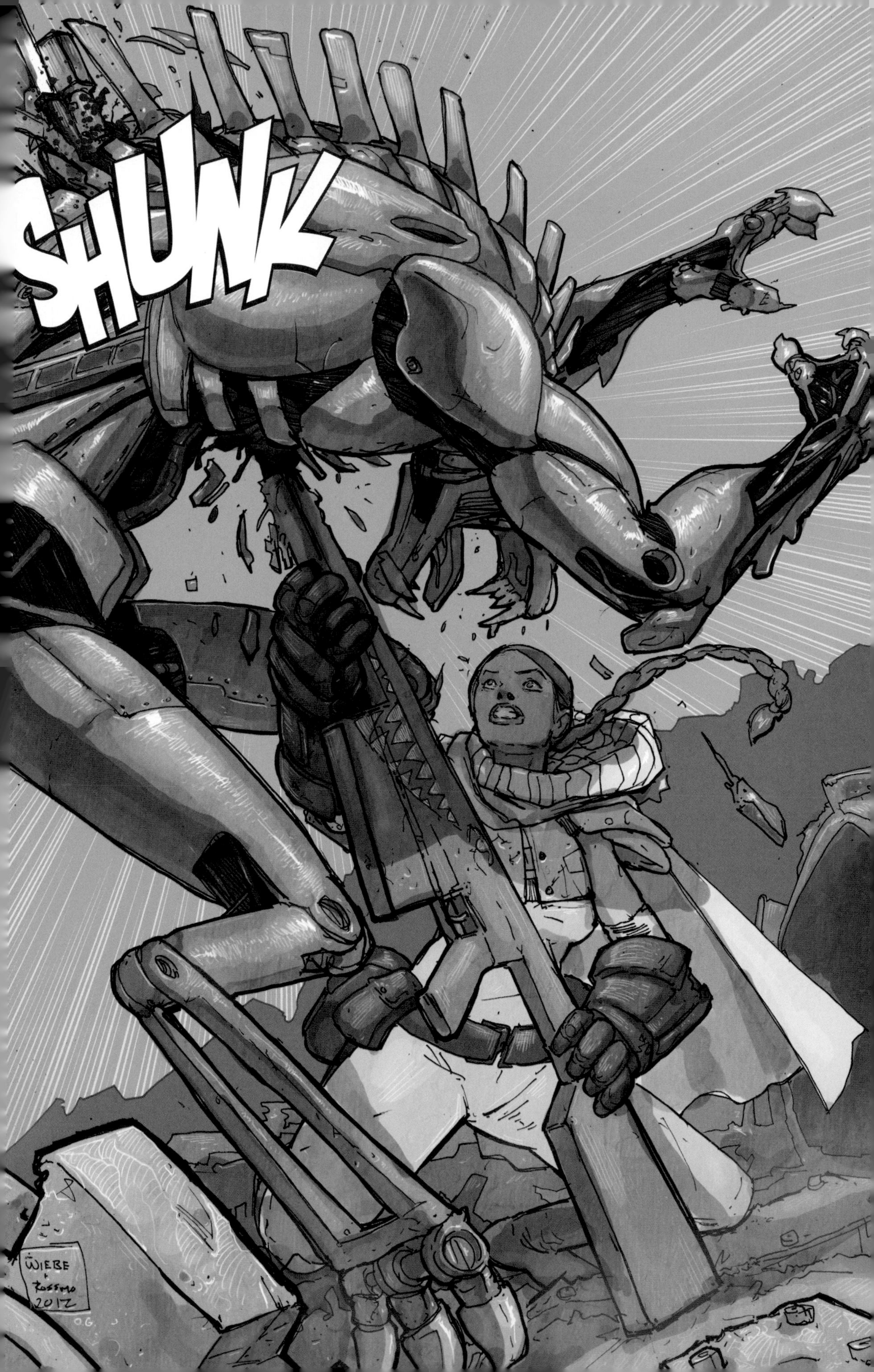
SHUNK
WIEBE + ROSSMO 2012

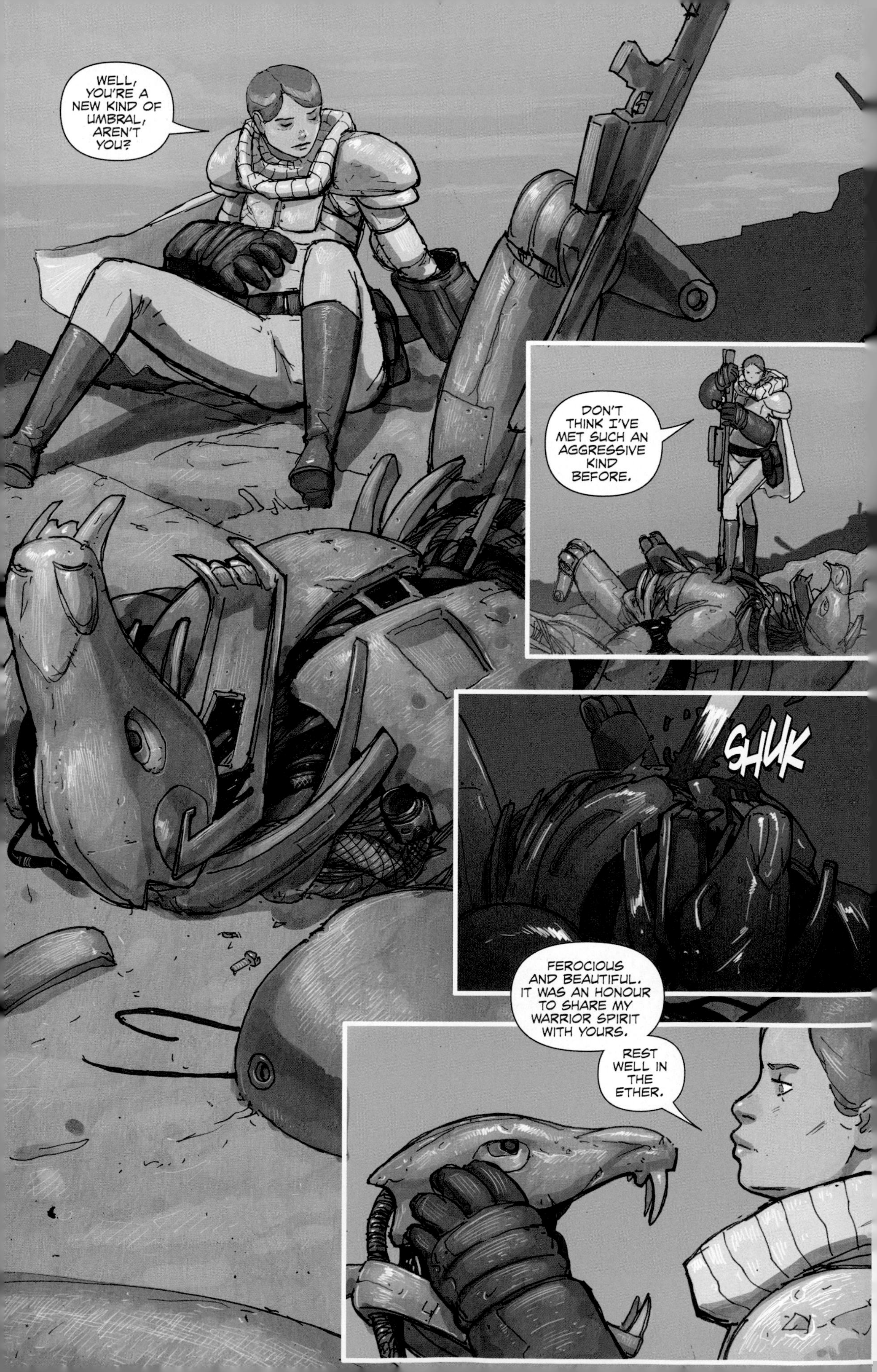
WELL, YOU'RE A NEW KIND OF UMBRAL, AREN'T YOU?
DON'T THINK I'VE MET SUCH AN AGGRESSIVE KIND BEFORE.
SHUK
FEROCIOUS AND BEAUTIFUL. IT WAS AN HONOUR TO SHARE MY WARRIOR SPIRIT WITH YOURS.
REST WELL IN THE ETHER.

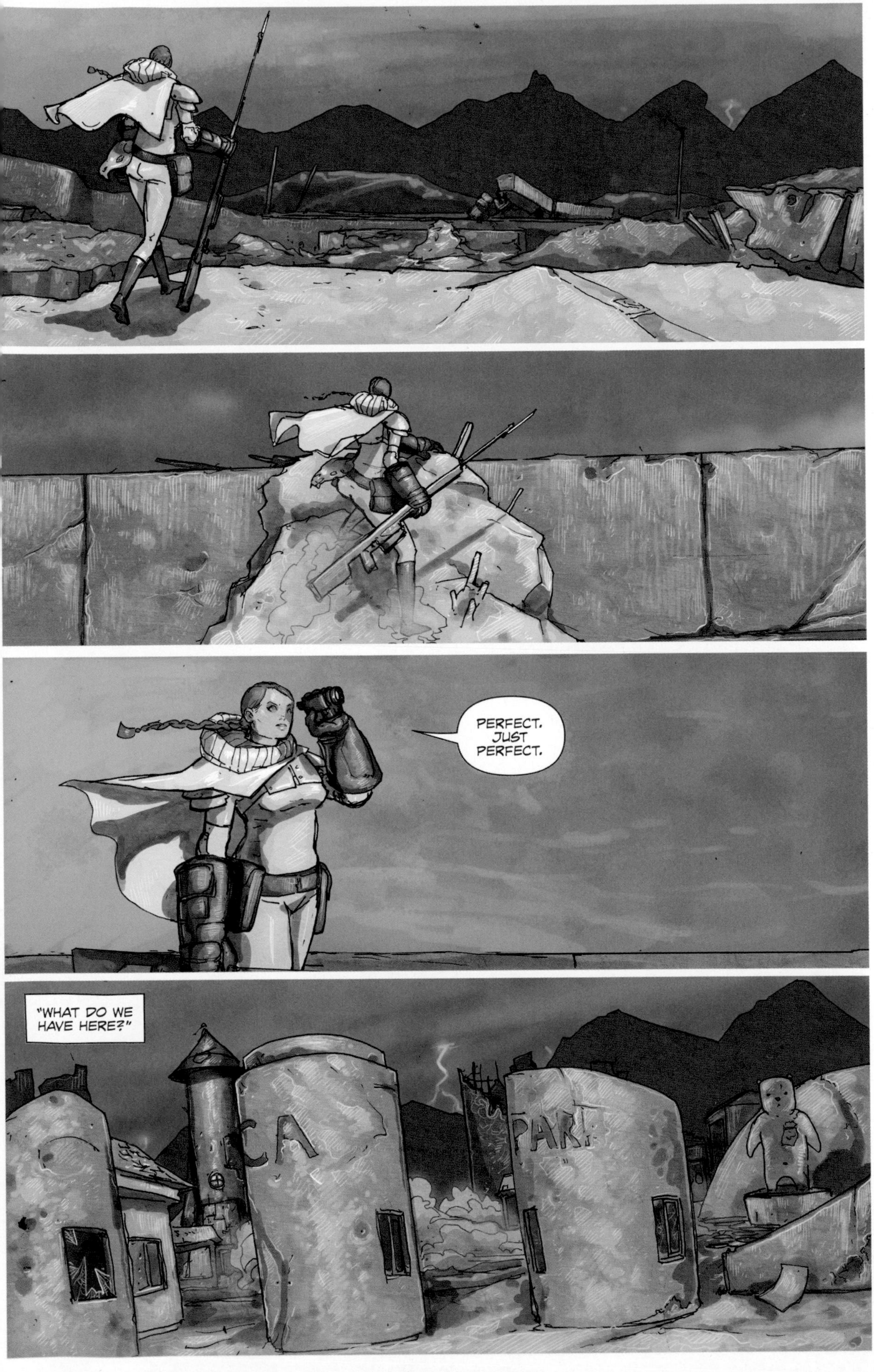
PERFECT. JUST PERFECT.
"WHAT DO WE HAVE HERE?"
CA
PAR

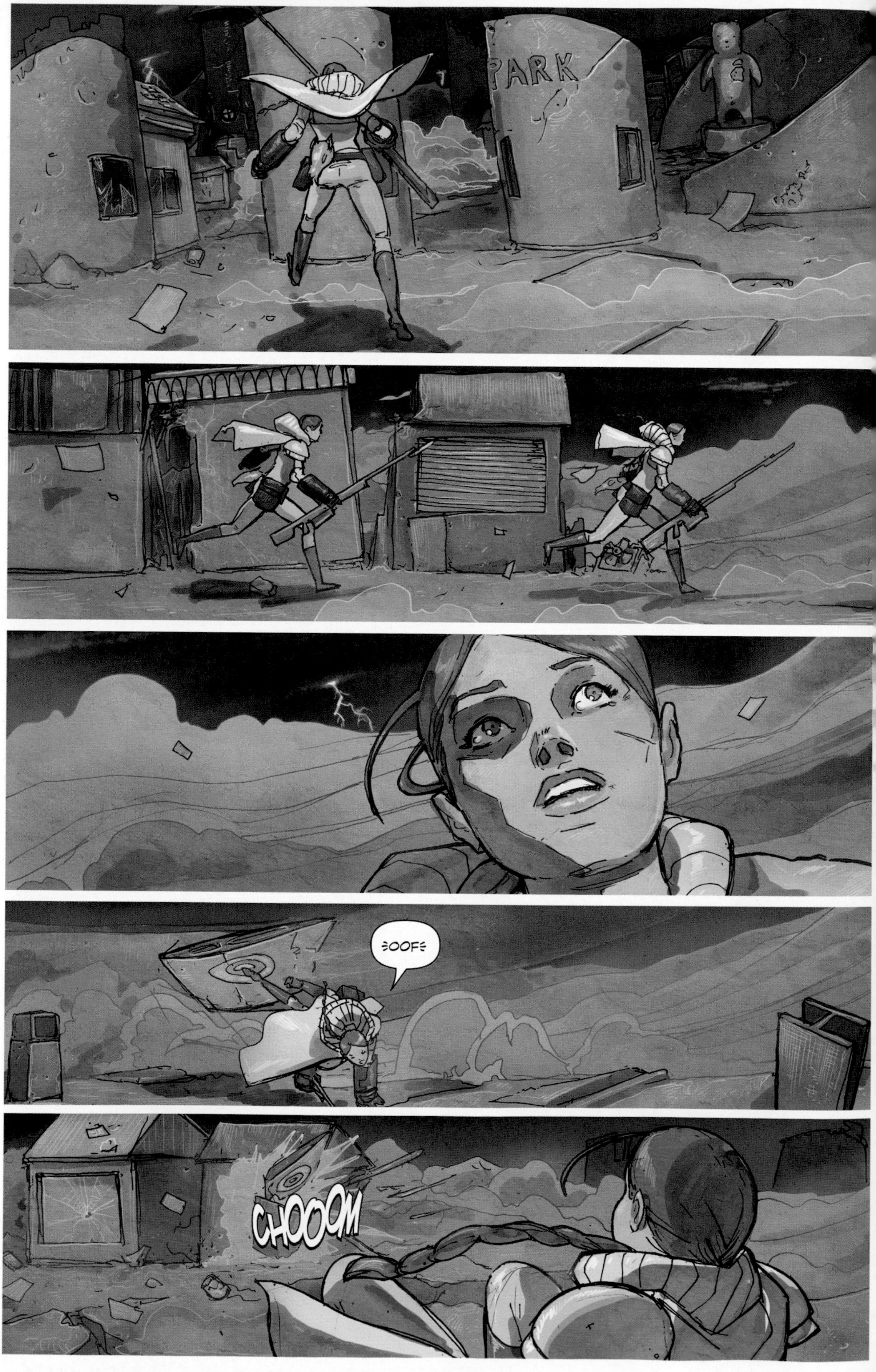
PARK
OOF
CHOOOM

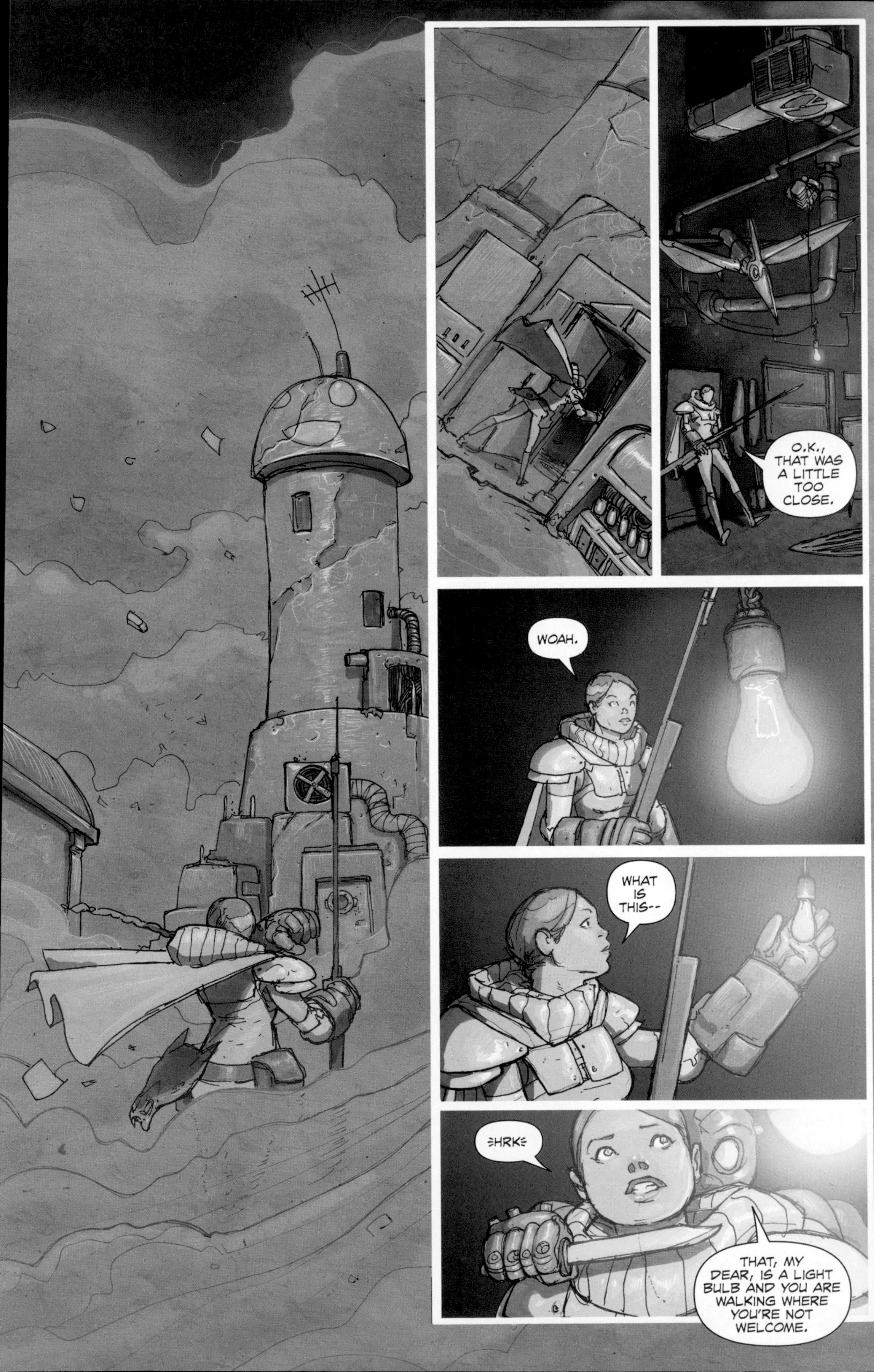
O.K., THAT WAS A LITTLE TOO CLOSE.
WOAH.
WHAT IS THIS--
≡HRK≡
THAT, MY DEAR, IS A LIGHT BULB AND YOU ARE WALKING WHERE YOU'RE NOT WELCOME.

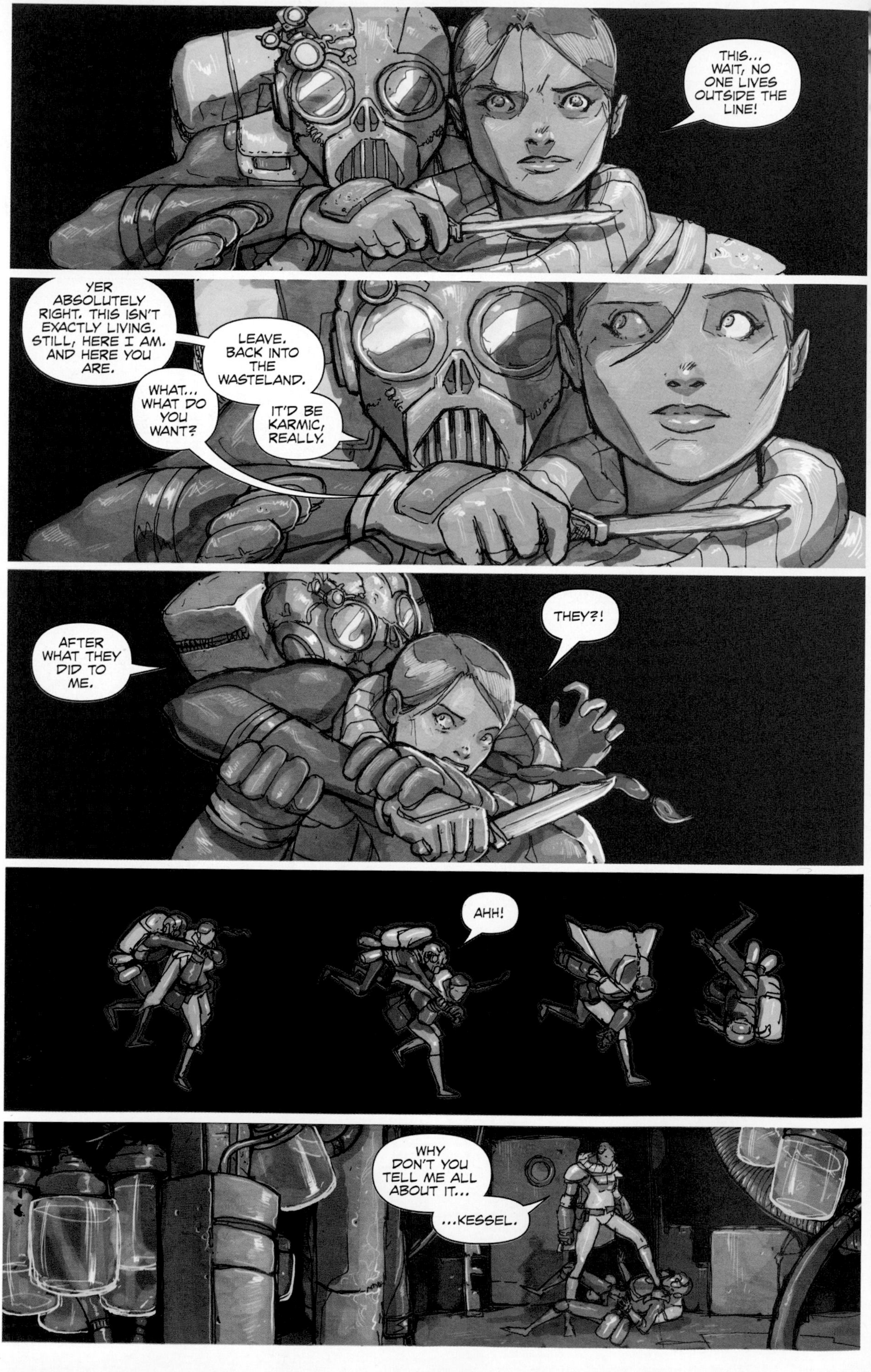
THIS... WAIT, NO ONE LIVES OUTSIDE THE LINE!
YER ABSOLUTELY RIGHT. THIS ISN'T EXACTLY LIVING. STILL, HERE I AM. AND HERE YOU ARE.
LEAVE. BACK INTO THE WASTELAND.
WHAT... WHAT DO YOU WANT?
IT'D BE KARMIC, REALLY.
AFTER WHAT THEY DID TO ME.
THEY?!
AHH!
WHY DON'T YOU TELL ME ALL ABOUT IT...
...KESSEL.

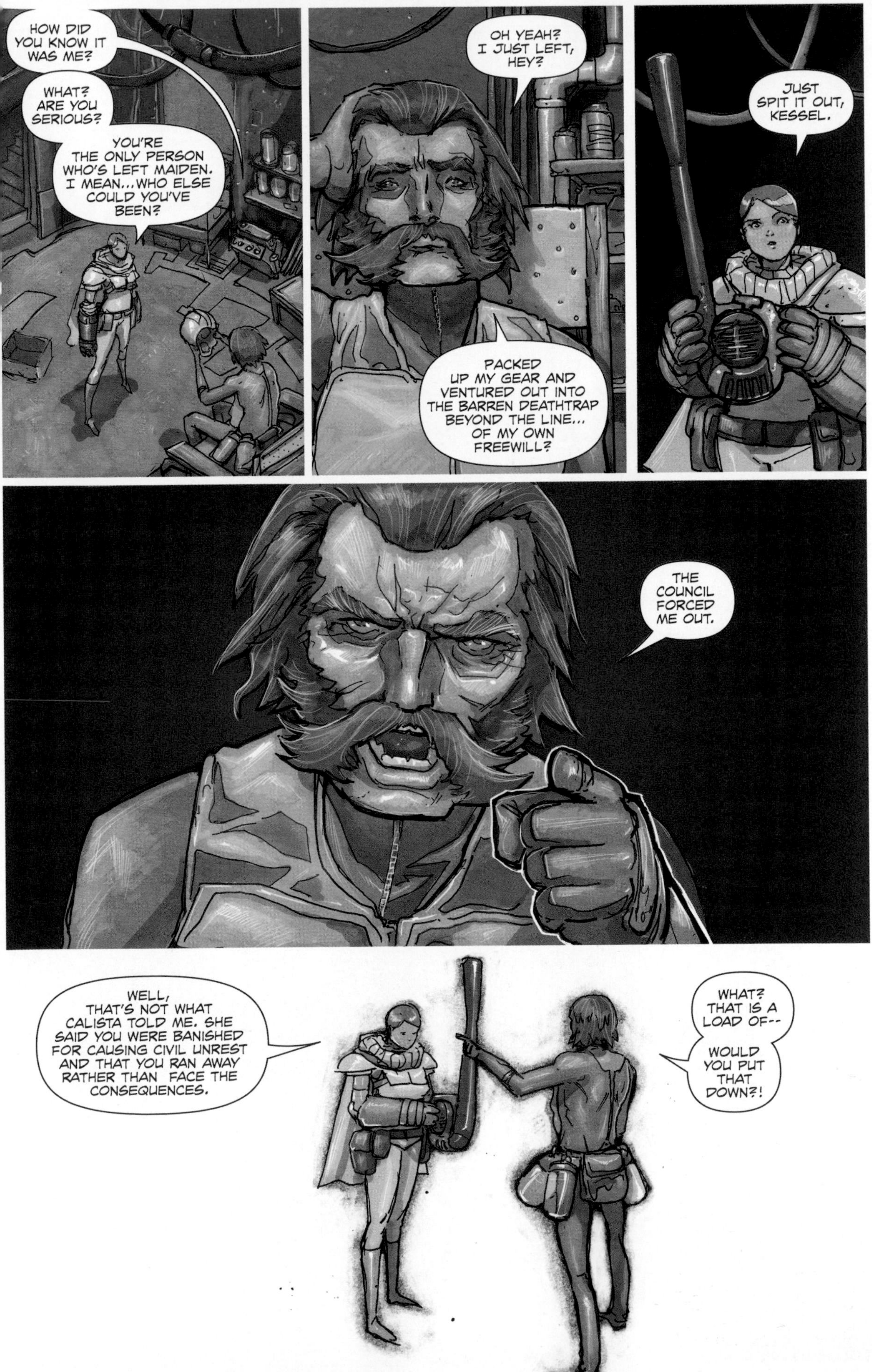
HOW DID YOU KNOW IT WAS ME?
WHAT? ARE YOU SERIOUS?
YOU'RE THE ONLY PERSON WHO'S LEFT MAIDEN. I MEAN...WHO ELSE COULD YOU'VE BEEN?
OH YEAH? I JUST LEFT, HEY?
PACKED UP MY GEAR AND VENTURED OUT INTO THE BARREN DEATHTRAP BEYOND THE LINE... OF MY OWN FREEWILL?
JUST SPIT IT OUT, KESSEL.
THE COUNCIL FORCED ME OUT.
WELL, THAT'S NOT WHAT CALISTA TOLD ME. SHE SAID YOU WERE BANISHED FOR CAUSING CIVIL UNREST AND THAT YOU RAN AWAY RATHER THAN FACE THE CONSEQUENCES.
WHAT? THAT IS A LOAD OF--
WOULD YOU PUT THAT DOWN?!

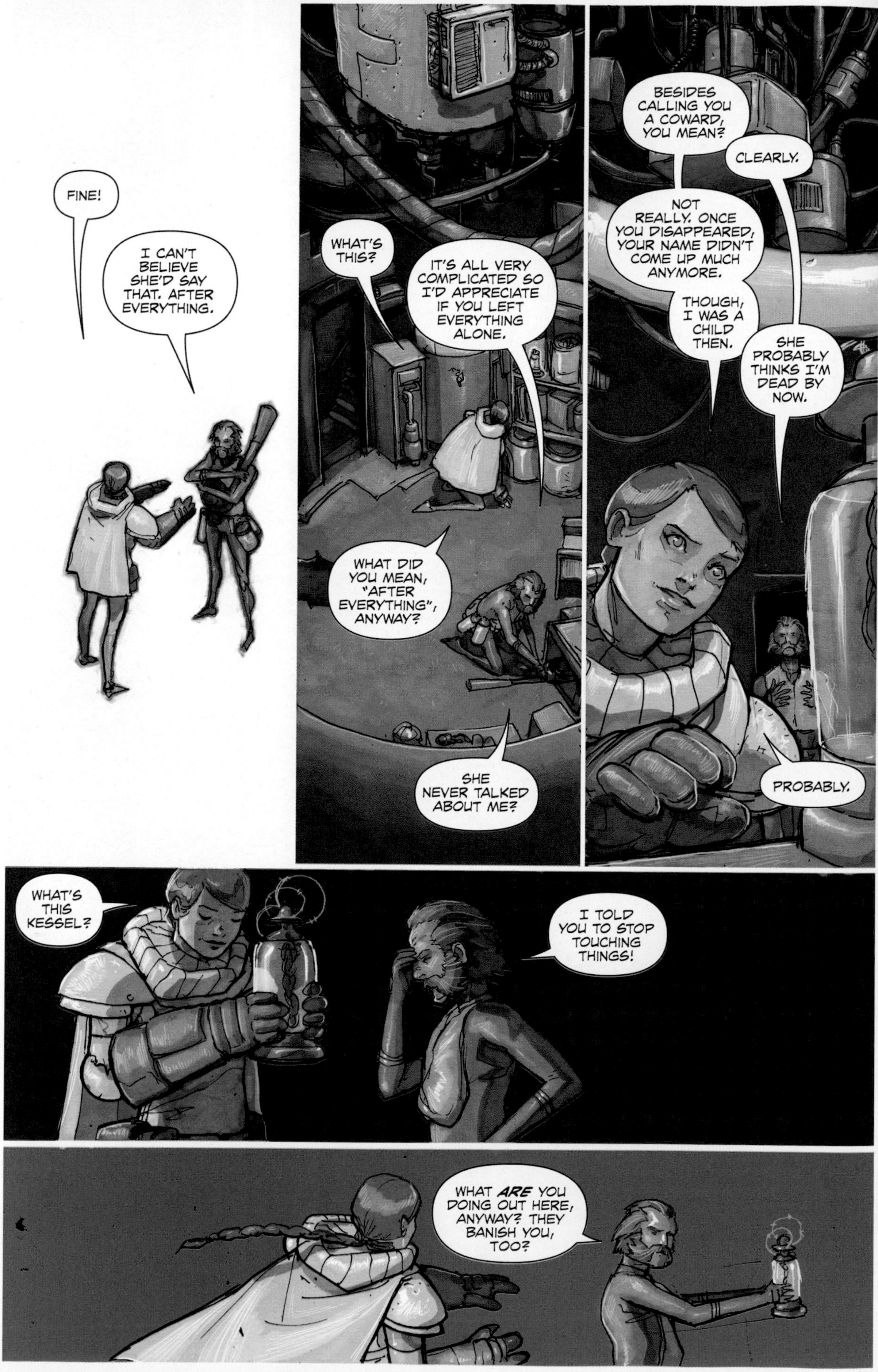
FINE!
I CAN'T BELIEVE SHE'D SAY THAT. AFTER EVERYTHING.
WHAT'S THIS?
IT'S ALL VERY COMPLICATED SO I'D APPRECIATE IF YOU LEFT EVERYTHING ALONE.
WHAT DID YOU MEAN, "AFTER EVERYTHING", ANYWAY?
SHE NEVER TALKED ABOUT ME?
BESIDES CALLING YOU A COWARD, YOU MEAN?
CLEARLY.
NOT REALLY. ONCE YOU DISAPPEARED, YOUR NAME DIDN'T COME UP MUCH ANYMORE.
THOUGH, I WAS A CHILD THEN.
SHE PROBABLY THINKS I'M DEAD BY NOW.
PROBABLY.
WHAT'S THIS KESSEL?
I TOLD YOU TO STOP TOUCHING THINGS!
WHAT ***ARE*** YOU DOING OUT HERE, ANYWAY? THEY BANISH YOU, TOO?

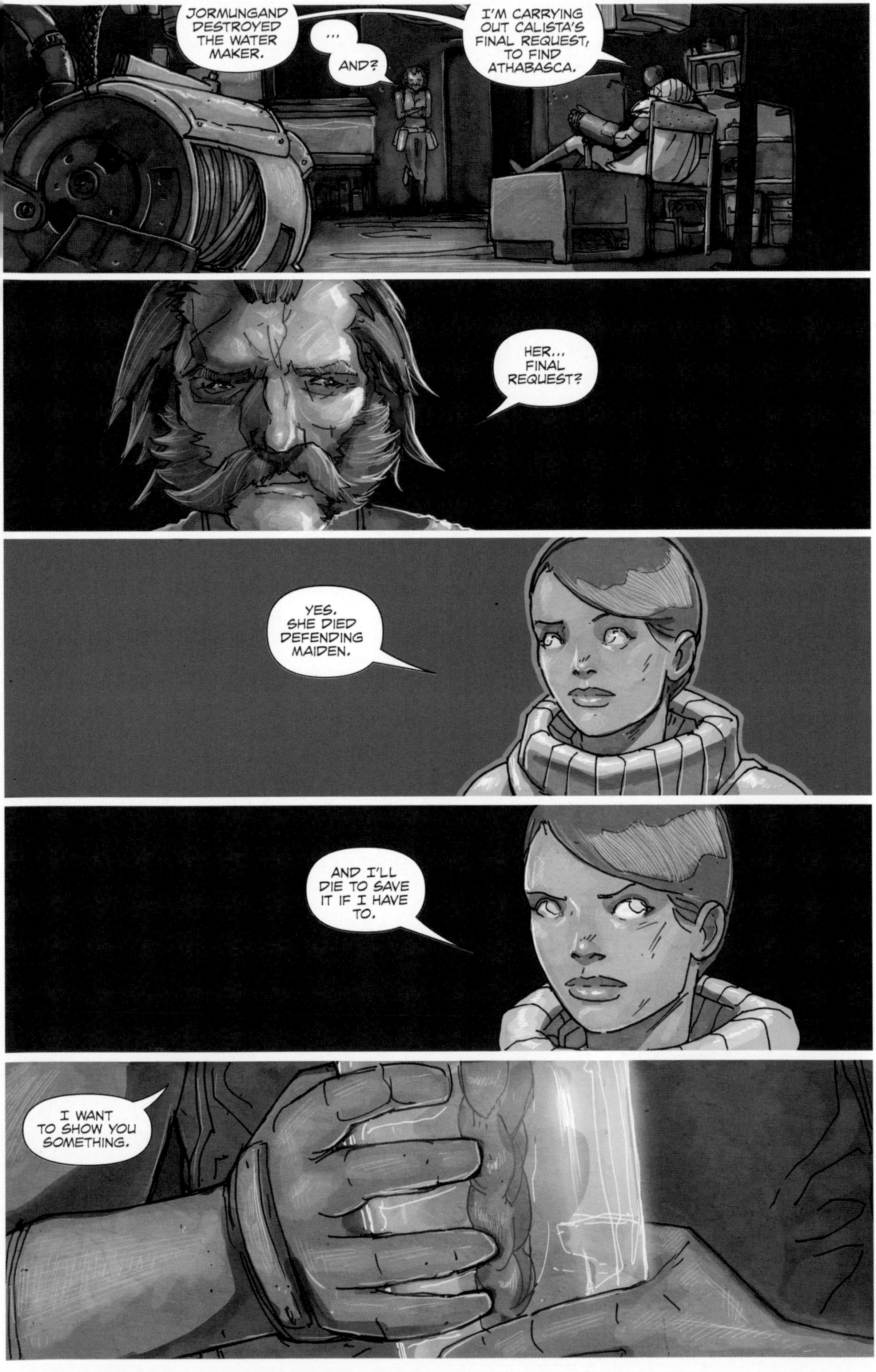

JORMUNGAND DESTROYED THE WATER MAKER.
...
AND?
I'M CARRYING OUT CALISTA'S FINAL REQUEST, TO FIND ATHABASCA.
HER... FINAL REQUEST?
YES. SHE DIED DEFENDING MAIDEN.
AND I'LL DIE TO SAVE IT IF I HAVE TO.
I WANT TO SHOW YOU SOMETHING.

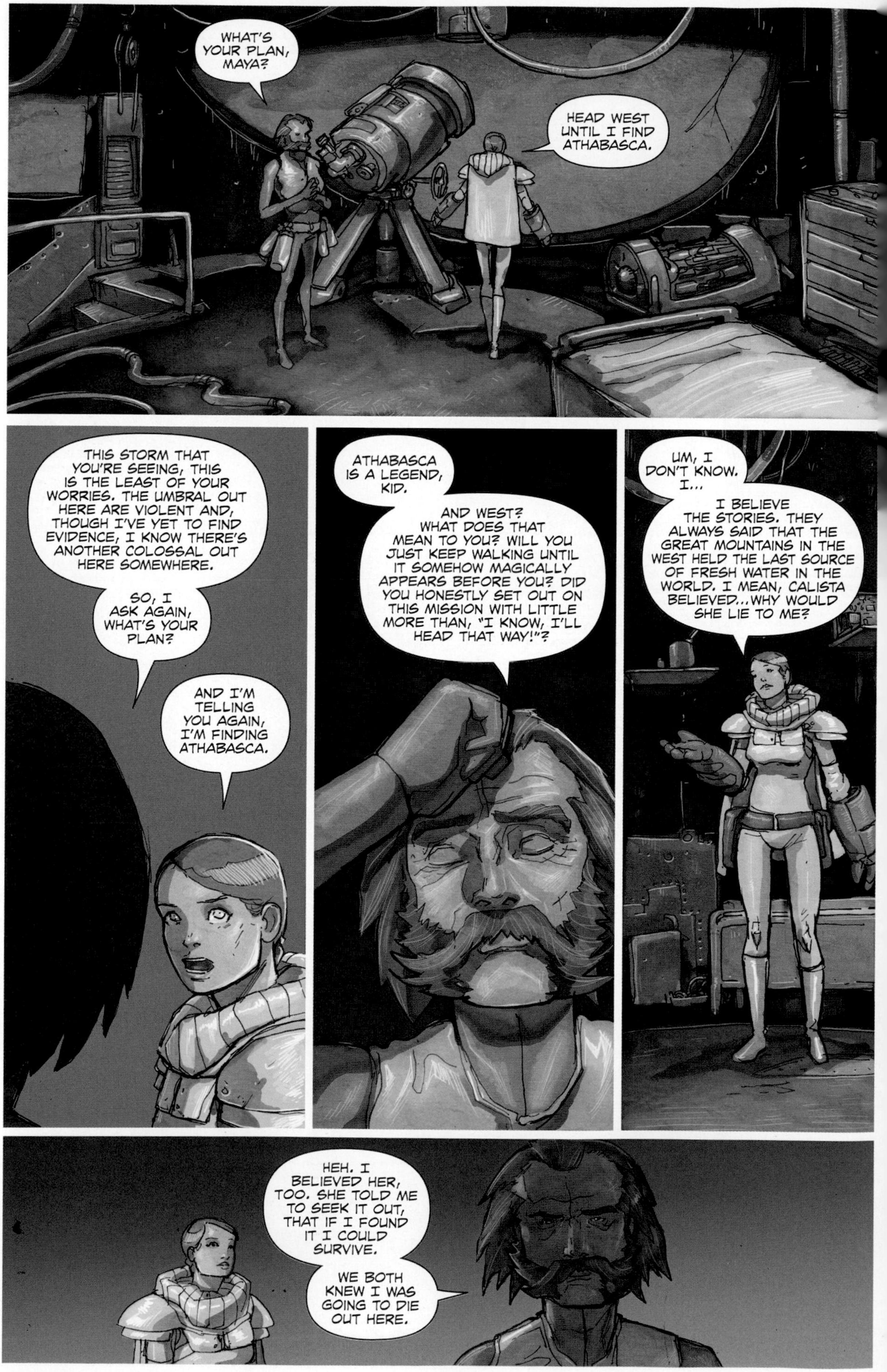
WHAT'S YOUR PLAN, MAYA?
HEAD WEST UNTIL I FIND ATHABASCA.
THIS STORM THAT YOU'RE SEEING, THIS IS THE LEAST OF YOUR WORRIES. THE UMBRAL OUT HERE ARE VIOLENT AND, THOUGH I'VE YET TO FIND EVIDENCE, I KNOW THERE'S ANOTHER COLOSSAL OUT HERE SOMEWHERE.
SO, I ASK AGAIN, WHAT'S YOUR PLAN?
AND I'M TELLING YOU AGAIN, I'M FINDING ATHABASCA.
ATHABASCA IS A LEGEND, KID.
AND WEST? WHAT DOES THAT MEAN TO YOU? WILL YOU JUST KEEP WALKING UNTIL IT SOMEHOW MAGICALLY APPEARS BEFORE YOU? DID YOU HONESTLY SET OUT ON THIS MISSION WITH LITTLE MORE THAN, "I KNOW, I'LL HEAD THAT WAY!"?
UM, I DON'T KNOW. I...
I BELIEVE THE STORIES. THEY ALWAYS SAID THAT THE GREAT MOUNTAINS IN THE WEST HELD THE LAST SOURCE OF FRESH WATER IN THE WORLD. I MEAN, CALISTA BELIEVED...WHY WOULD SHE LIE TO ME?
HEH. I BELIEVED HER, TOO. SHE TOLD ME TO SEEK IT OUT, THAT IF I FOUND IT I COULD SURVIVE.
WE BOTH KNEW I WAS GOING TO DIE OUT HERE.

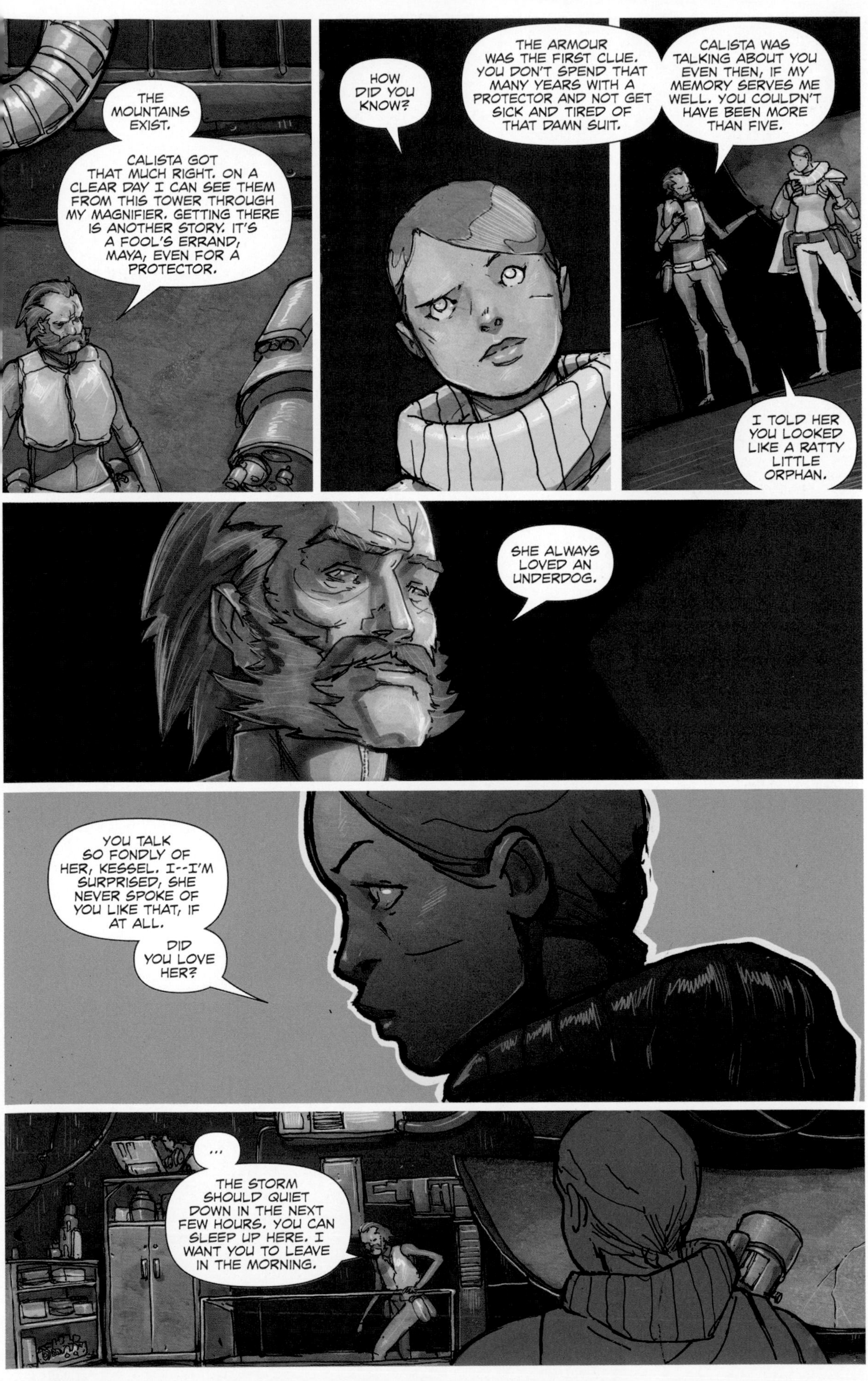
THE MOUNTAINS EXIST.
CALISTA GOT THAT MUCH RIGHT. ON A CLEAR DAY I CAN SEE THEM FROM THIS TOWER THROUGH MY MAGNIFIER. GETTING THERE IS ANOTHER STORY. IT'S A FOOL'S ERRAND, MAYA, EVEN FOR A PROTECTOR.
HOW DID YOU KNOW?
THE ARMOUR WAS THE FIRST CLUE. YOU DON'T SPEND THAT MANY YEARS WITH A PROTECTOR AND NOT GET SICK AND TIRED OF THAT DAMN SUIT.
CALISTA WAS TALKING ABOUT YOU EVEN THEN, IF MY MEMORY SERVES ME WELL. YOU COULDN'T HAVE BEEN MORE THAN FIVE.
I TOLD HER YOU LOOKED LIKE A RATTY LITTLE ORPHAN.
SHE ALWAYS LOVED AN UNDERDOG.
YOU TALK SO FONDLY OF HER, KESSEL. I--I'M SURPRISED, SHE NEVER SPOKE OF YOU LIKE THAT, IF AT ALL.
DID YOU LOVE HER?
...
THE STORM SHOULD QUIET DOWN IN THE NEXT FEW HOURS. YOU CAN SLEEP UP HERE. I WANT YOU TO LEAVE IN THE MORNING.

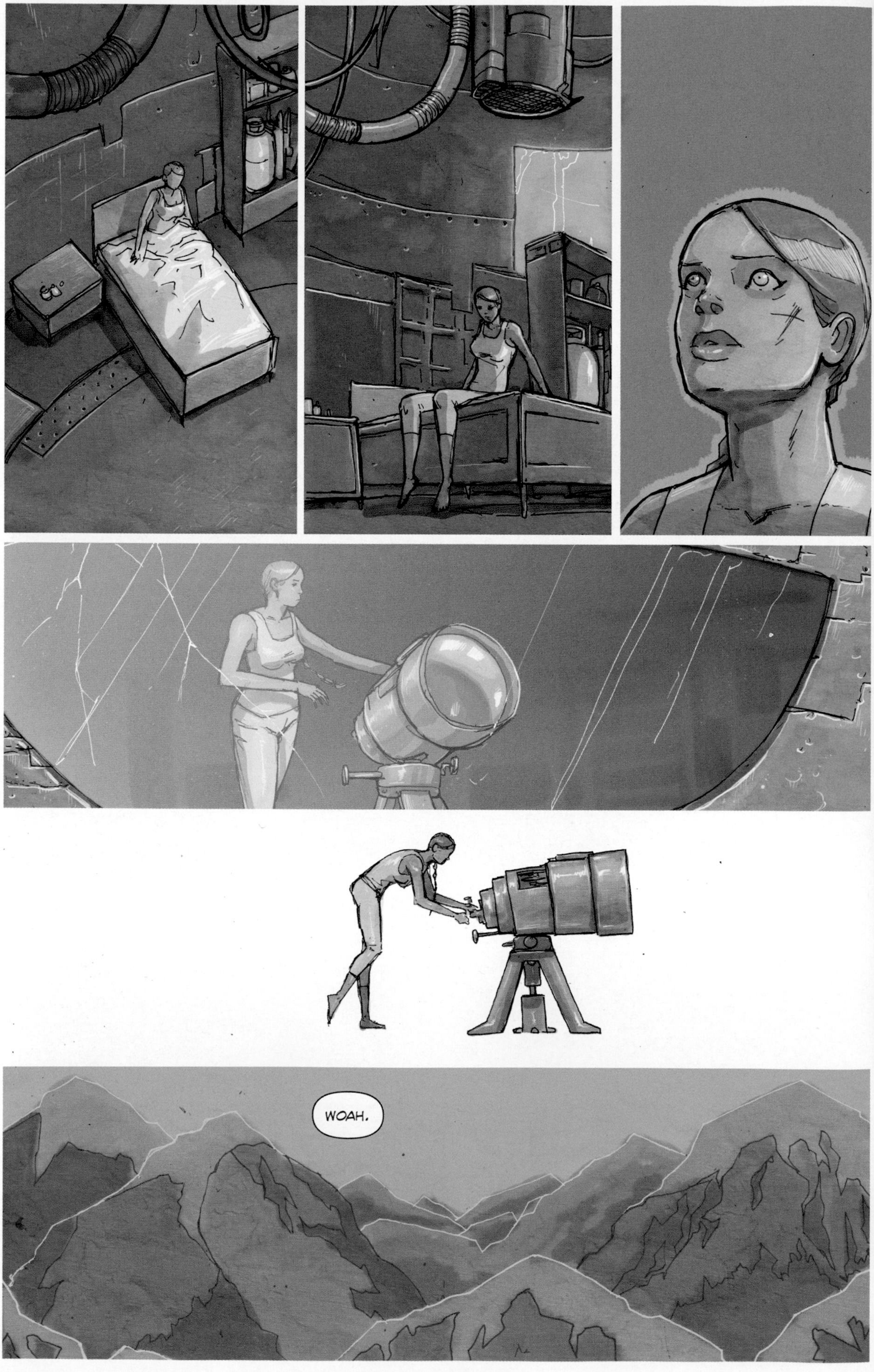
WOAH.

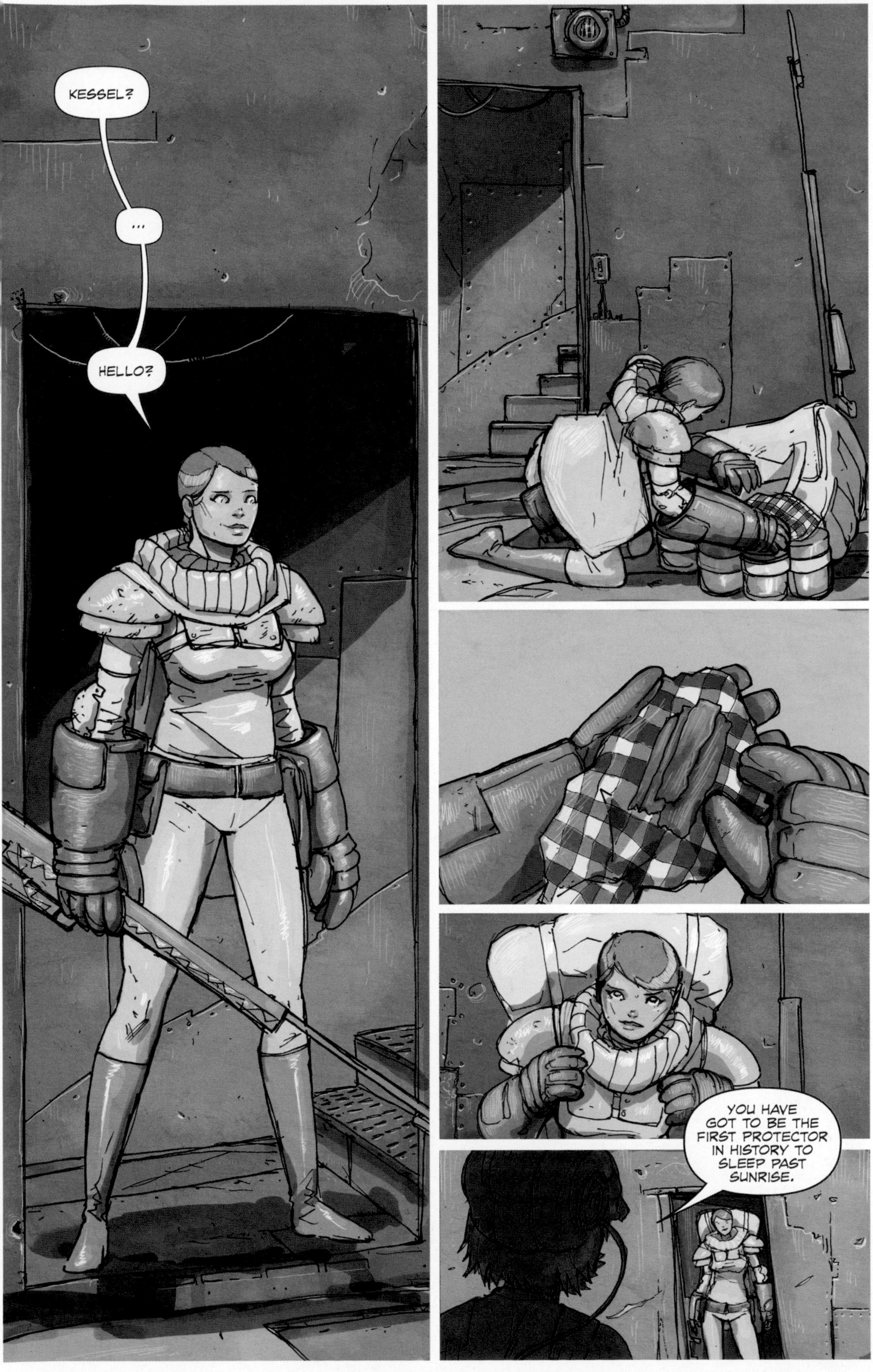
KESSEL?
...
HELLO?
YOU HAVE GOT TO BE THE FIRST PROTECTOR IN HISTORY TO SLEEP PAST SUNRISE.

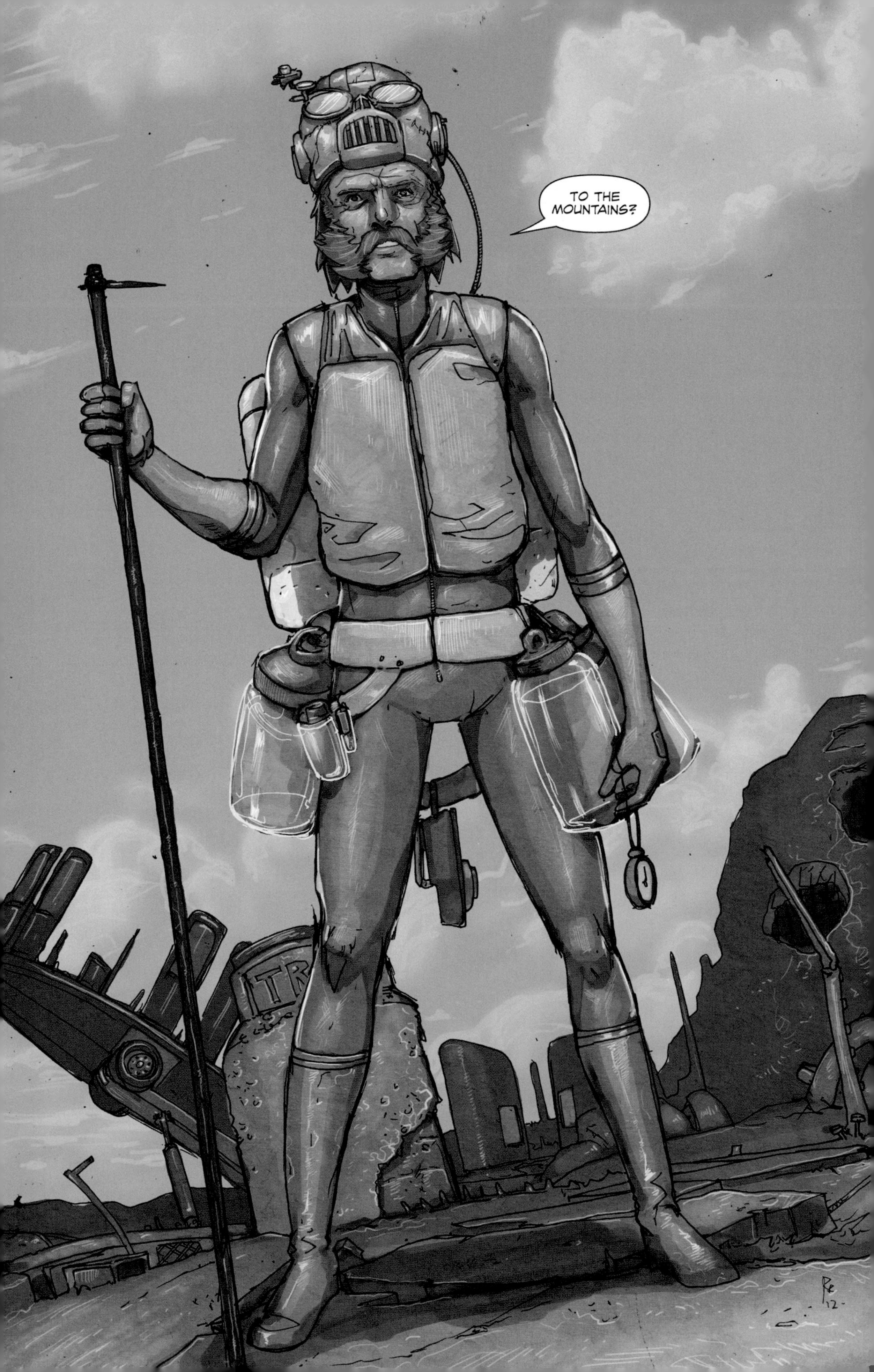
TO THE MOUNTAINS?

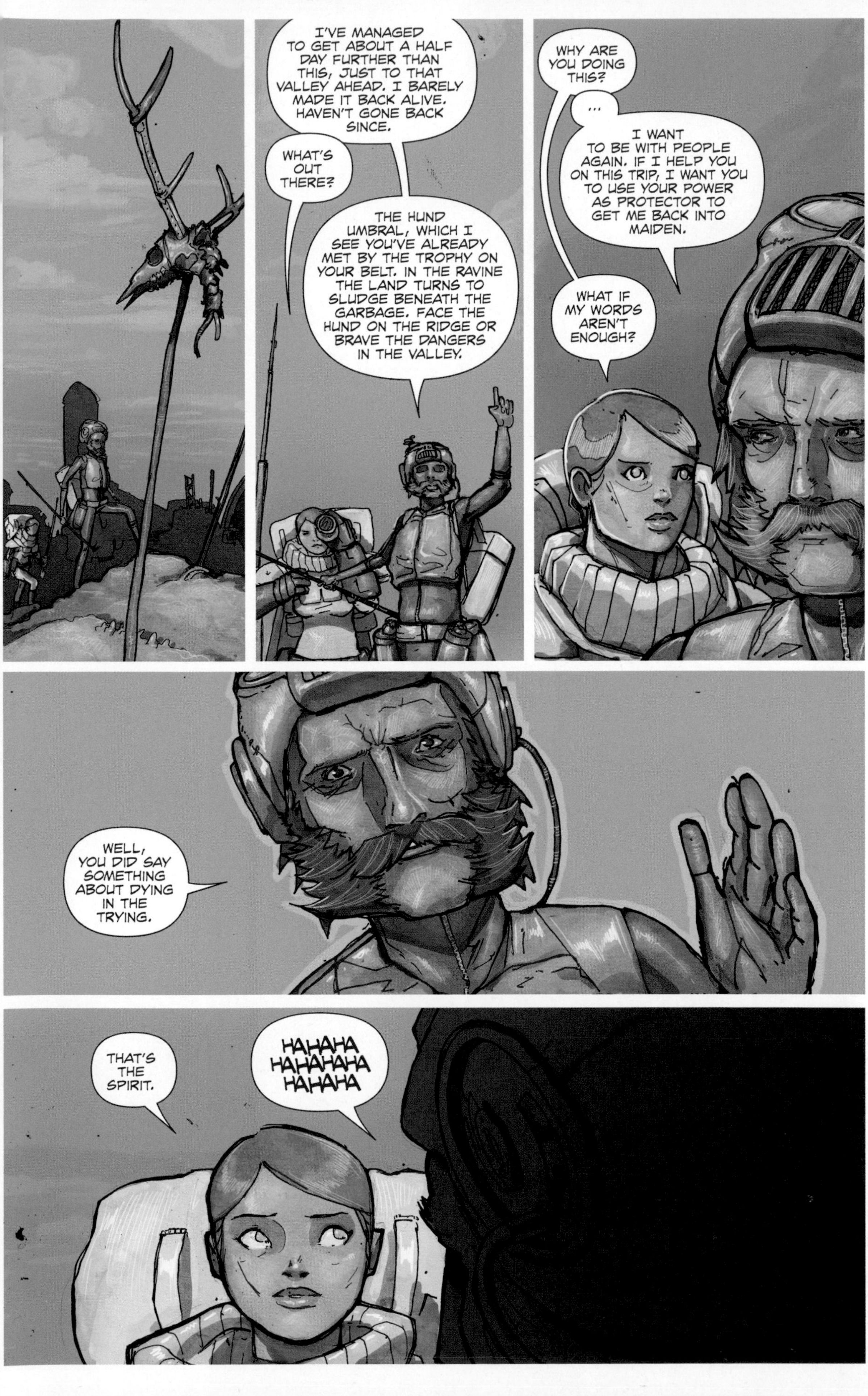

I'VE MANAGED TO GET ABOUT A HALF DAY FURTHER THAN THIS, JUST TO THAT VALLEY AHEAD. I BARELY MADE IT BACK ALIVE. HAVEN'T GONE BACK SINCE.
WHAT'S OUT THERE?
THE HUND UMBRAL, WHICH I SEE YOU'VE ALREADY MET BY THE TROPHY ON YOUR BELT. IN THE RAVINE THE LAND TURNS TO SLUDGE BENEATH THE GARBAGE. FACE THE HUND ON THE RIDGE OR BRAVE THE DANGERS IN THE VALLEY.
WHY ARE YOU DOING THIS?
...
I WANT TO BE WITH PEOPLE AGAIN. IF I HELP YOU ON THIS TRIP, I WANT YOU TO USE YOUR POWER AS PROTECTOR TO GET ME BACK INTO MAIDEN.
WHAT IF MY WORDS AREN'T ENOUGH?
WELL, YOU DID SAY SOMETHING ABOUT DYING IN THE TRYING.
THAT'S THE SPIRIT.
HAHAHA HAHAHAHA HAHAHA

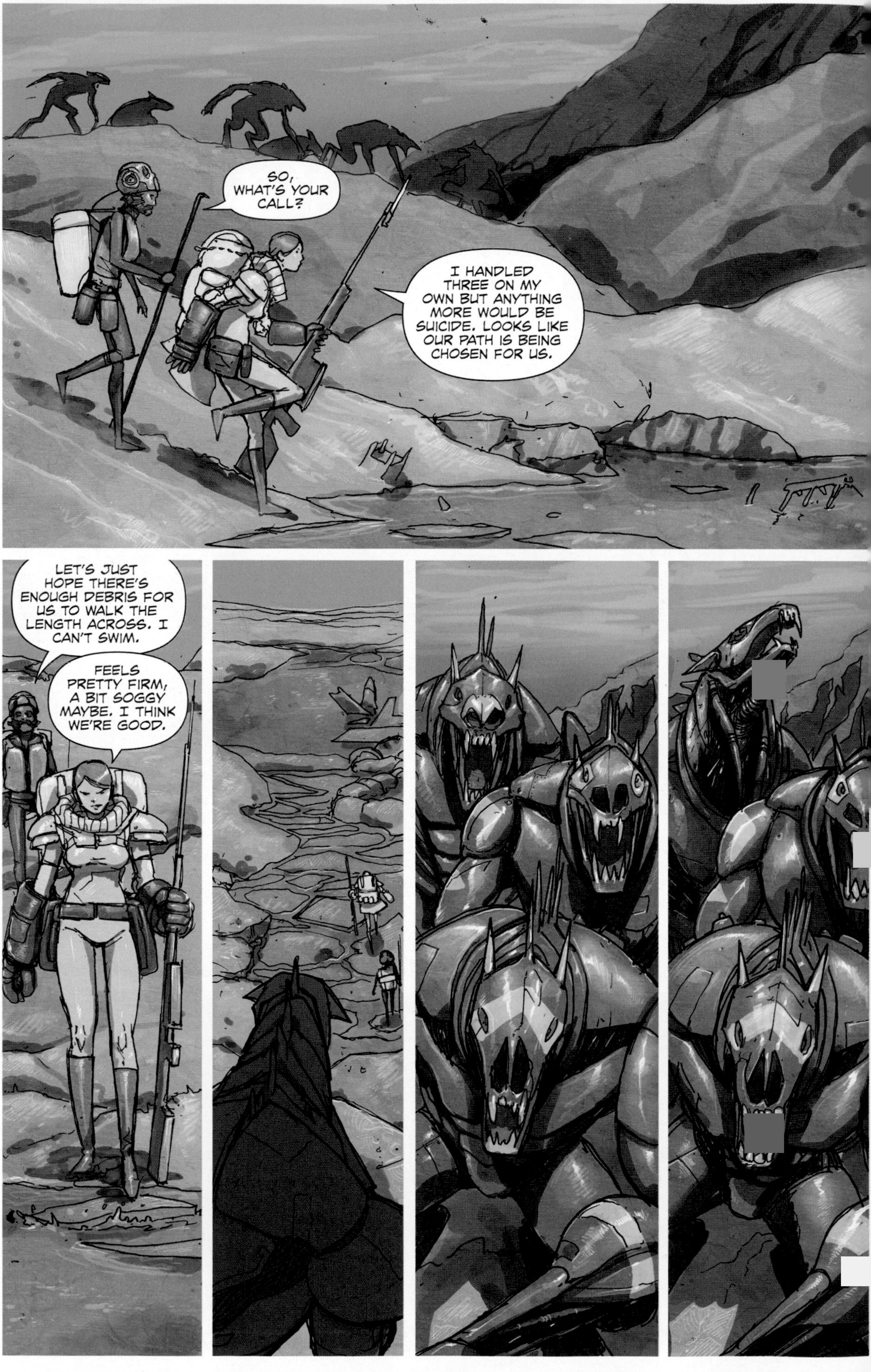
SO, WHAT'S YOUR CALL?
I HANDLED THREE ON MY OWN BUT ANYTHING MORE WOULD BE SUICIDE. LOOKS LIKE OUR PATH IS BEING CHOSEN FOR US.
LET'S JUST HOPE THERE'S ENOUGH DEBRIS FOR US TO WALK THE LENGTH ACROSS. I CAN'T SWIM.
FEELS PRETTY FIRM, A BIT SOGGY MAYBE. I THINK WE'RE GOOD.

THREE

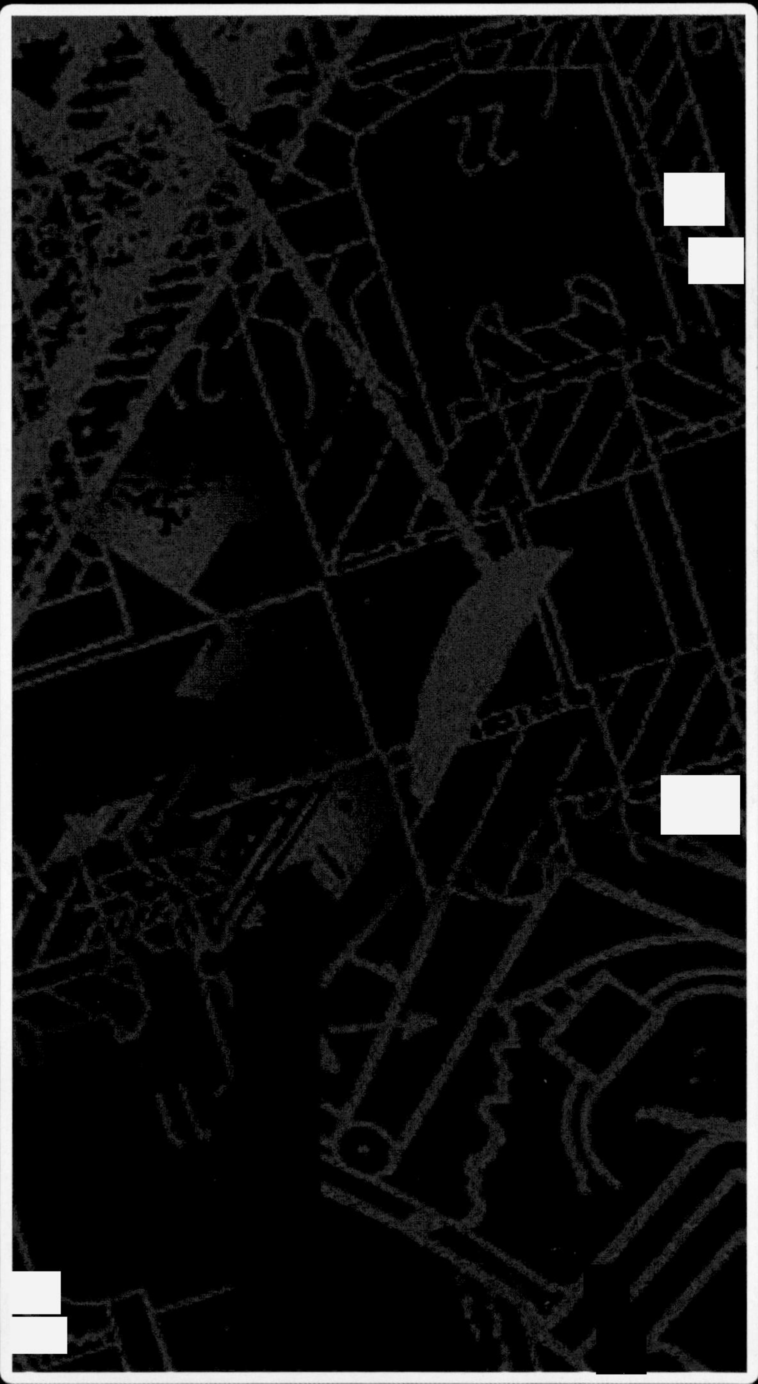

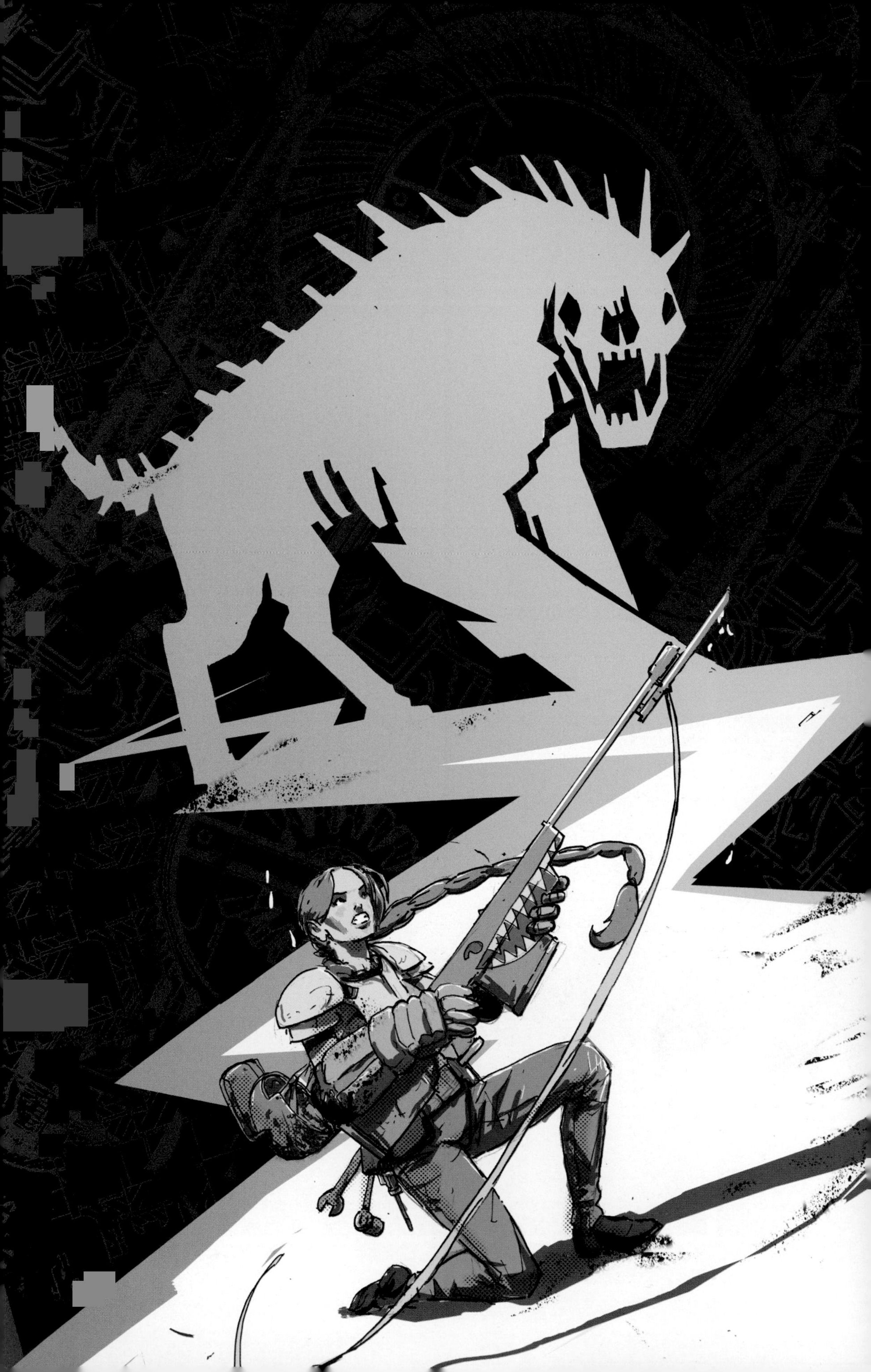

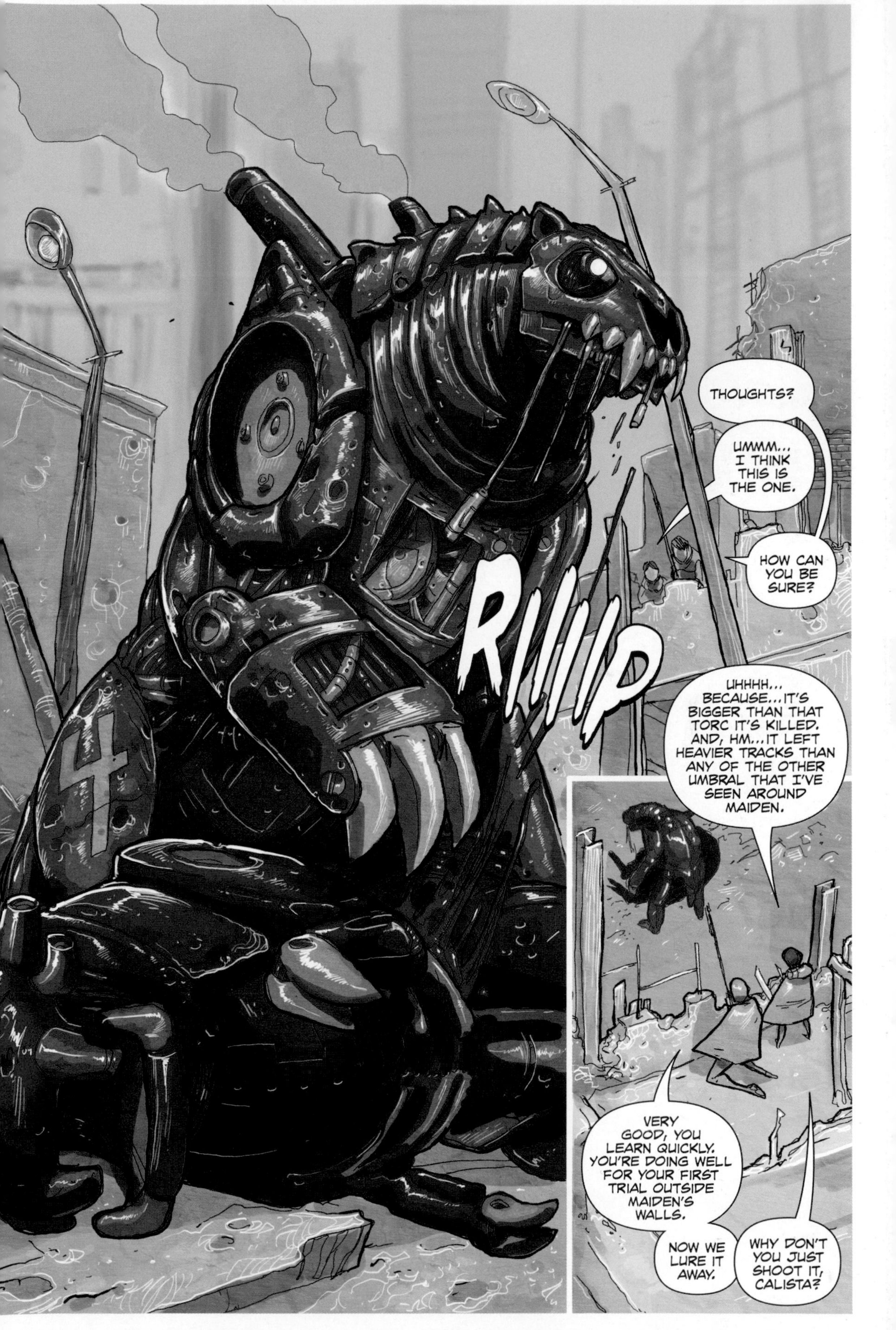
THOUGHTS?
UMMM... I THINK THIS IS THE ONE.
HOW CAN YOU BE SURE?
RIIIIP
UHHHH... BECAUSE...IT'S BIGGER THAN THAT TORC IT'S KILLED. AND, HM...IT LEFT HEAVIER TRACKS THAN ANY OF THE OTHER UMBRAL THAT I'VE SEEN AROUND MAIDEN.
VERY GOOD, YOU LEARN QUICKLY. YOU'RE DOING WELL FOR YOUR FIRST TRIAL OUTSIDE MAIDEN'S WALLS.
NOW WE LURE IT AWAY.
WHY DON'T YOU JUST SHOOT IT, CALISTA?

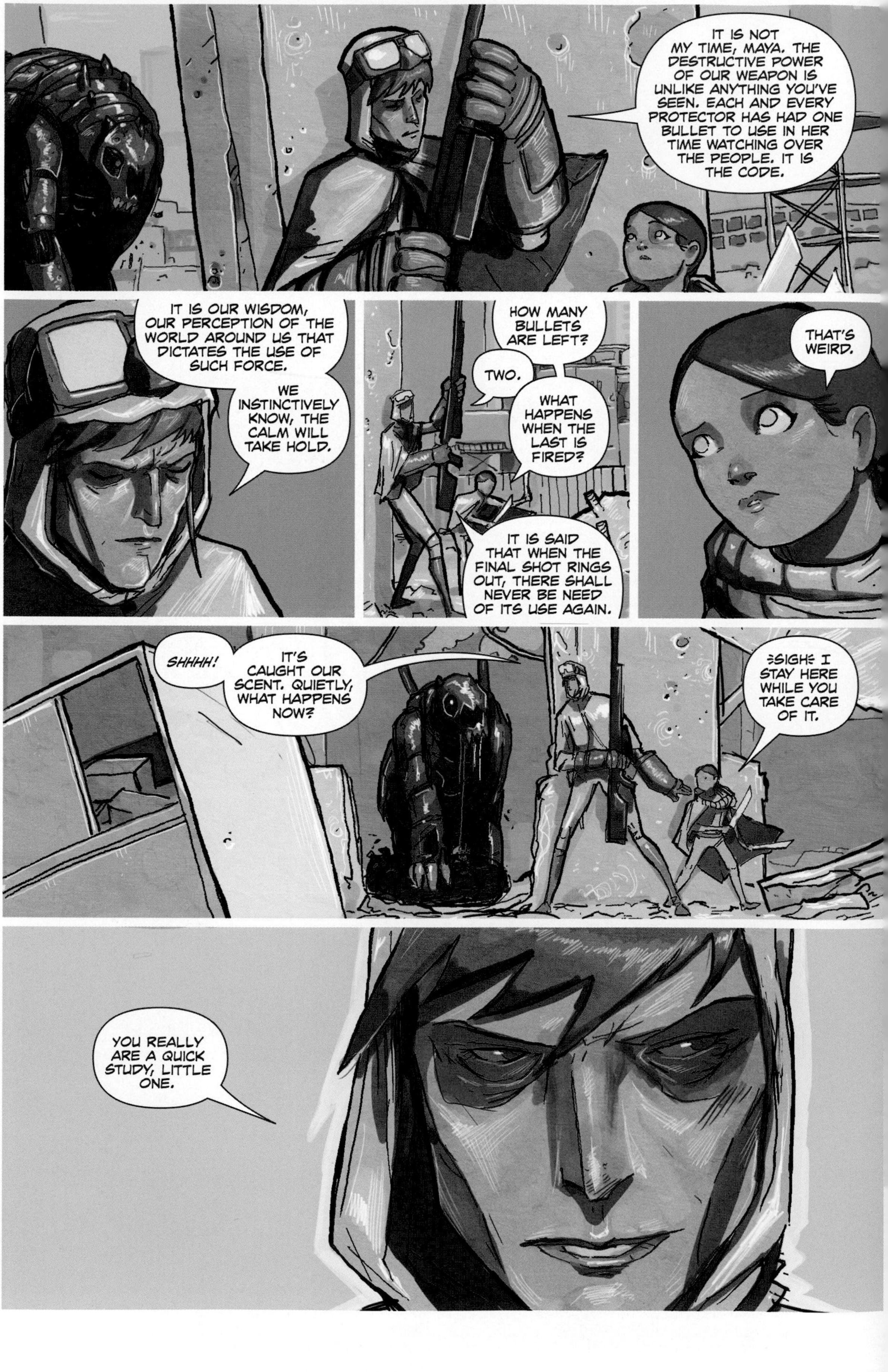
IT IS NOT MY TIME, MAYA. THE DESTRUCTIVE POWER OF OUR WEAPON IS UNLIKE ANYTHING YOU'VE SEEN. EACH AND EVERY PROTECTOR HAS HAD ONE BULLET TO USE IN HER TIME WATCHING OVER THE PEOPLE. IT IS THE CODE.
IT IS OUR WISDOM, OUR PERCEPTION OF THE WORLD AROUND US THAT DICTATES THE USE OF SUCH FORCE.
WE INSTINCTIVELY KNOW, THE CALM WILL TAKE HOLD.
HOW MANY BULLETS ARE LEFT?
TWO.
WHAT HAPPENS WHEN THE LAST IS FIRED?
IT IS SAID THAT WHEN THE FINAL SHOT RINGS OUT, THERE SHALL NEVER BE NEED OF ITS USE AGAIN.
THAT'S WEIRD.
SHHHH!
IT'S CAUGHT OUR SCENT. QUIETLY, WHAT HAPPENS NOW?
=SIGH= I STAY HERE WHILE YOU TAKE CARE OF IT.
YOU REALLY ARE A QUICK STUDY, LITTLE ONE.

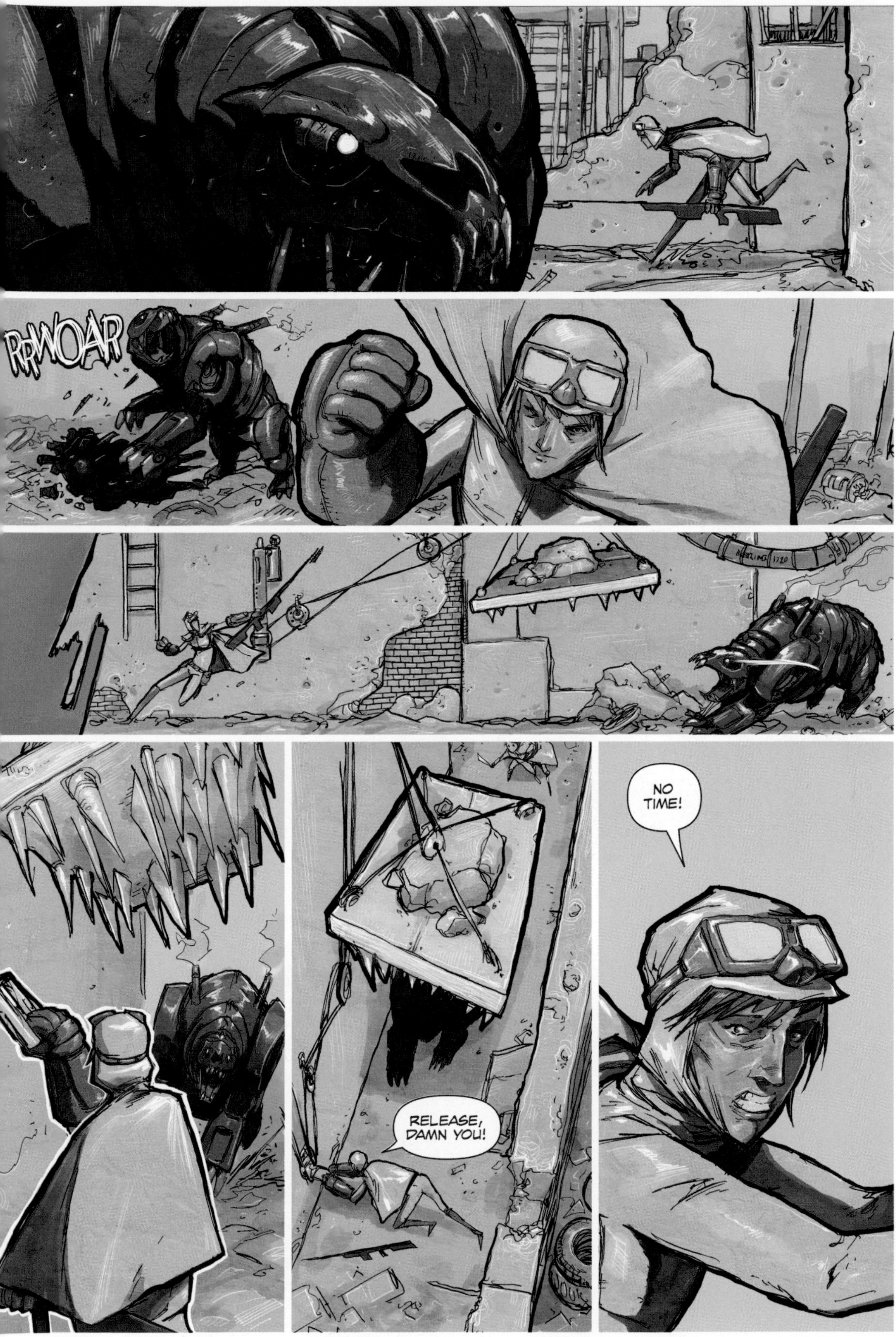
RRWOAR
RELEASE, DAMN YOU!
NO TIME!

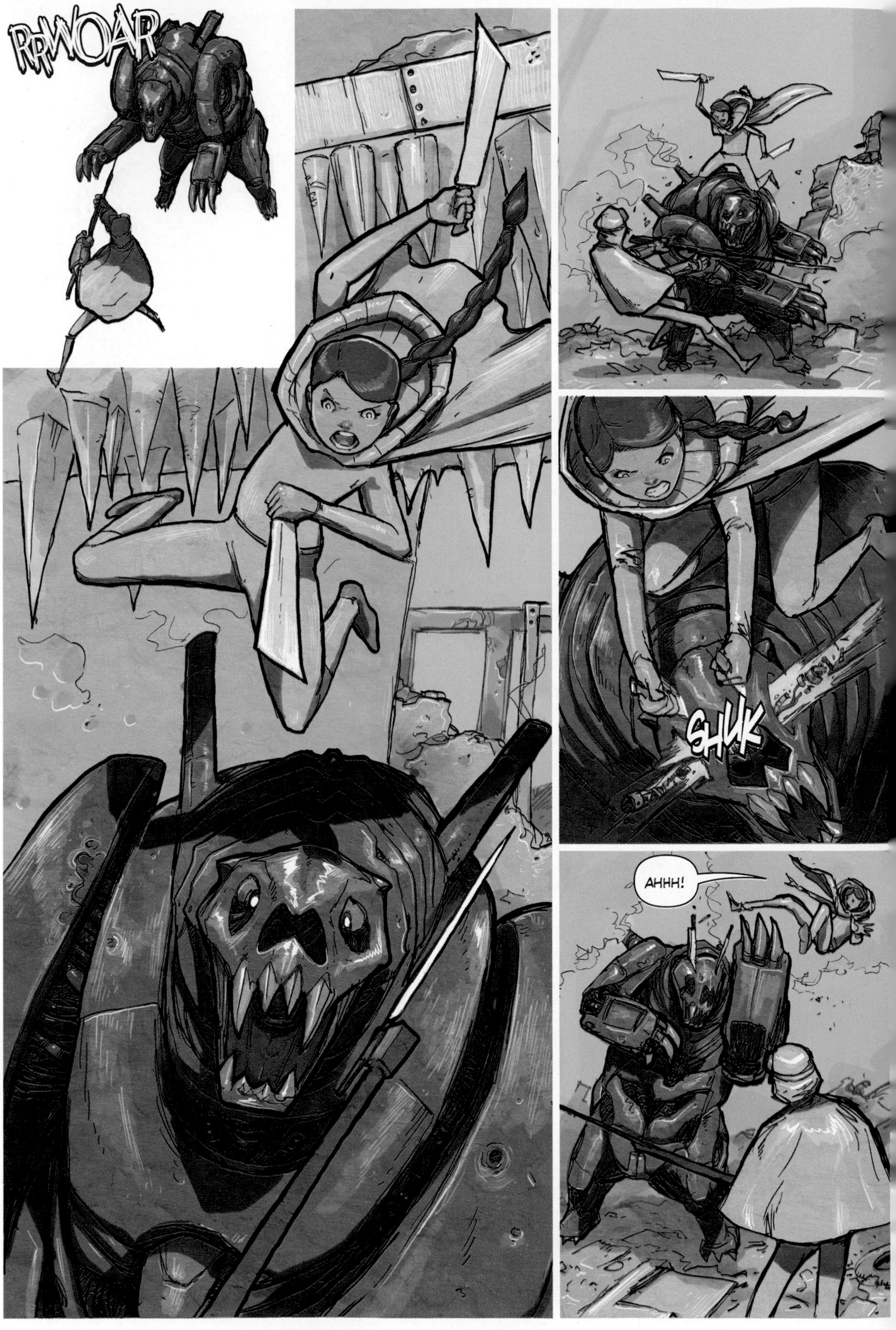
RRWOAR
SHUK
AHHH!

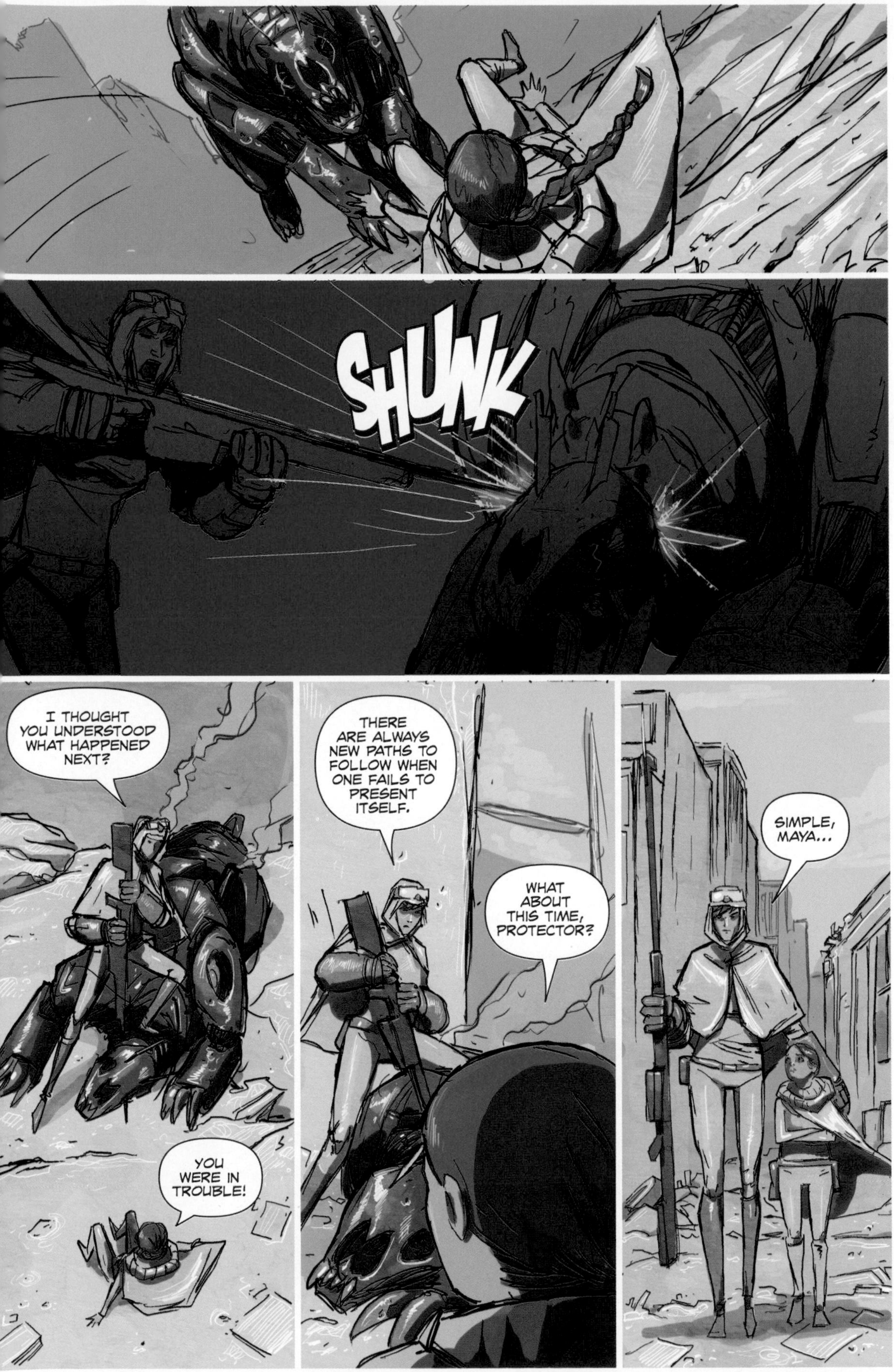
SHUNK
I THOUGHT YOU UNDERSTOOD WHAT HAPPENED NEXT?
YOU WERE IN TROUBLE!
THERE ARE ALWAYS NEW PATHS TO FOLLOW WHEN ONE FAILS TO PRESENT ITSELF.
WHAT ABOUT THIS TIME, PROTECTOR?
SIMPLE, MAYA...

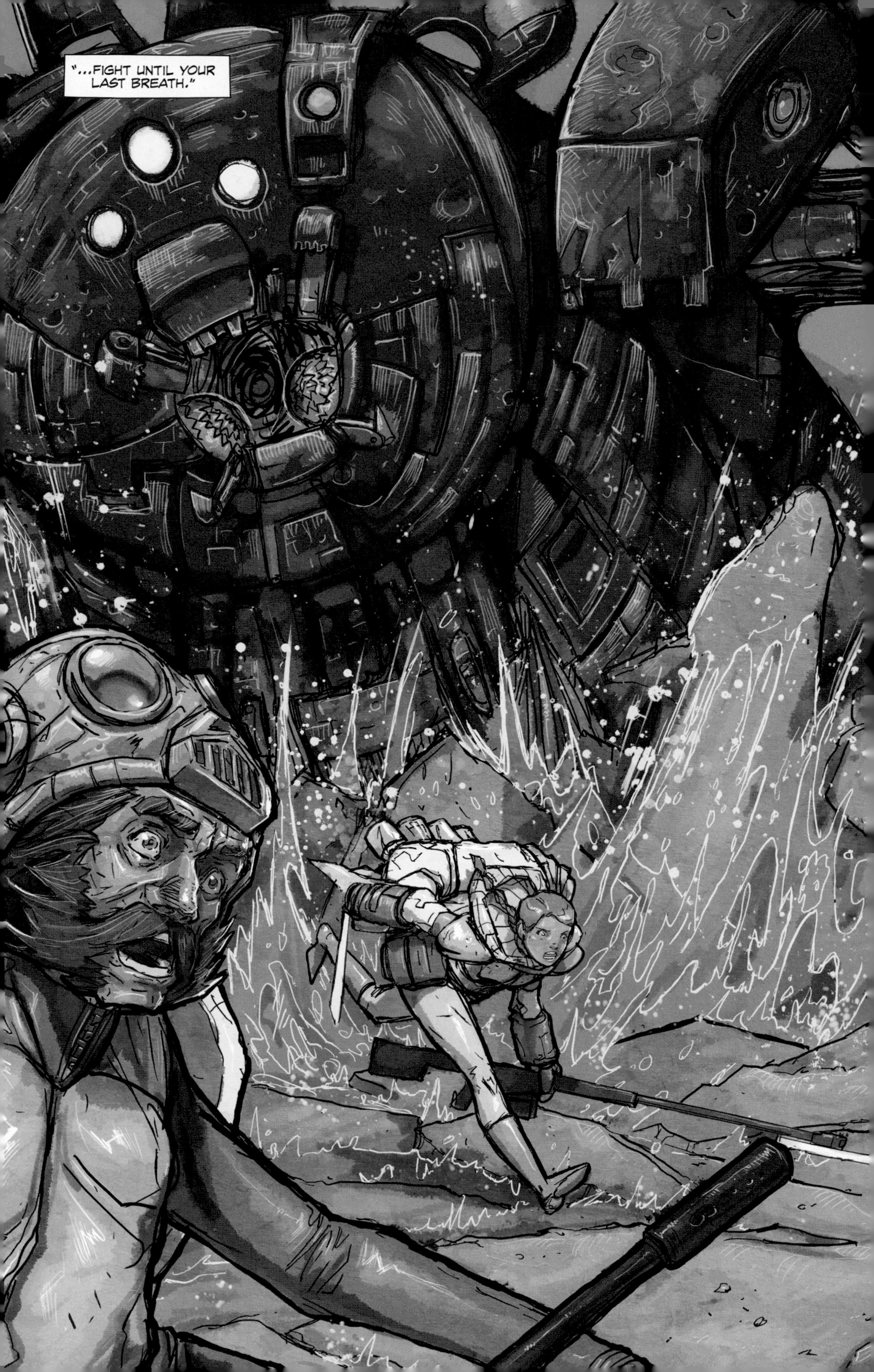
"...FIGHT UNTIL YOUR LAST BREATH."

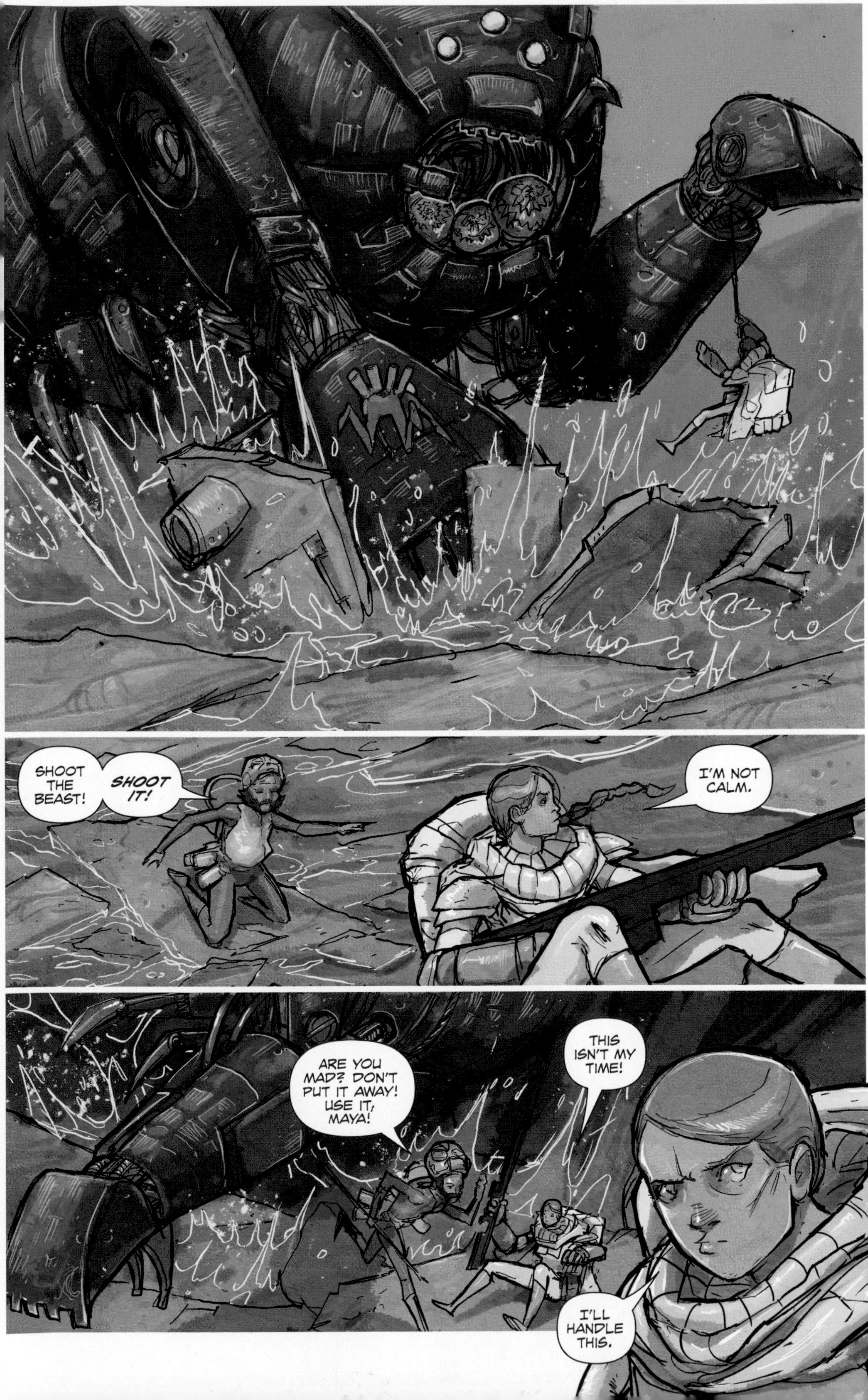
SHOOT THE BEAST!
SHOOT IT!
I'M NOT CALM.
ARE YOU MAD? DON'T PUT IT AWAY! USE IT, MAYA!
THIS ISN'T MY TIME!
I'LL HANDLE THIS.

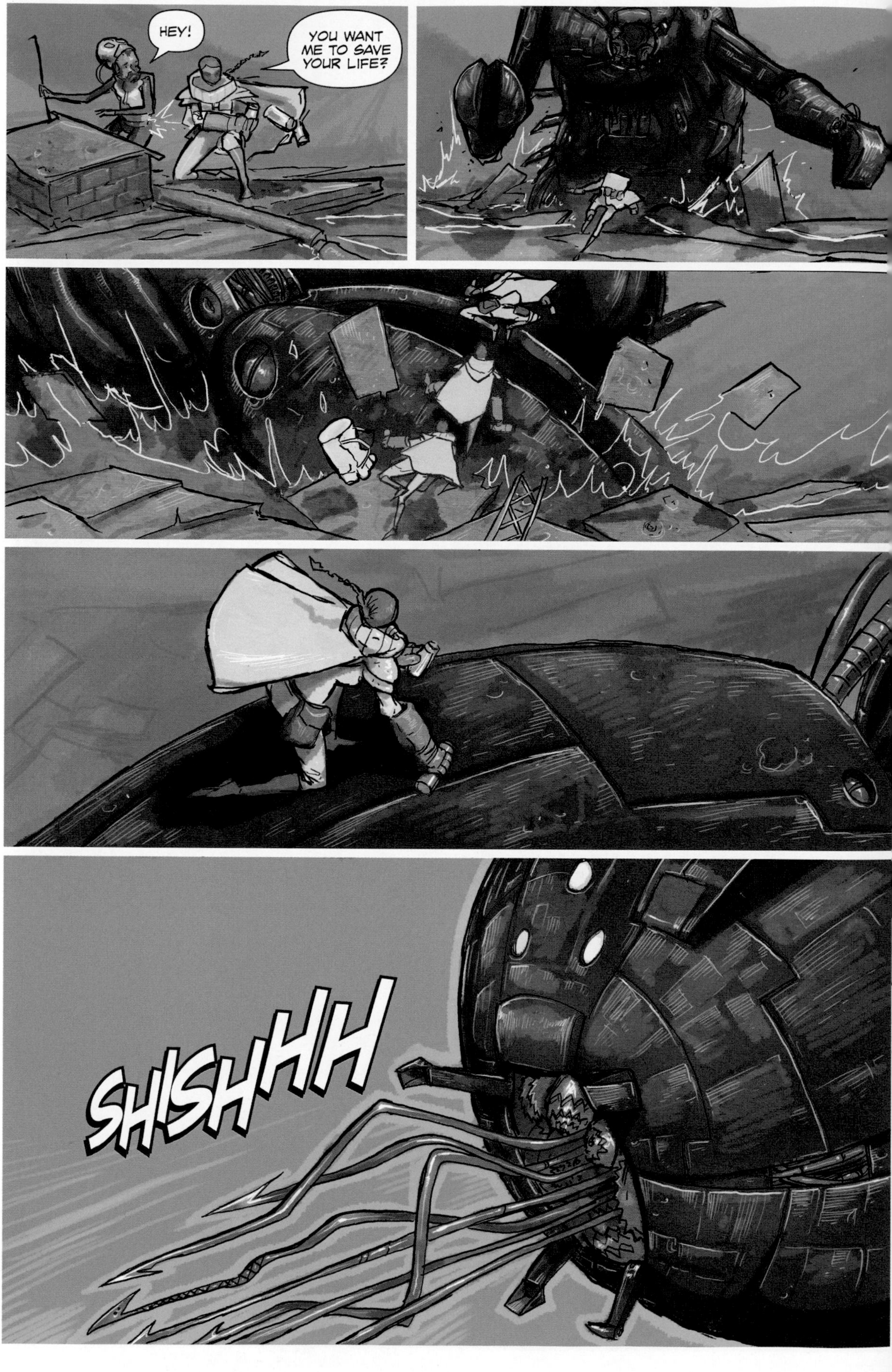
HEY!
YOU WANT ME TO SAVE YOUR LIFE?
SHISHHH

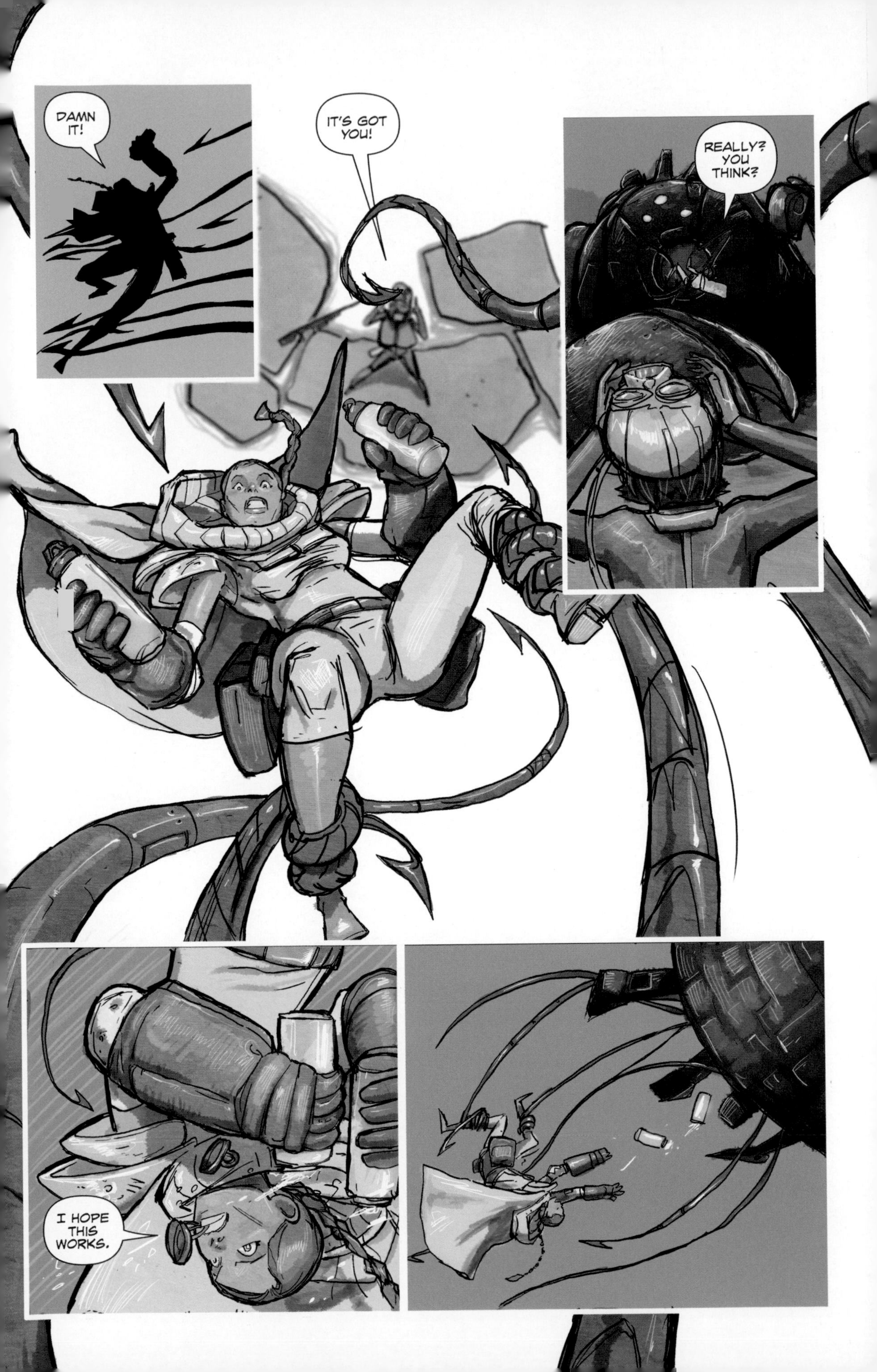
DAMN IT!
IT'S GOT YOU!
REALLY? YOU THINK?
I HOPE THIS WORKS.

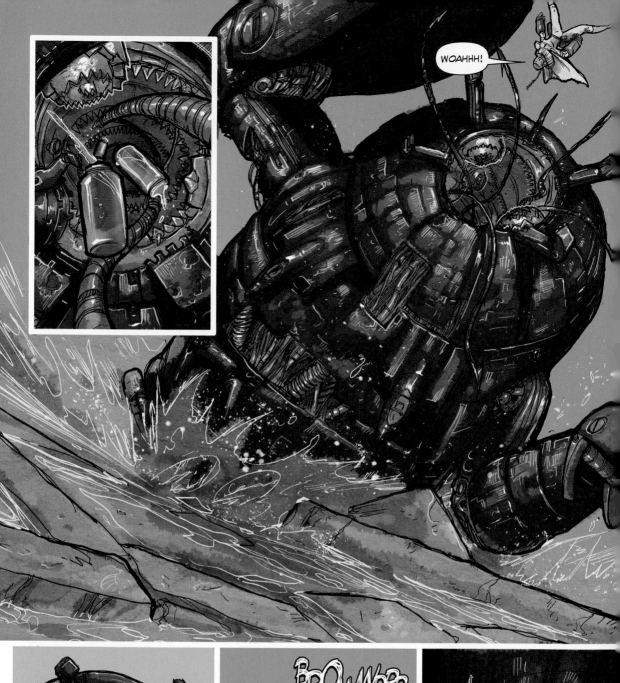

WOAHHH!

BROWWRRR

SPLOOSH

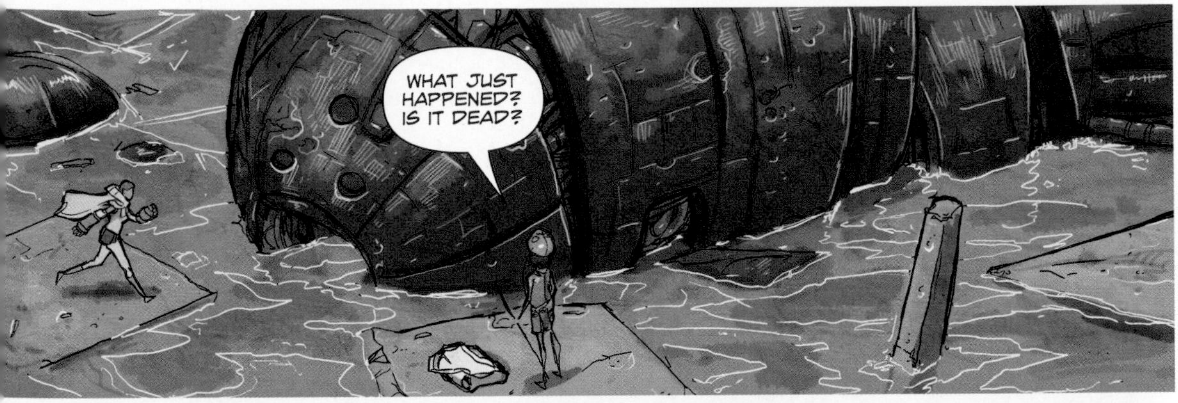
WHAT JUST HAPPENED? IS IT DEAD?

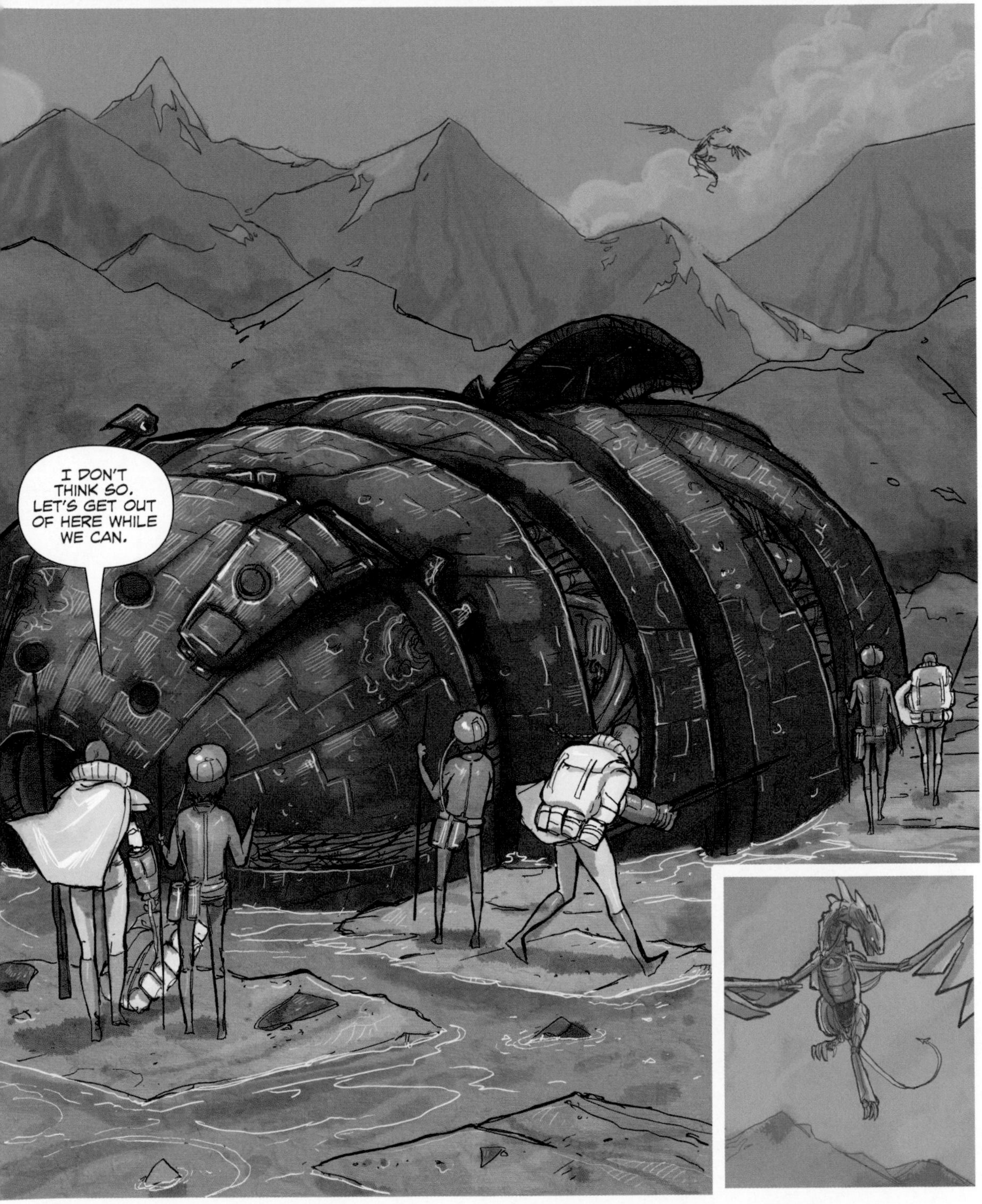
I DON'T THINK SO. LET'S GET OUT OF HERE WHILE WE CAN.

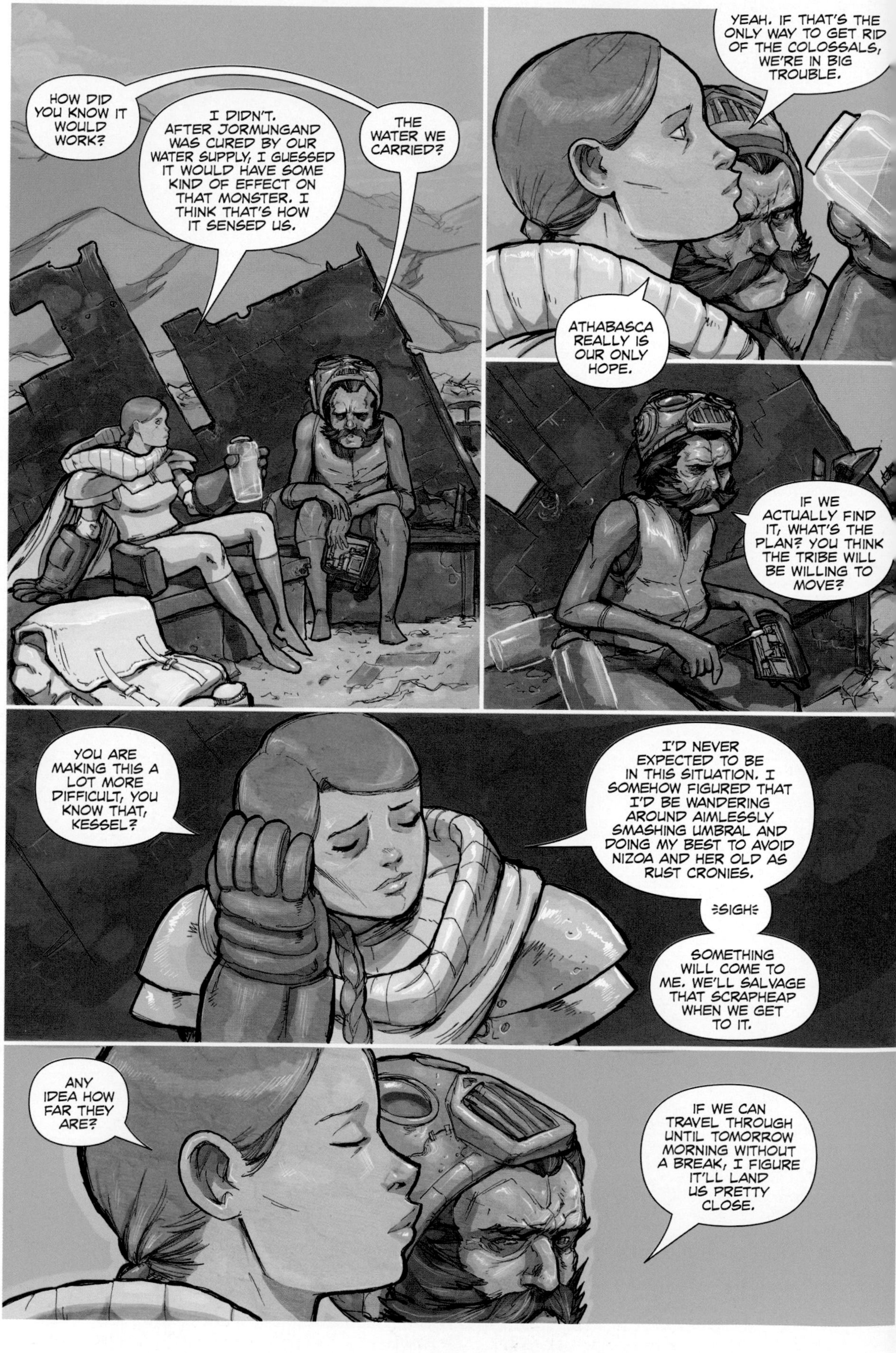
HOW DID YOU KNOW IT WOULD WORK?
I DIDN'T. AFTER JORMUNGAND WAS CURED BY OUR WATER SUPPLY, I GUESSED IT WOULD HAVE SOME KIND OF EFFECT ON THAT MONSTER. I THINK THAT'S HOW IT SENSED US.
THE WATER WE CARRIED?
YEAH. IF THAT'S THE ONLY WAY TO GET RID OF THE COLOSSALS, WE'RE IN BIG TROUBLE.
ATHABASCA REALLY IS OUR ONLY HOPE.
IF WE ACTUALLY FIND IT, WHAT'S THE PLAN? YOU THINK THE TRIBE WILL BE WILLING TO MOVE?
YOU ARE MAKING THIS A LOT MORE DIFFICULT, YOU KNOW THAT, KESSEL?
I'D NEVER EXPECTED TO BE IN THIS SITUATION. I SOMEHOW FIGURED THAT I'D BE WANDERING AROUND AIMLESSLY SMASHING UMBRAL AND DOING MY BEST TO AVOID NIZOA AND HER OLD AS RUST CRONIES.
SIGH
SOMETHING WILL COME TO ME. WE'LL SALVAGE THAT SCRAPHEAP WHEN WE GET TO IT.
ANY IDEA HOW FAR THEY ARE?
IF WE CAN TRAVEL THROUGH UNTIL TOMORROW MORNING WITHOUT A BREAK, I FIGURE IT'LL LAND US PRETTY CLOSE.

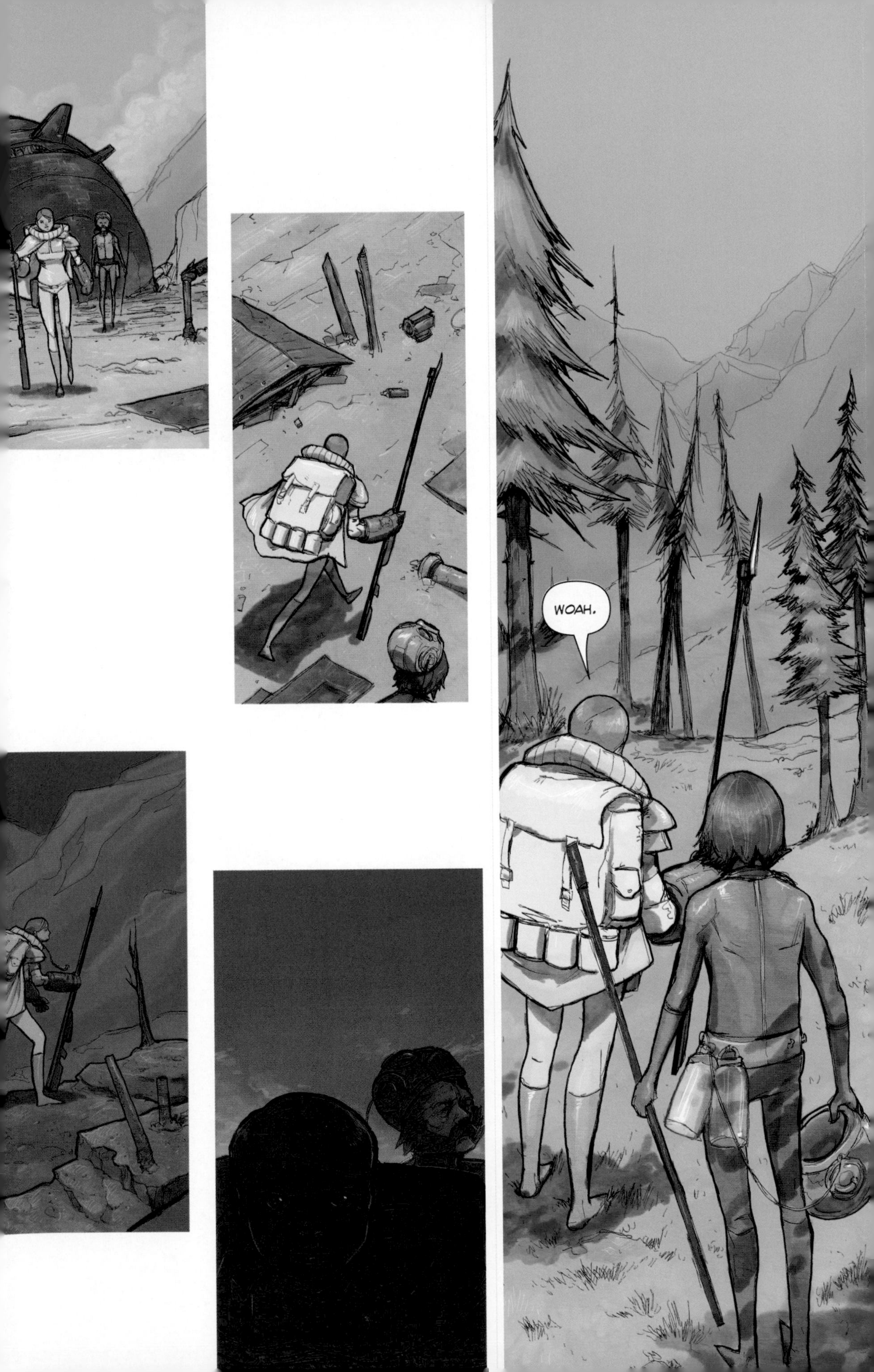
WOAH.

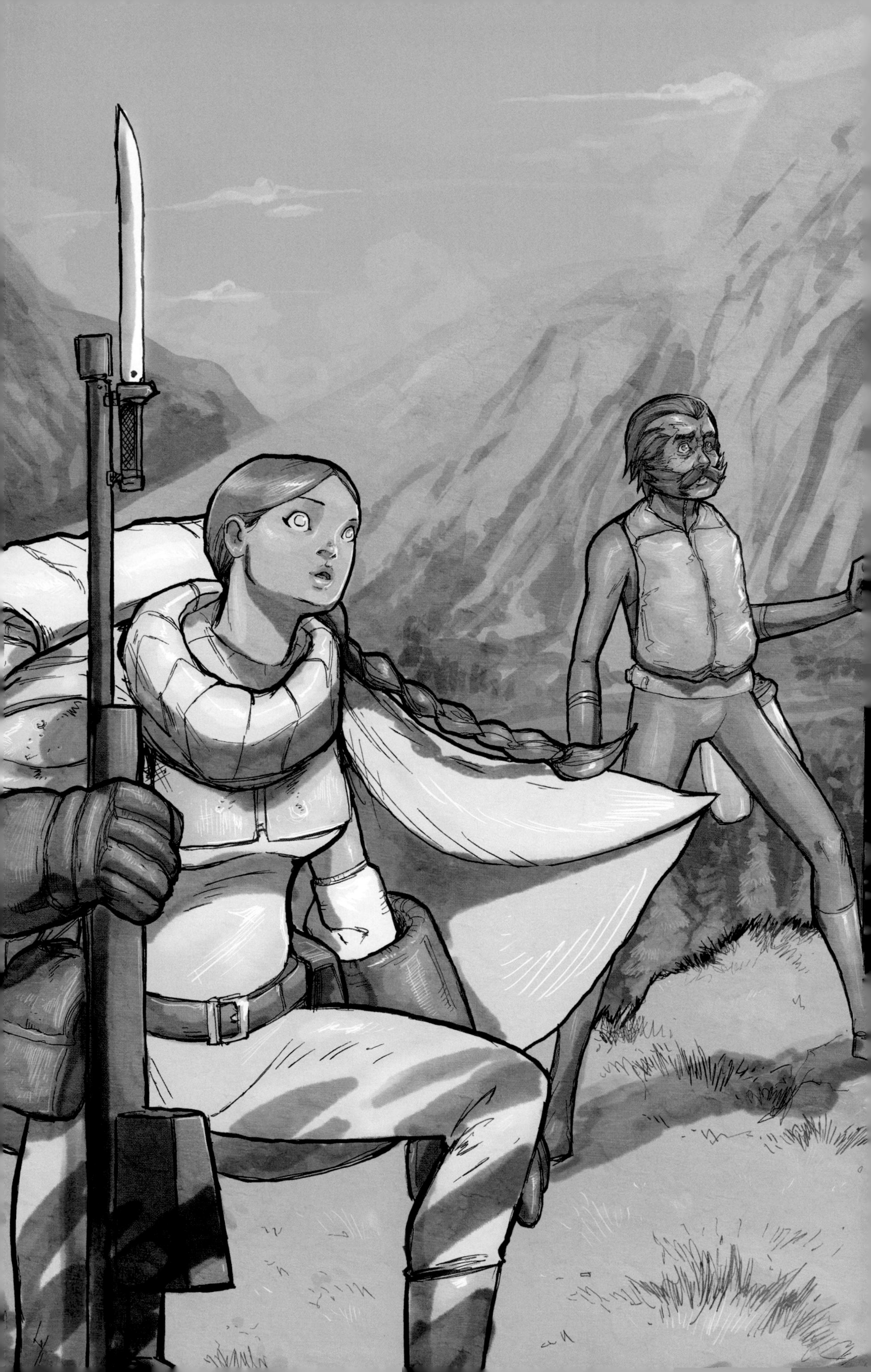

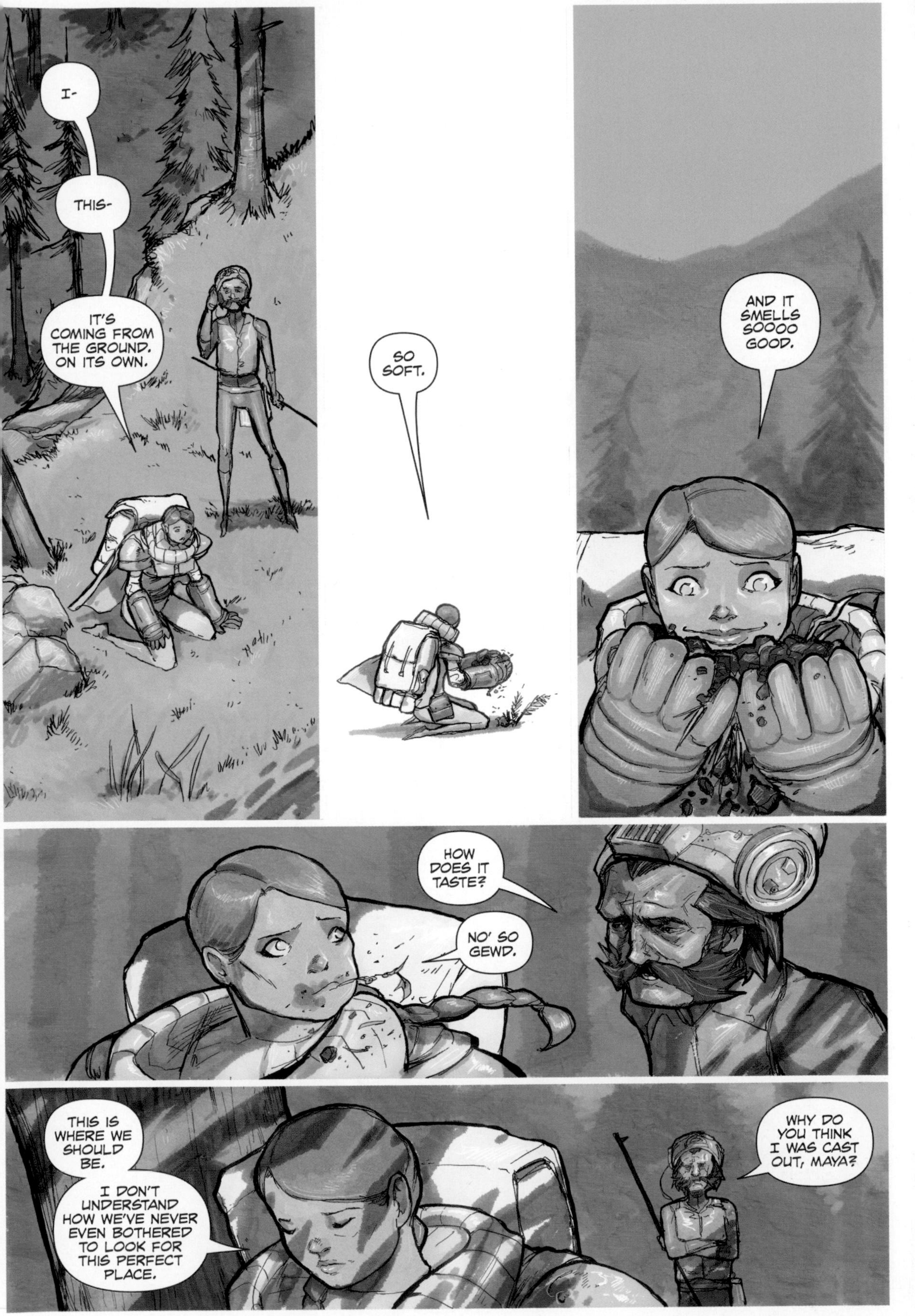
I-
THIS-
IT'S COMING FROM THE GROUND. ON ITS OWN.
SO SOFT.
AND IT SMELLS SOOOO GOOD.
HOW DOES IT TASTE?
NO' SO GEWD.
THIS IS WHERE WE SHOULD BE.
I DON'T UNDERSTAND HOW WE'VE NEVER EVEN BOTHERED TO LOOK FOR THIS PERFECT PLACE.
WHY DO YOU THINK I WAS CAST OUT, MAYA?

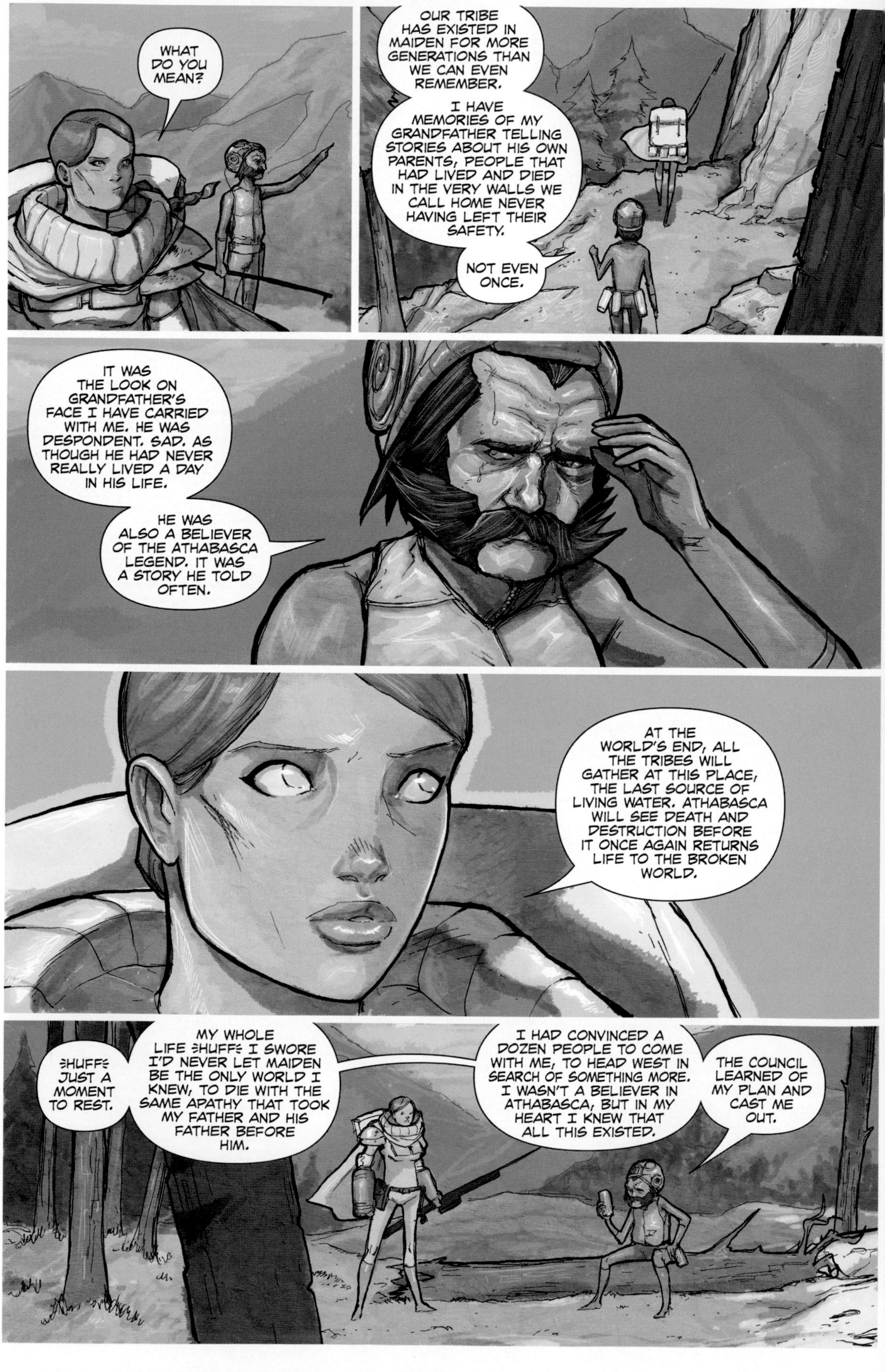
WHAT DO YOU MEAN?
OUR TRIBE HAS EXISTED IN MAIDEN FOR MORE GENERATIONS THAN WE CAN EVEN REMEMBER.
I HAVE MEMORIES OF MY GRANDFATHER TELLING STORIES ABOUT HIS OWN PARENTS, PEOPLE THAT HAD LIVED AND DIED IN THE VERY WALLS WE CALL HOME NEVER HAVING LEFT THEIR SAFETY.
NOT EVEN ONCE.
IT WAS THE LOOK ON GRANDFATHER'S FACE I HAVE CARRIED WITH ME. HE WAS DESPONDENT. SAD. AS THOUGH HE HAD NEVER REALLY LIVED A DAY IN HIS LIFE.
HE WAS ALSO A BELIEVER OF THE ATHABASCA LEGEND. IT WAS A STORY HE TOLD OFTEN.
AT THE WORLD'S END, ALL THE TRIBES WILL GATHER AT THIS PLACE, THE LAST SOURCE OF LIVING WATER. ATHABASCA WILL SEE DEATH AND DESTRUCTION BEFORE IT ONCE AGAIN RETURNS LIFE TO THE BROKEN WORLD.
=HUFF= JUST A MOMENT TO REST.
MY WHOLE LIFE =HUFF= I SWORE I'D NEVER LET MAIDEN BE THE ONLY WORLD I KNEW, TO DIE WITH THE SAME APATHY THAT TOOK MY FATHER AND HIS FATHER BEFORE HIM.
I HAD CONVINCED A DOZEN PEOPLE TO COME WITH ME, TO HEAD WEST IN SEARCH OF SOMETHING MORE. I WASN'T A BELIEVER IN ATHABASCA, BUT IN MY HEART I KNEW THAT ALL THIS EXISTED.
THE COUNCIL LEARNED OF MY PLAN AND CAST ME OUT.

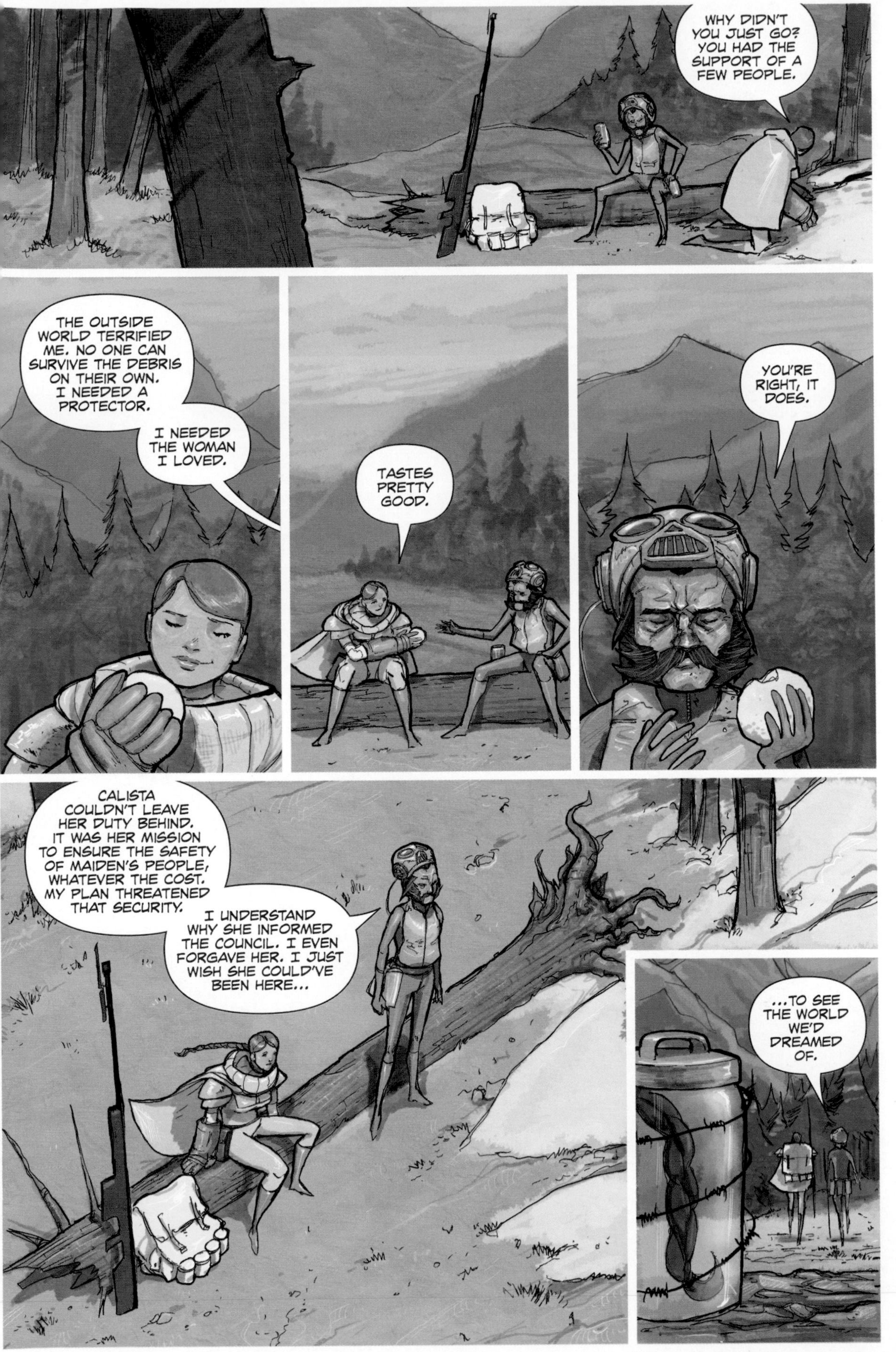
WHY DIDN'T YOU JUST GO? YOU HAD THE SUPPORT OF A FEW PEOPLE.
THE OUTSIDE WORLD TERRIFIED ME. NO ONE CAN SURVIVE THE DEBRIS ON THEIR OWN. I NEEDED A PROTECTOR.
I NEEDED THE WOMAN I LOVED.
TASTES PRETTY GOOD.
YOU'RE RIGHT, IT DOES.
CALISTA COULDN'T LEAVE HER DUTY BEHIND. IT WAS HER MISSION TO ENSURE THE SAFETY OF MAIDEN'S PEOPLE, WHATEVER THE COST. MY PLAN THREATENED THAT SECURITY.
I UNDERSTAND WHY SHE INFORMED THE COUNCIL. I EVEN FORGAVE HER. I JUST WISH SHE COULD'VE BEEN HERE...
...TO SEE THE WORLD WE'D DREAMED OF.

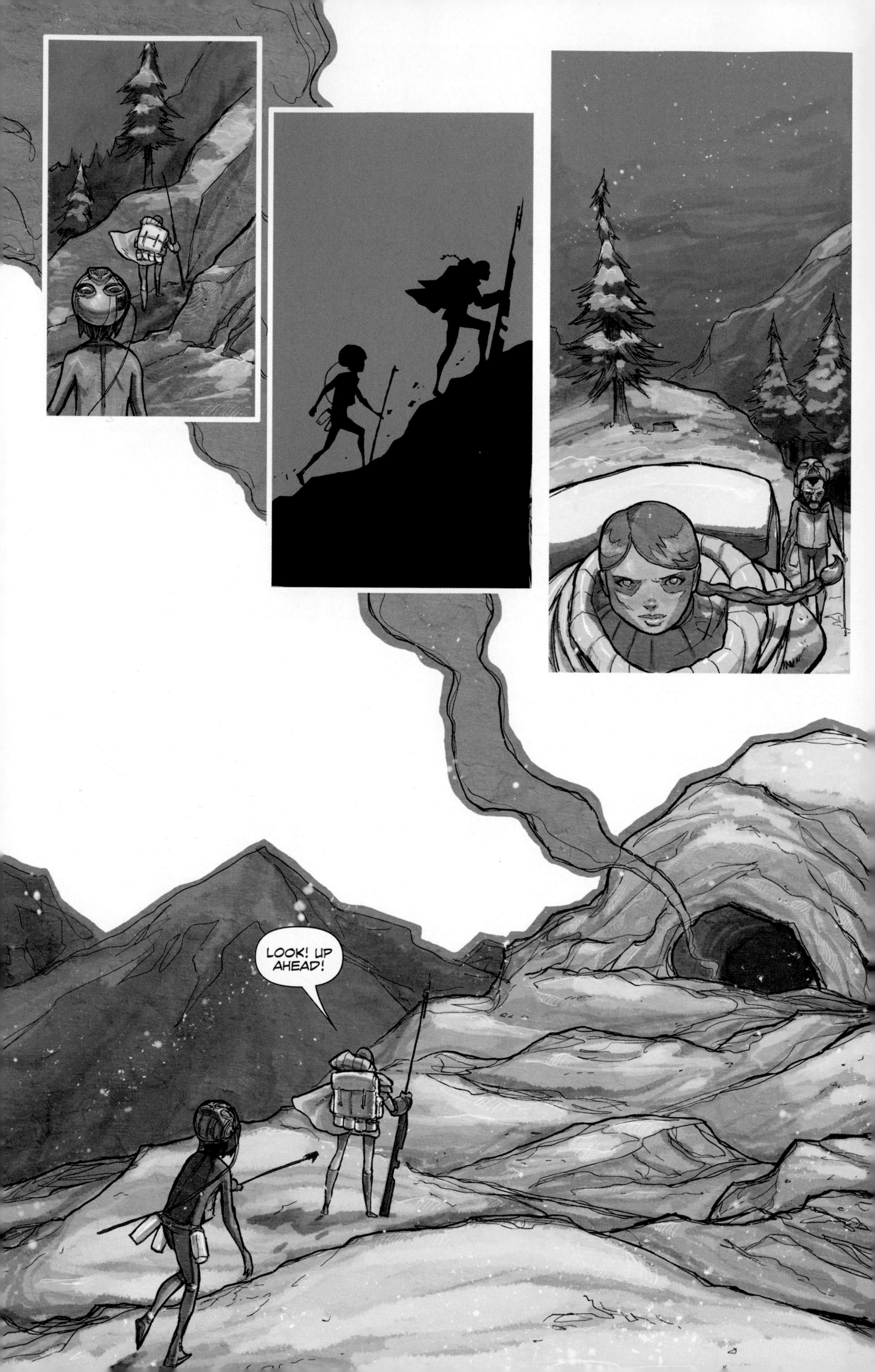
LOOK! UP AHEAD!

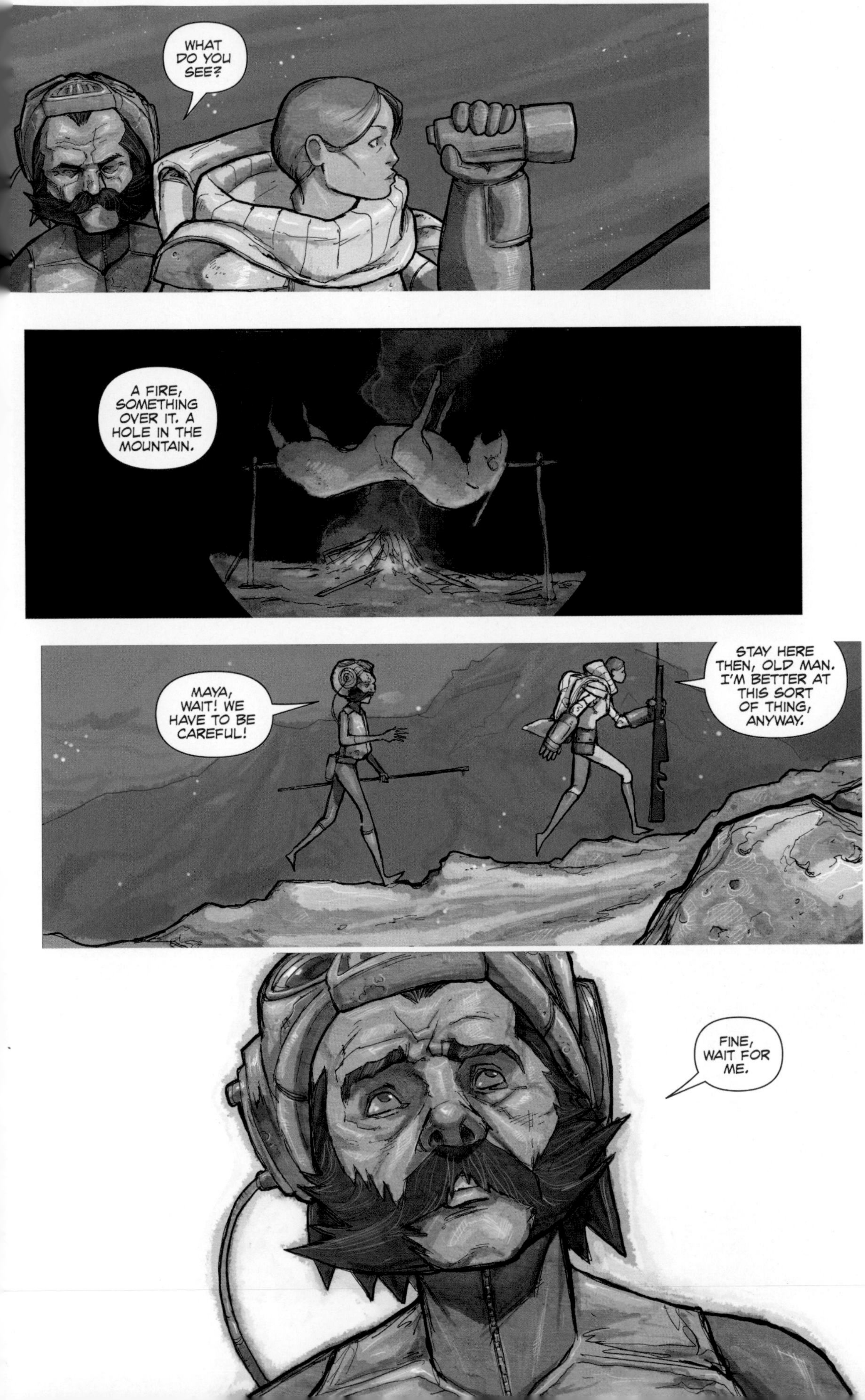
WHAT DO YOU SEE?
A FIRE, SOMETHING OVER IT. A HOLE IN THE MOUNTAIN.
MAYA, WAIT! WE HAVE TO BE CAREFUL!
STAY HERE THEN, OLD MAN. I'M BETTER AT THIS SORT OF THING, ANYWAY.
FINE, WAIT FOR ME.

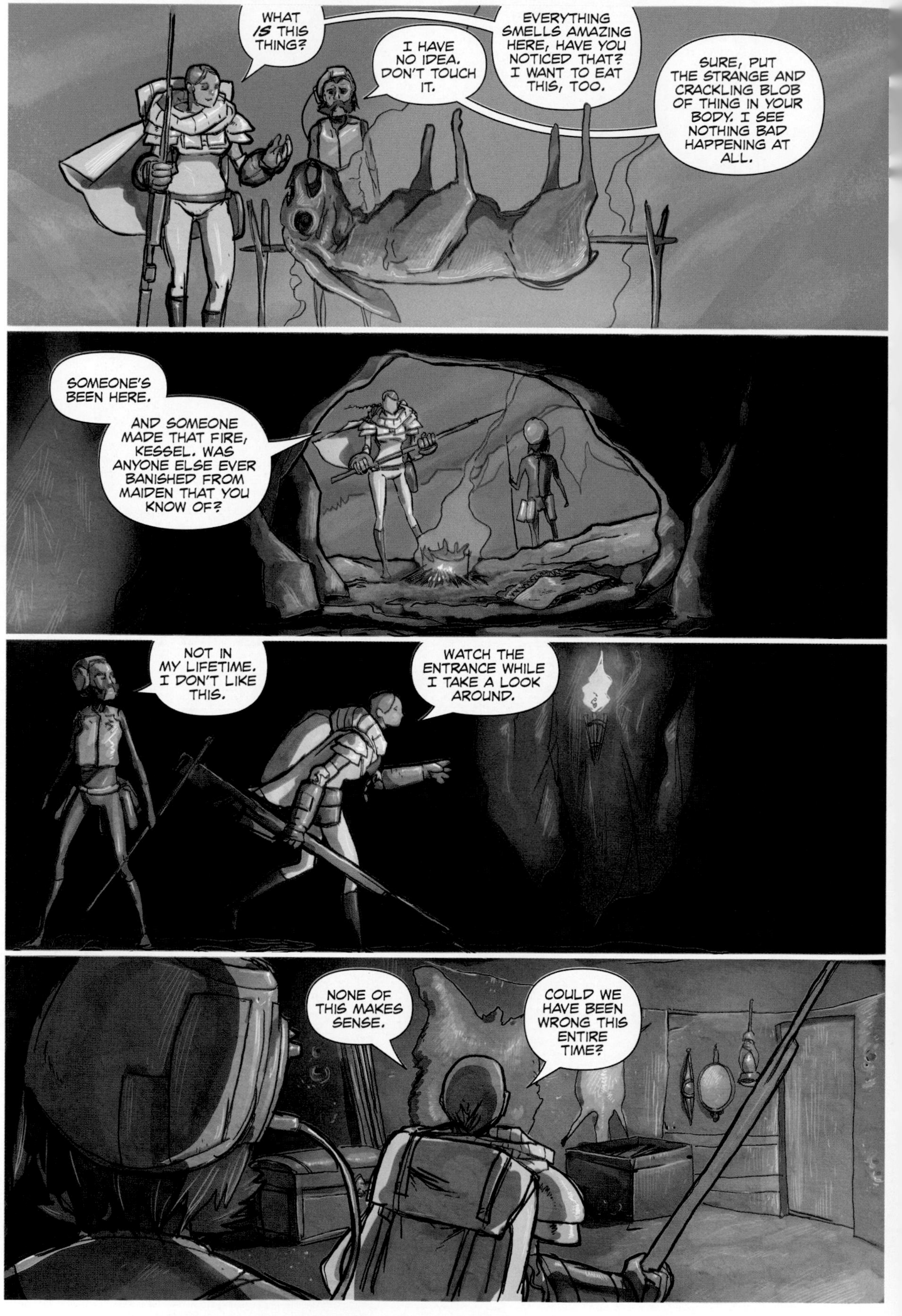
WHAT *IS* THIS THING?
I HAVE NO IDEA. DON'T TOUCH IT.
EVERYTHING SMELLS AMAZING HERE, HAVE YOU NOTICED THAT? I WANT TO EAT THIS, TOO.
SURE, PUT THE STRANGE AND CRACKLING BLOB OF THING IN YOUR BODY. I SEE NOTHING BAD HAPPENING AT ALL.
SOMEONE'S BEEN HERE.
AND SOMEONE MADE THAT FIRE, KESSEL. WAS ANYONE ELSE EVER BANISHED FROM MAIDEN THAT YOU KNOW OF?
NOT IN MY LIFETIME. I DON'T LIKE THIS.
WATCH THE ENTRANCE WHILE I TAKE A LOOK AROUND.
NONE OF THIS MAKES SENSE.
COULD WE HAVE BEEN WRONG THIS ENTIRE TIME?

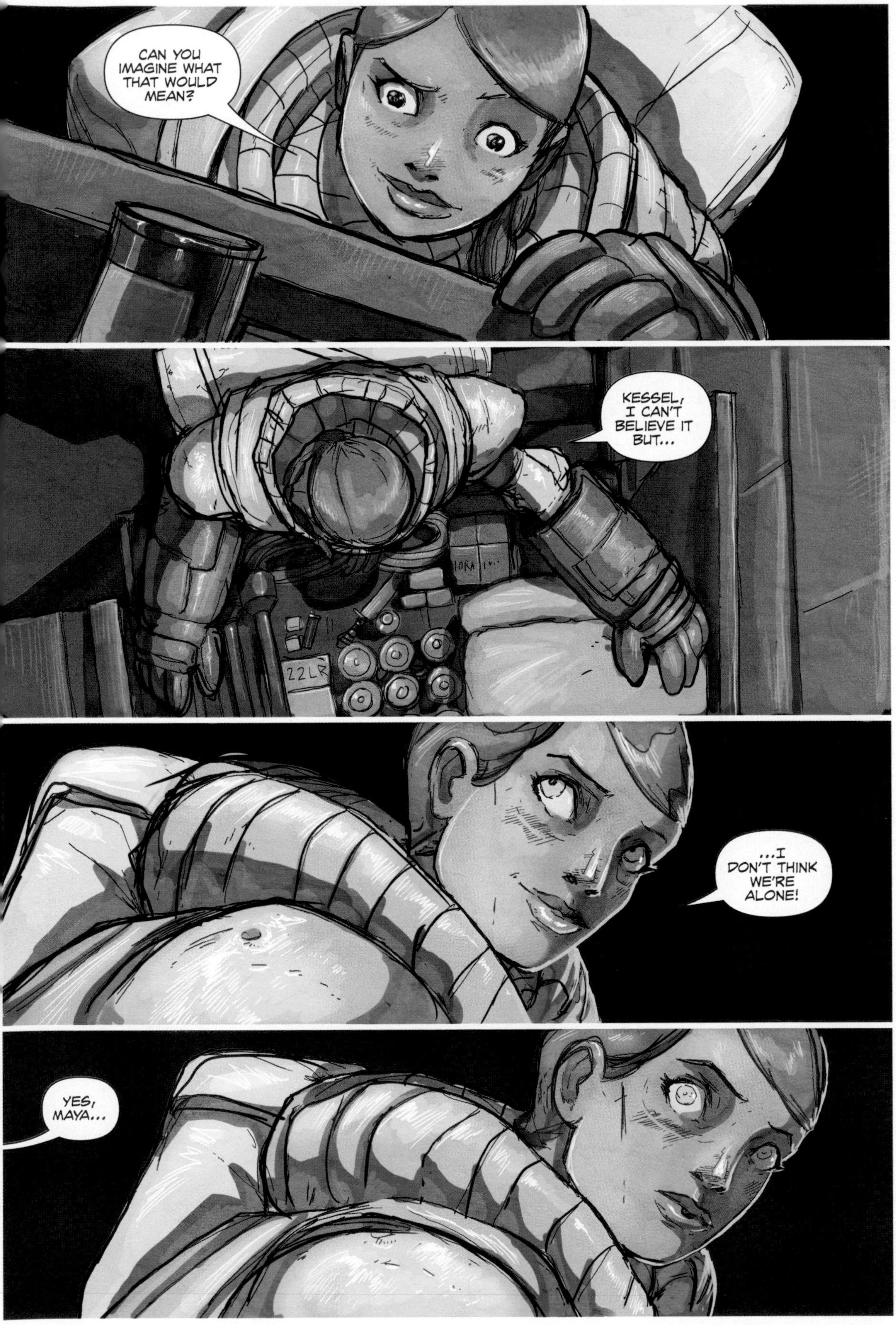
CAN YOU IMAGINE WHAT THAT WOULD MEAN?
KESSEL, I CAN'T BELIEVE IT BUT...
22LR
...I DON'T THINK WE'RE ALONE!
YES, MAYA...

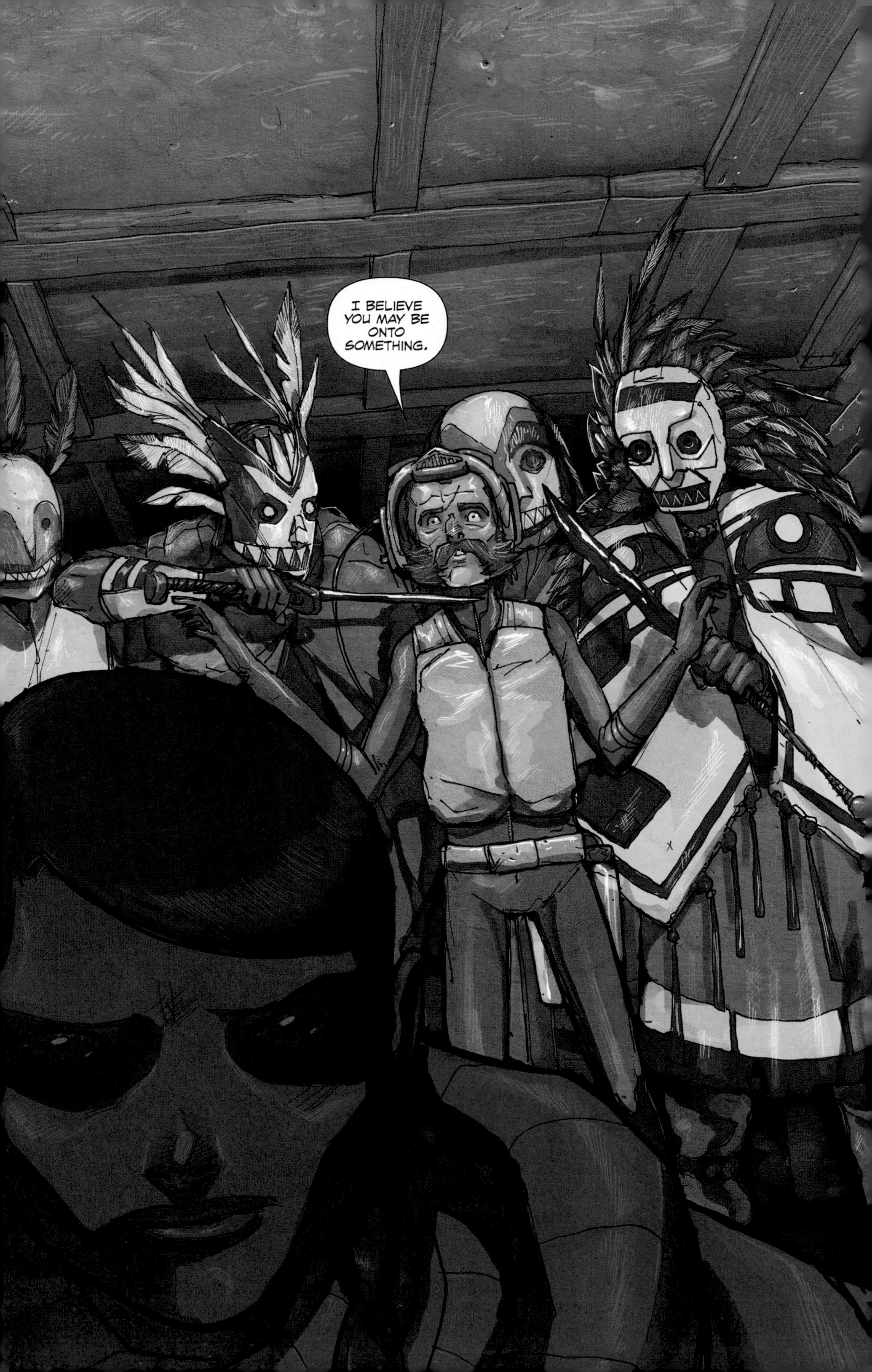
I BELIEVE YOU MAY BE ONTO SOMETHING.

FOUR

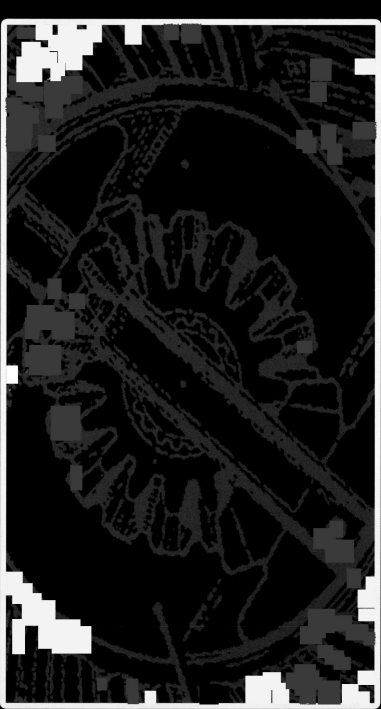

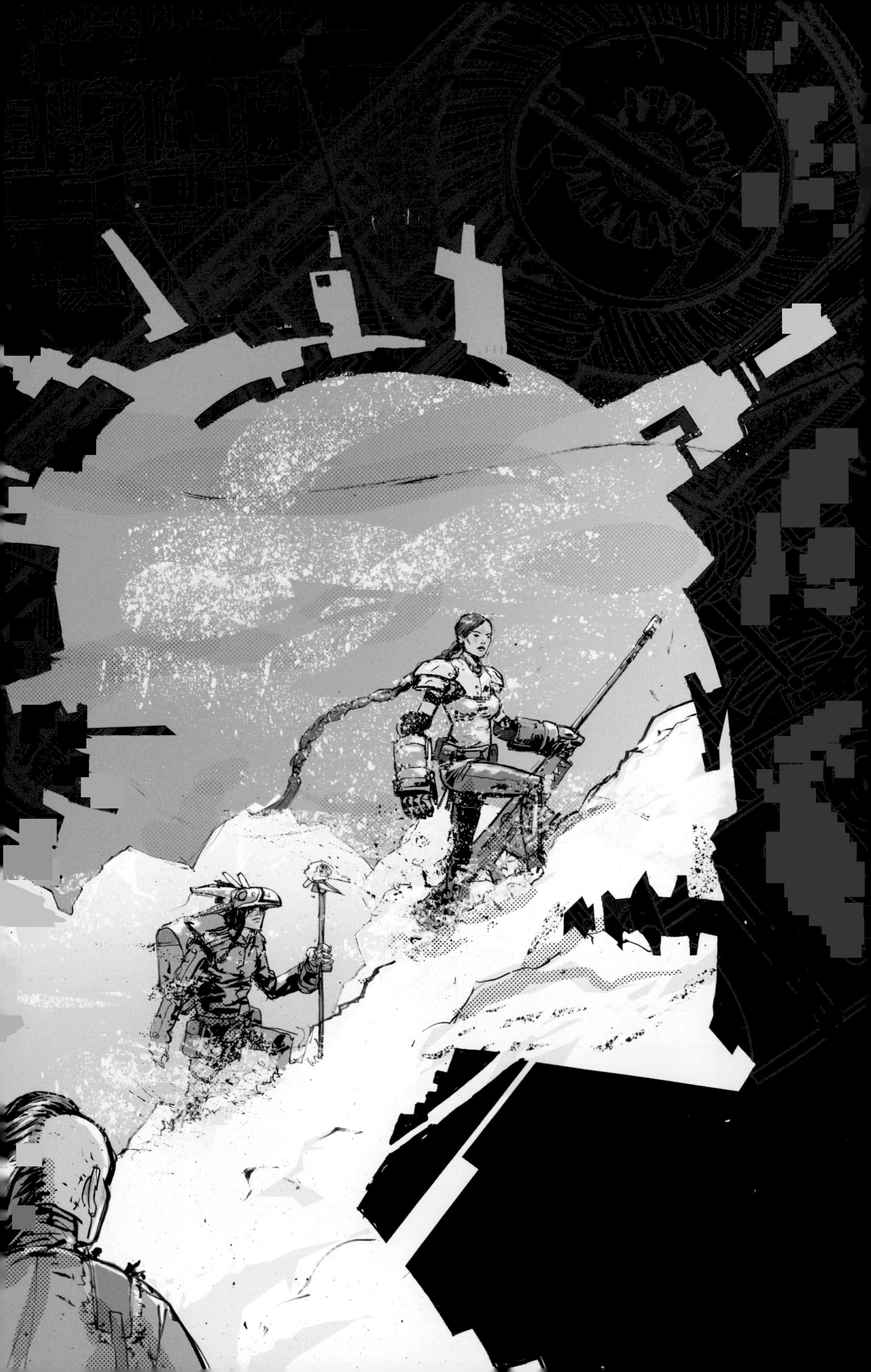

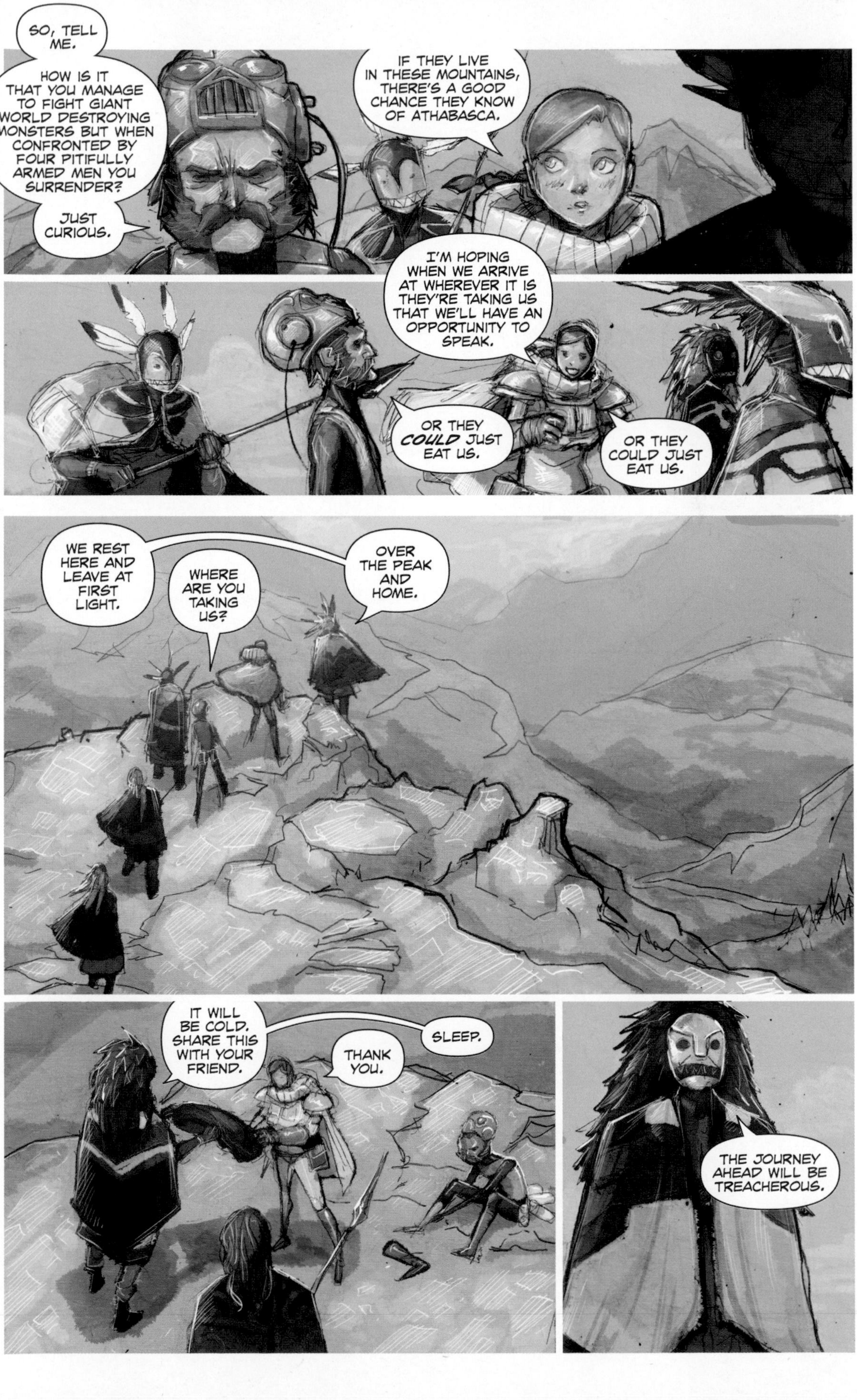
SO, TELL ME.
HOW IS IT THAT YOU MANAGE TO FIGHT GIANT WORLD DESTROYING MONSTERS BUT WHEN CONFRONTED BY FOUR PITIFULLY ARMED MEN YOU SURRENDER?
JUST CURIOUS.
IF THEY LIVE IN THESE MOUNTAINS, THERE'S A GOOD CHANCE THEY KNOW OF ATHABASCA.
I'M HOPING WHEN WE ARRIVE AT WHEREVER IT IS THEY'RE TAKING US THAT WE'LL HAVE AN OPPORTUNITY TO SPEAK.
OR THEY *COULD* JUST EAT US.
OR THEY COULD JUST EAT US.
WE REST HERE AND LEAVE AT FIRST LIGHT.
WHERE ARE YOU TAKING US?
OVER THE PEAK AND HOME.
IT WILL BE COLD. SHARE THIS WITH YOUR FRIEND.
THANK YOU.
SLEEP.
THE JOURNEY AHEAD WILL BE TREACHEROUS.

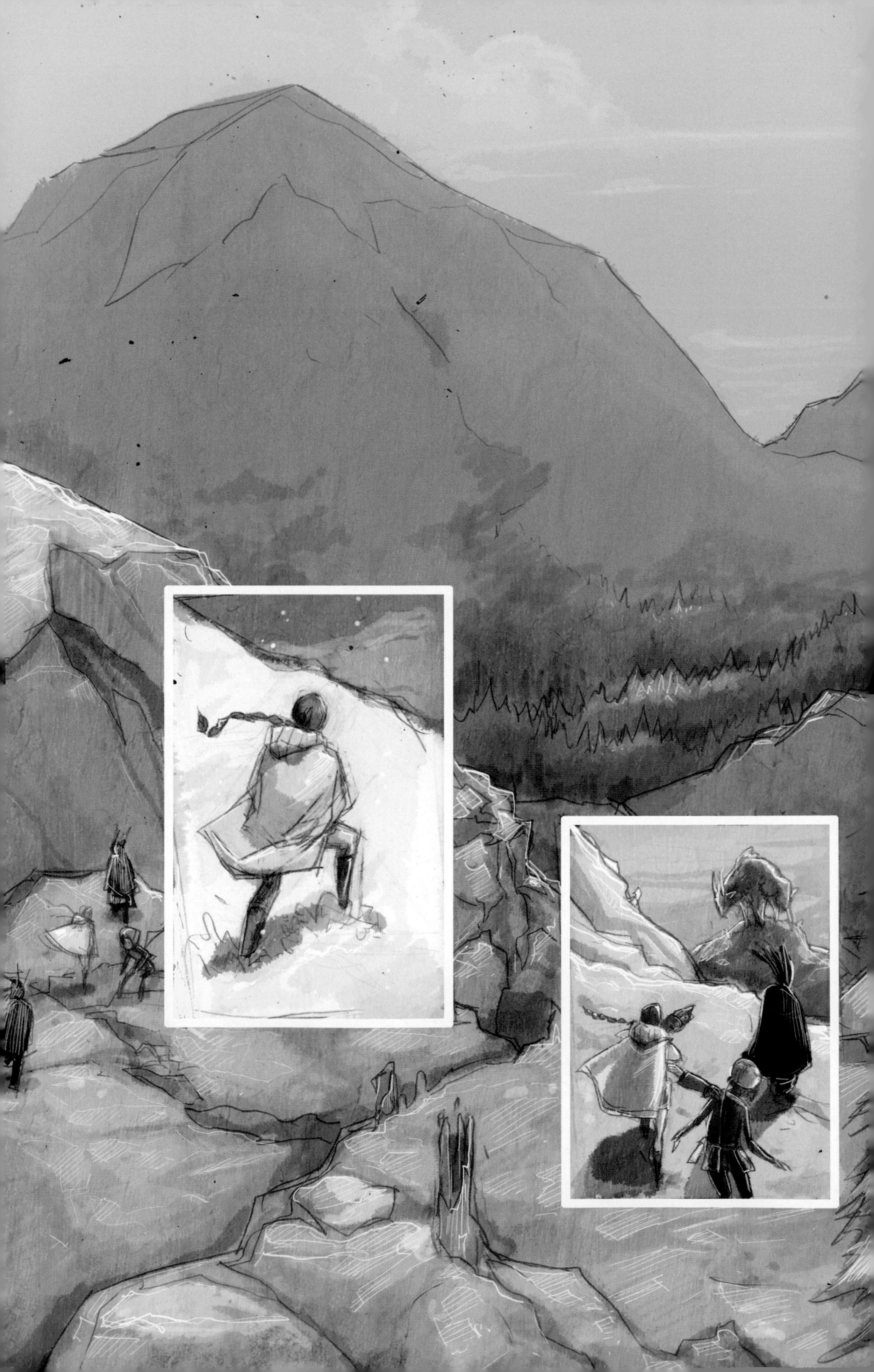

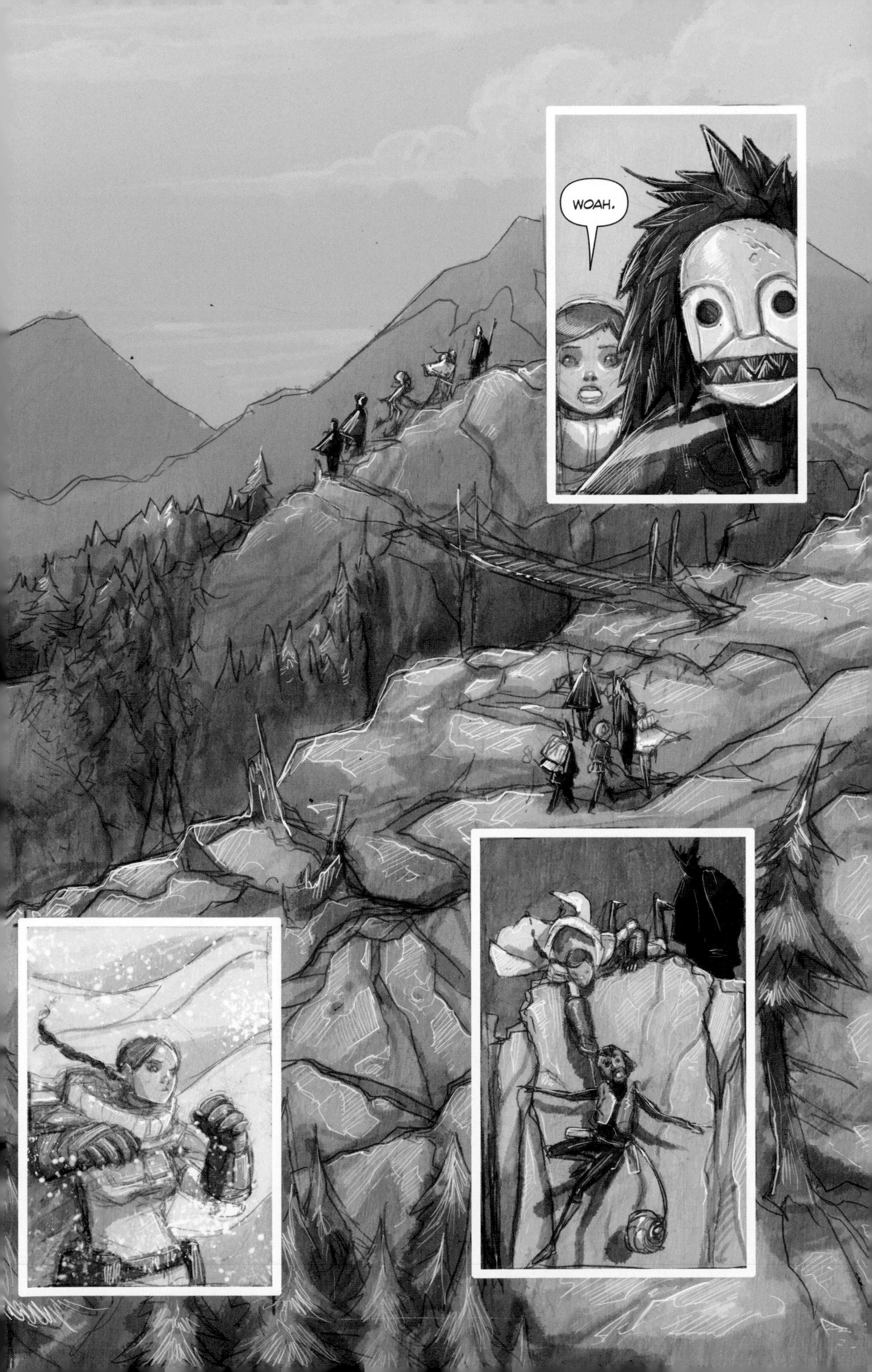
WOAH.

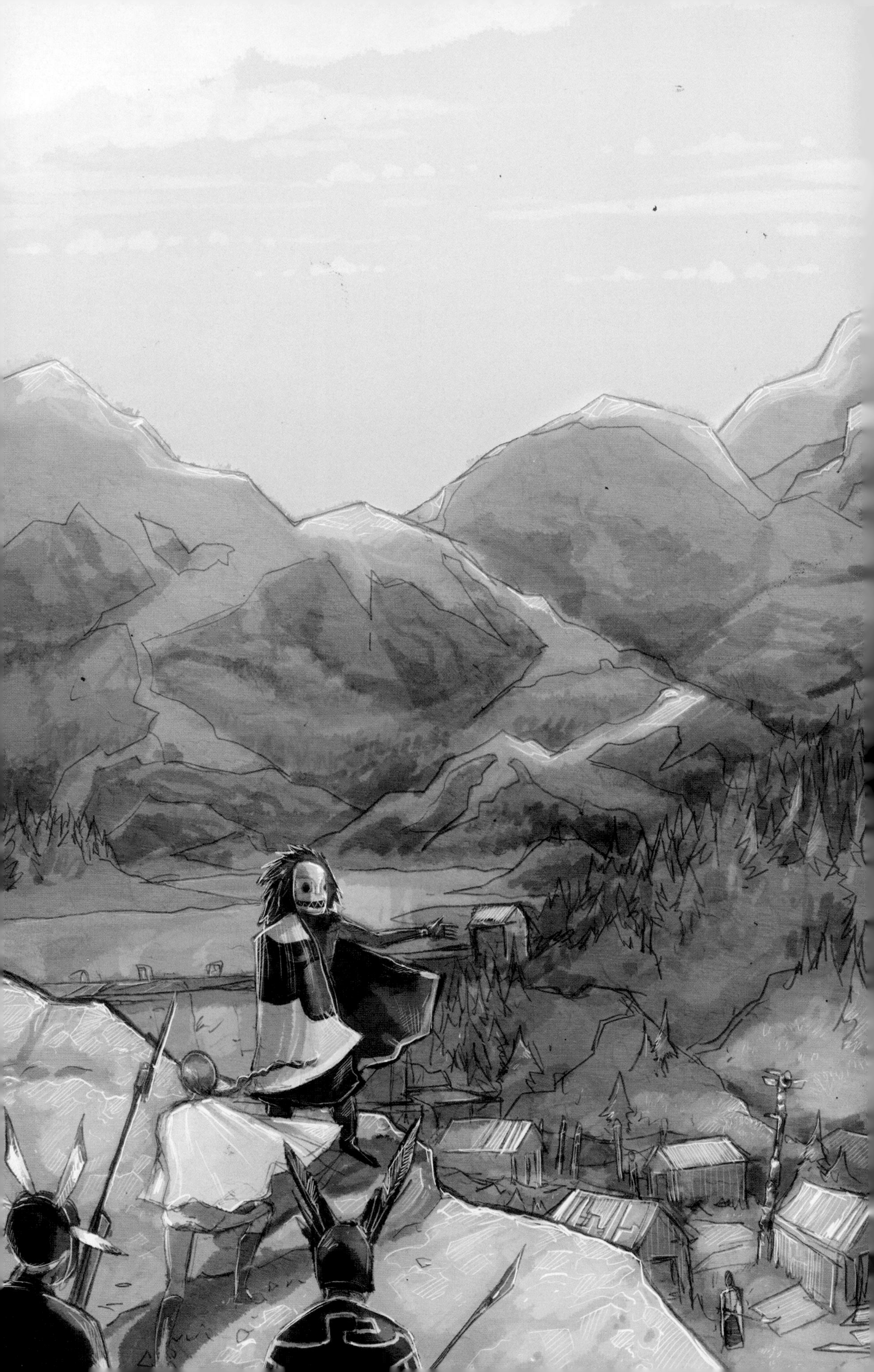

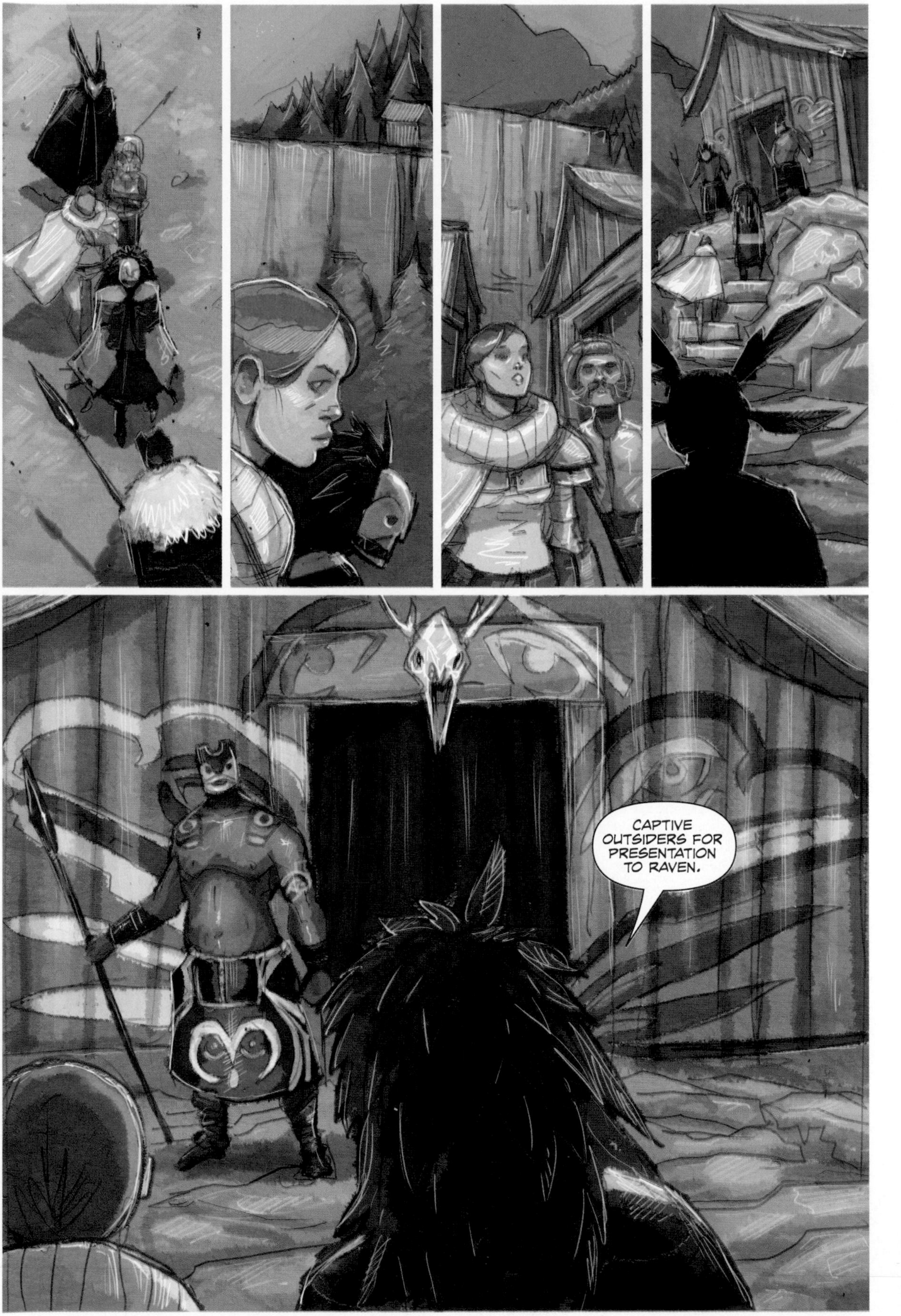
CAPTIVE OUTSIDERS FOR PRESENTATION TO RAVEN.

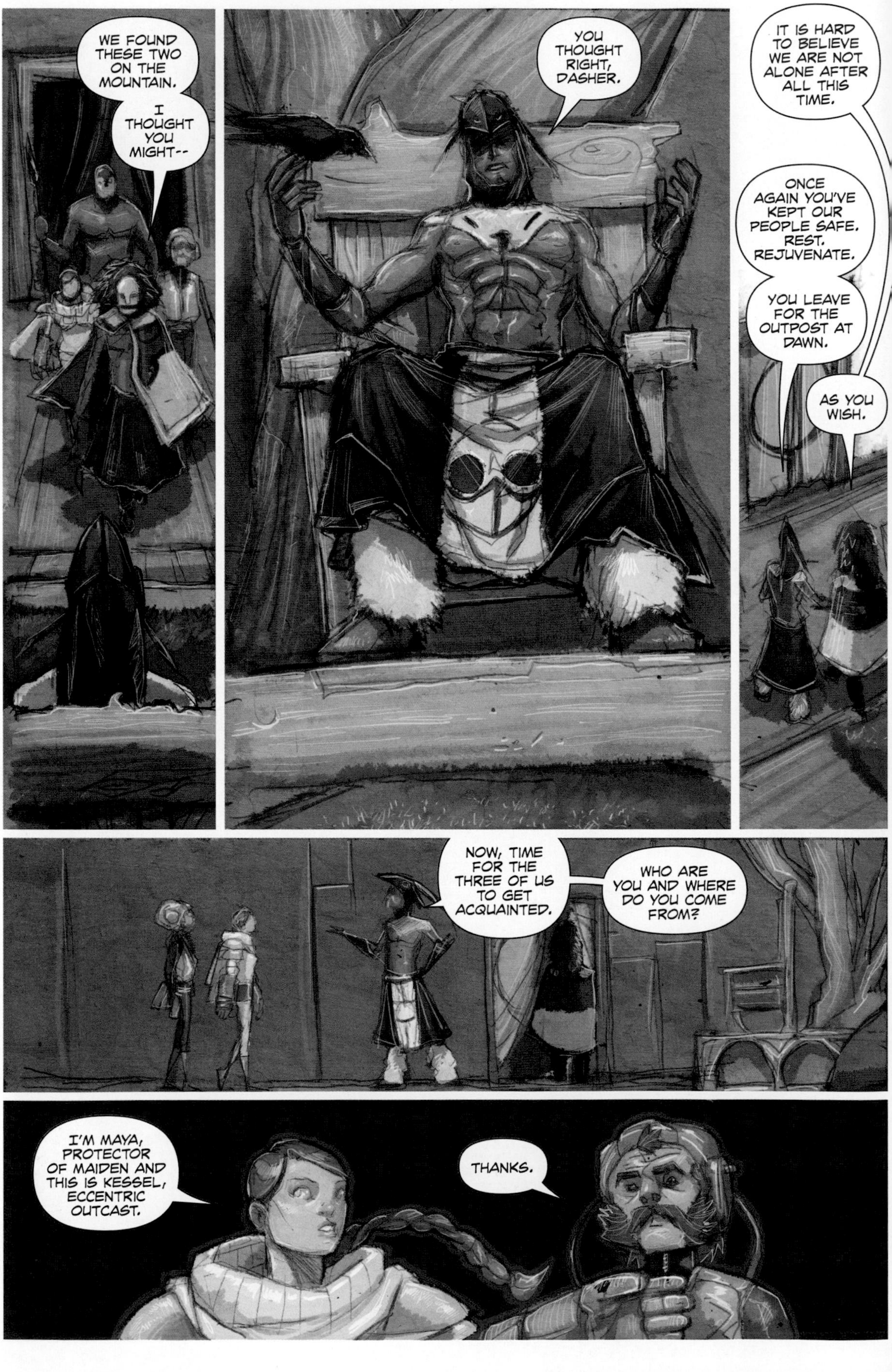
WE FOUND THESE TWO ON THE MOUNTAIN.
I THOUGHT YOU MIGHT--
YOU THOUGHT RIGHT, DASHER.
IT IS HARD TO BELIEVE WE ARE NOT ALONE AFTER ALL THIS TIME.
ONCE AGAIN YOU'VE KEPT OUR PEOPLE SAFE. REST. REJUVENATE.
YOU LEAVE FOR THE OUTPOST AT DAWN.
AS YOU WISH.
NOW, TIME FOR THE THREE OF US TO GET ACQUAINTED.
WHO ARE YOU AND WHERE DO YOU COME FROM?
I'M MAYA, PROTECTOR OF MAIDEN AND THIS IS KESSEL, ECCENTRIC OUTCAST.
THANKS.

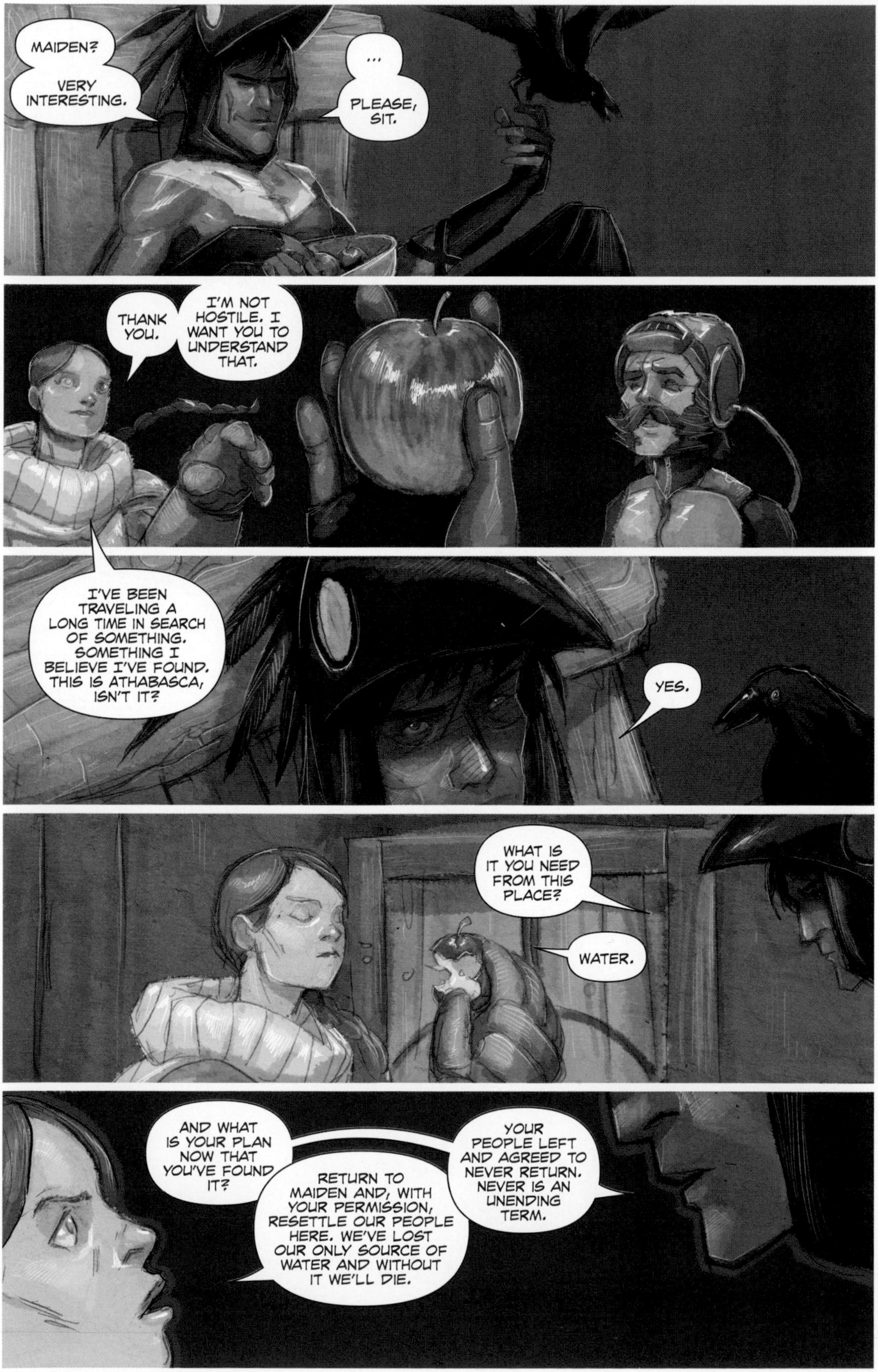
MAIDEN?
VERY INTERESTING.
...
PLEASE, SIT.
THANK YOU.
I'M NOT HOSTILE. I WANT YOU TO UNDERSTAND THAT.
I'VE BEEN TRAVELING A LONG TIME IN SEARCH OF SOMETHING. SOMETHING I BELIEVE I'VE FOUND. THIS IS ATHABASCA, ISN'T IT?
YES.
WHAT IS IT YOU NEED FROM THIS PLACE?
WATER.
AND WHAT IS YOUR PLAN NOW THAT YOU'VE FOUND IT?
RETURN TO MAIDEN AND, WITH YOUR PERMISSION, RESETTLE OUR PEOPLE HERE. WE'VE LOST OUR ONLY SOURCE OF WATER AND WITHOUT IT WE'LL DIE.
YOUR PEOPLE LEFT AND AGREED TO NEVER RETURN. NEVER IS AN UNENDING TERM.

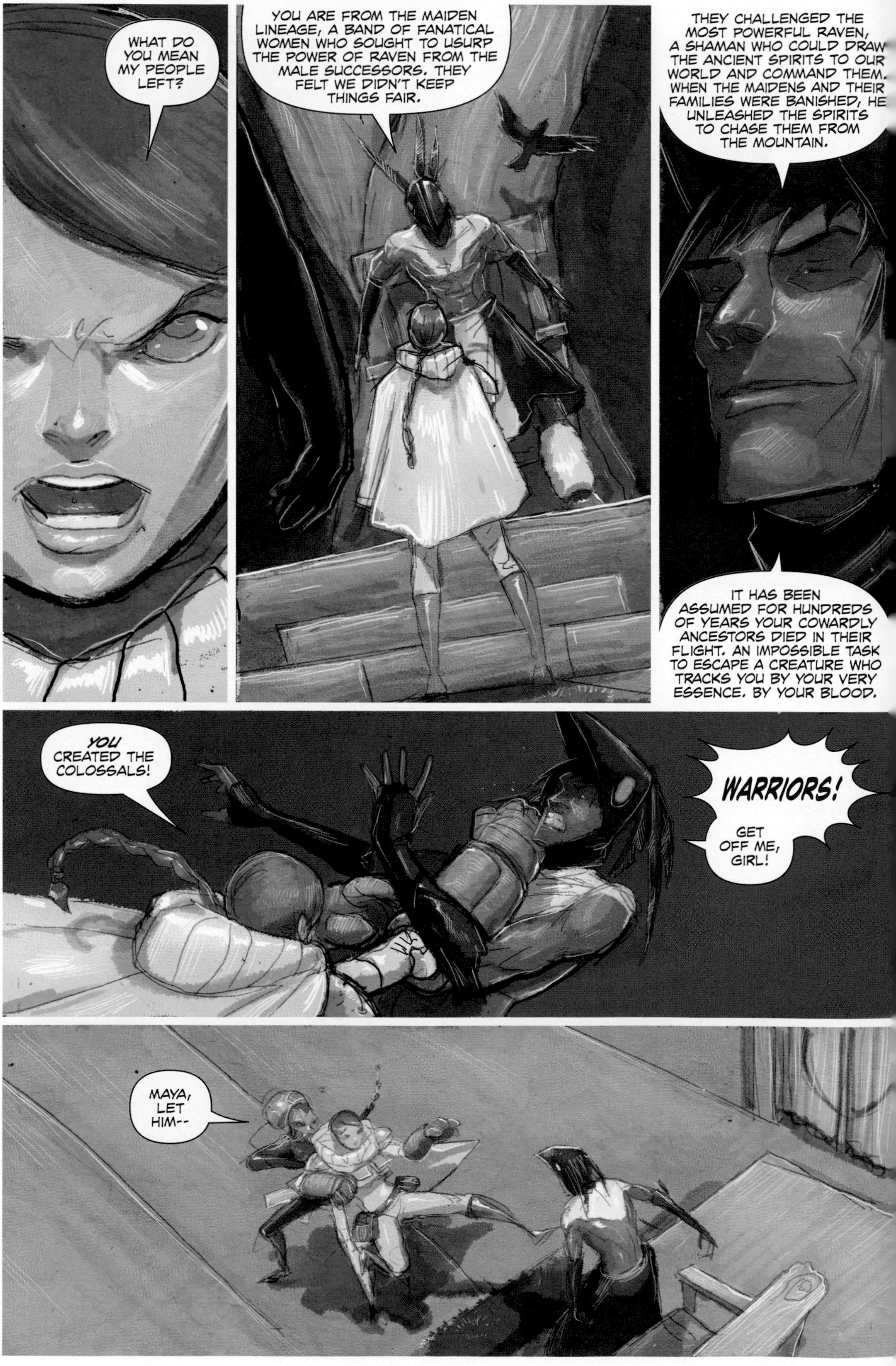
WHAT DO YOU MEAN MY PEOPLE LEFT?
YOU ARE FROM THE MAIDEN LINEAGE, A BAND OF FANATICAL WOMEN WHO SOUGHT TO USURP THE POWER OF RAVEN FROM THE MALE SUCCESSORS. THEY FELT WE DIDN'T KEEP THINGS FAIR.
THEY CHALLENGED THE MOST POWERFUL RAVEN, A SHAMAN WHO COULD DRAW THE ANCIENT SPIRITS TO OUR WORLD AND COMMAND THEM. WHEN THE MAIDENS AND THEIR FAMILIES WERE BANISHED, HE UNLEASHED THE SPIRITS TO CHASE THEM FROM THE MOUNTAIN.
IT HAS BEEN ASSUMED FOR HUNDREDS OF YEARS YOUR COWARDLY ANCESTORS DIED IN THEIR FLIGHT. AN IMPOSSIBLE TASK TO ESCAPE A CREATURE WHO TRACKS YOU BY YOUR VERY ESSENCE. BY YOUR BLOOD.
YOU CREATED THE COLOSSALS!
WARRIORS!
GET OFF ME, GIRL!
MAYA, LET HIM--

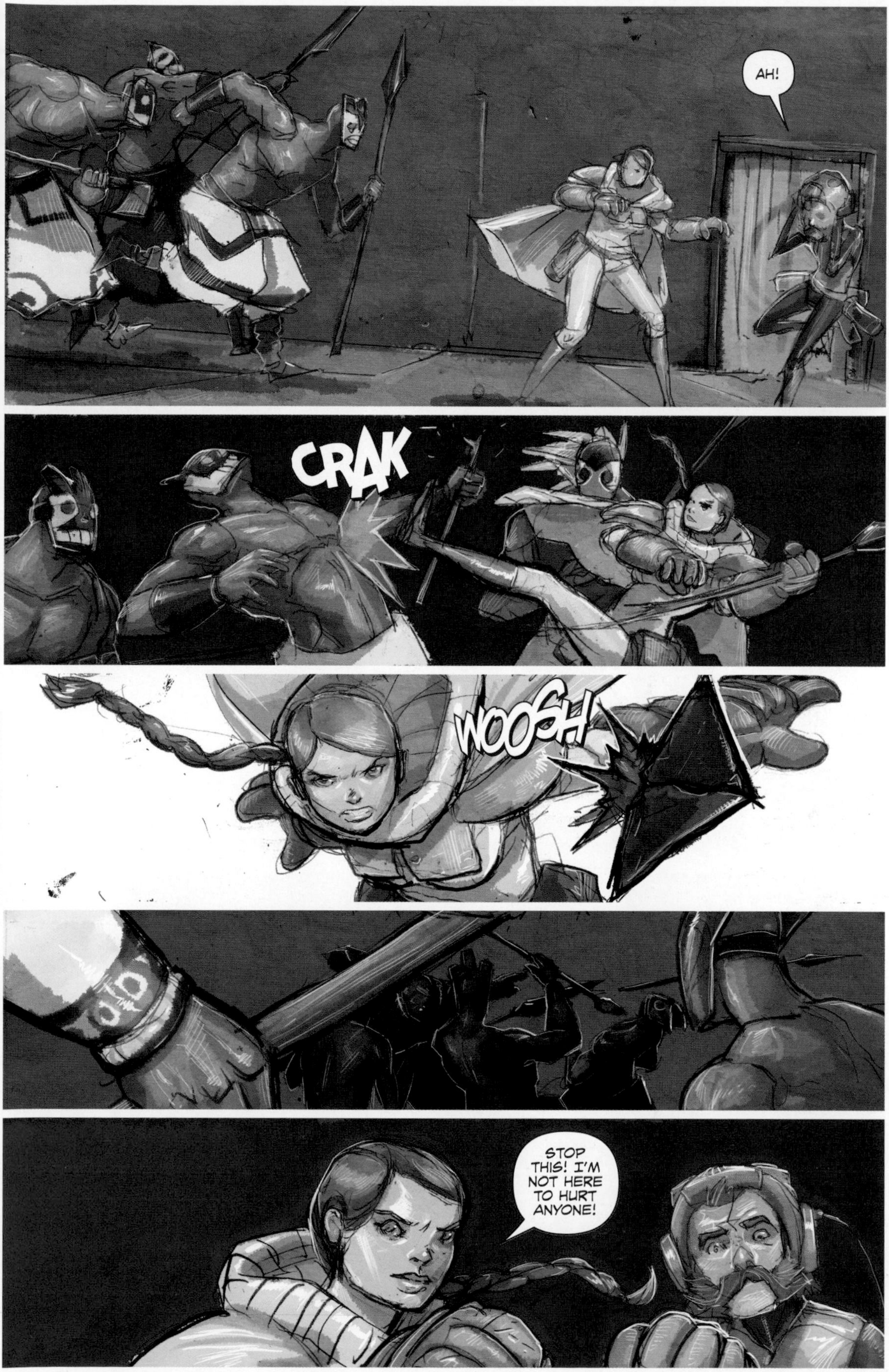
AH!
CRAK
WOOSH
STOP THIS! I'M NOT HERE TO HURT ANYONE!

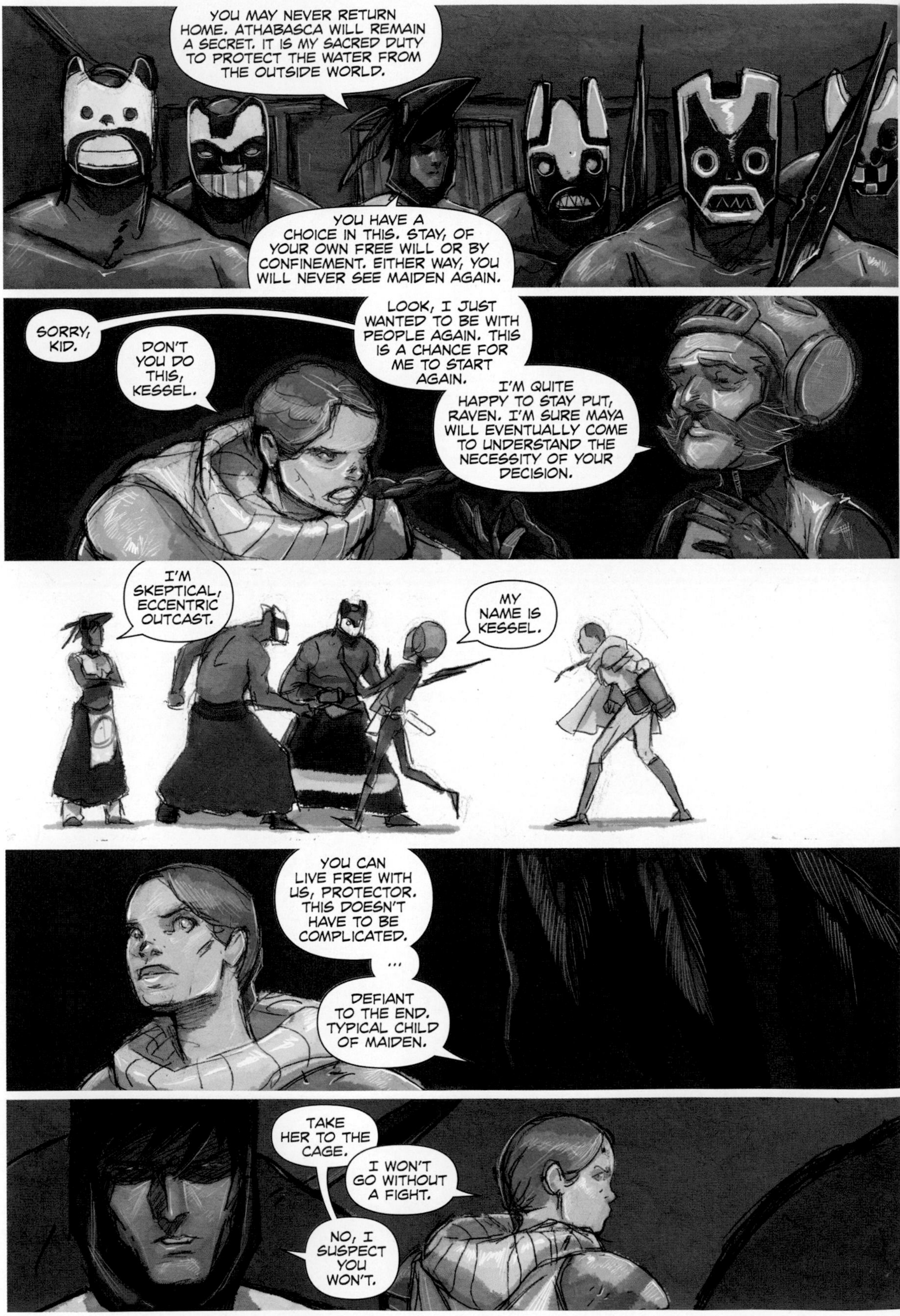
YOU MAY NEVER RETURN HOME. ATHABASCA WILL REMAIN A SECRET. IT IS MY SACRED DUTY TO PROTECT THE WATER FROM THE OUTSIDE WORLD.
YOU HAVE A CHOICE IN THIS. STAY, OF YOUR OWN FREE WILL OR BY CONFINEMENT. EITHER WAY, YOU WILL NEVER SEE MAIDEN AGAIN.
SORRY, KID.
LOOK, I JUST WANTED TO BE WITH PEOPLE AGAIN. THIS IS A CHANCE FOR ME TO START AGAIN.
DON'T YOU DO THIS, KESSEL.
I'M QUITE HAPPY TO STAY PUT, RAVEN. I'M SURE MAYA WILL EVENTUALLY COME TO UNDERSTAND THE NECESSITY OF YOUR DECISION.
I'M SKEPTICAL, ECCENTRIC OUTCAST.
MY NAME IS KESSEL.
YOU CAN LIVE FREE WITH US, PROTECTOR. THIS DOESN'T HAVE TO BE COMPLICATED.
...
DEFIANT TO THE END. TYPICAL CHILD OF MAIDEN.
TAKE HER TO THE CAGE.
I WON'T GO WITHOUT A FIGHT.
NO, I SUSPECT YOU WON'T.

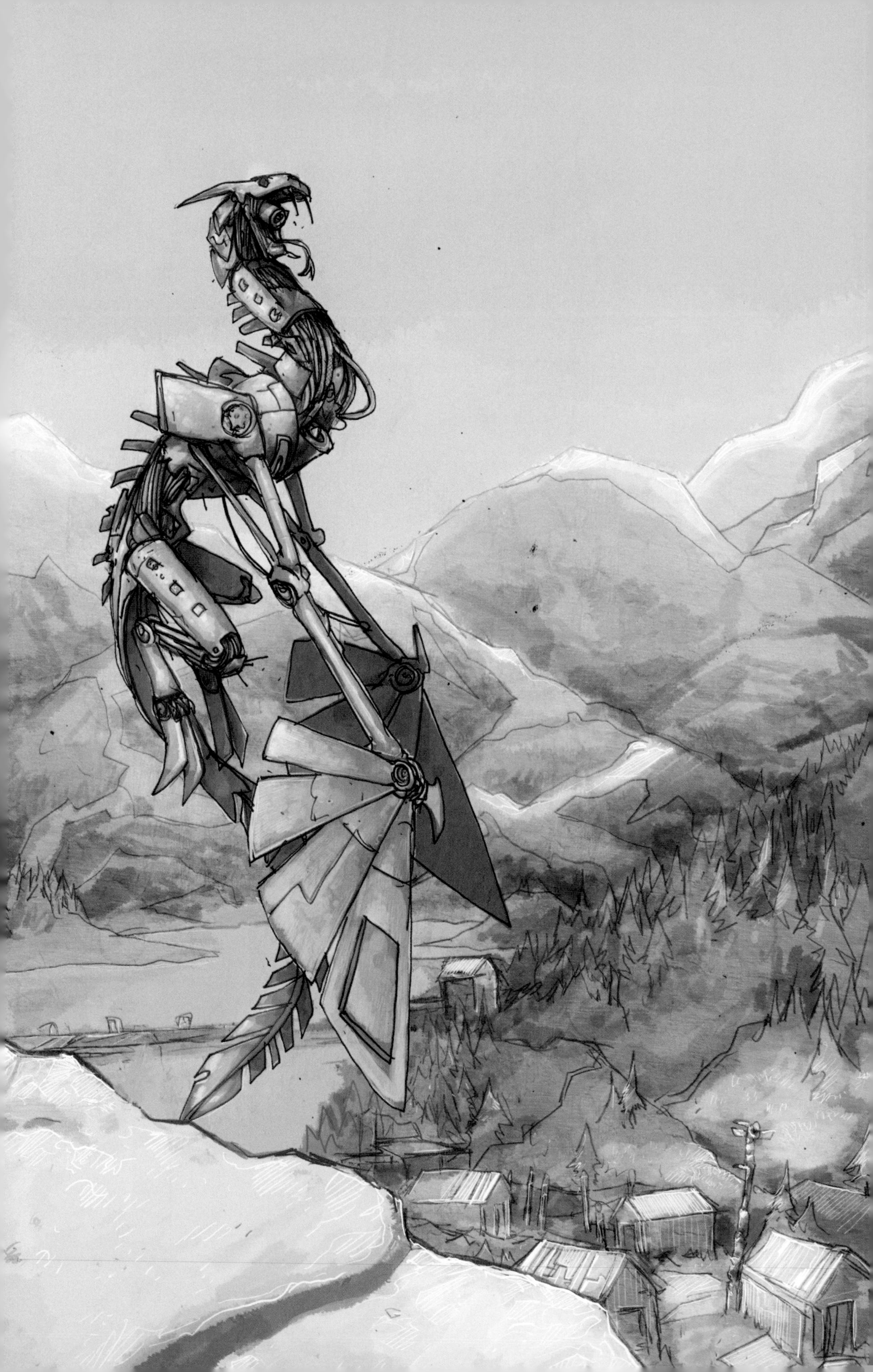

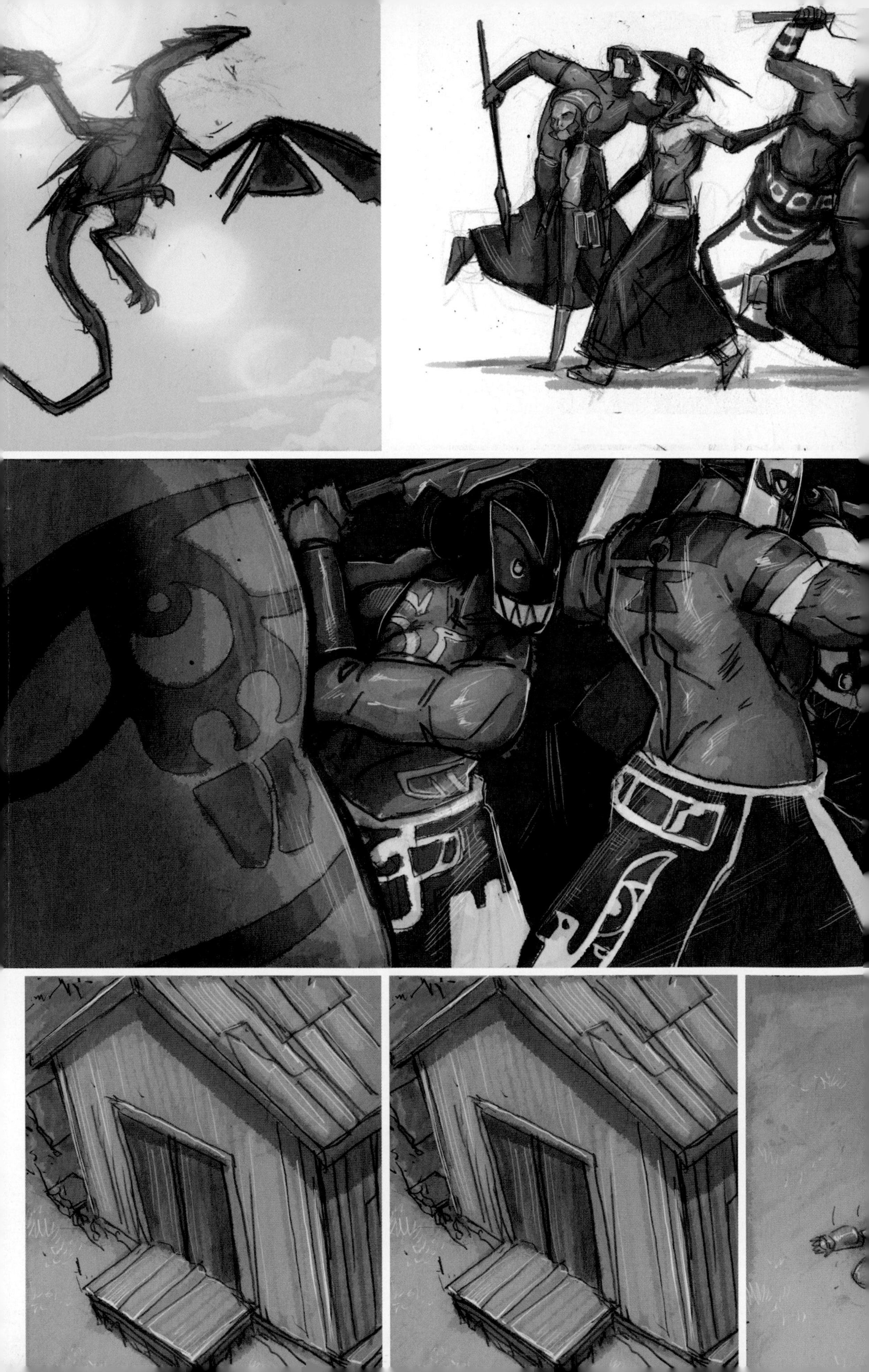

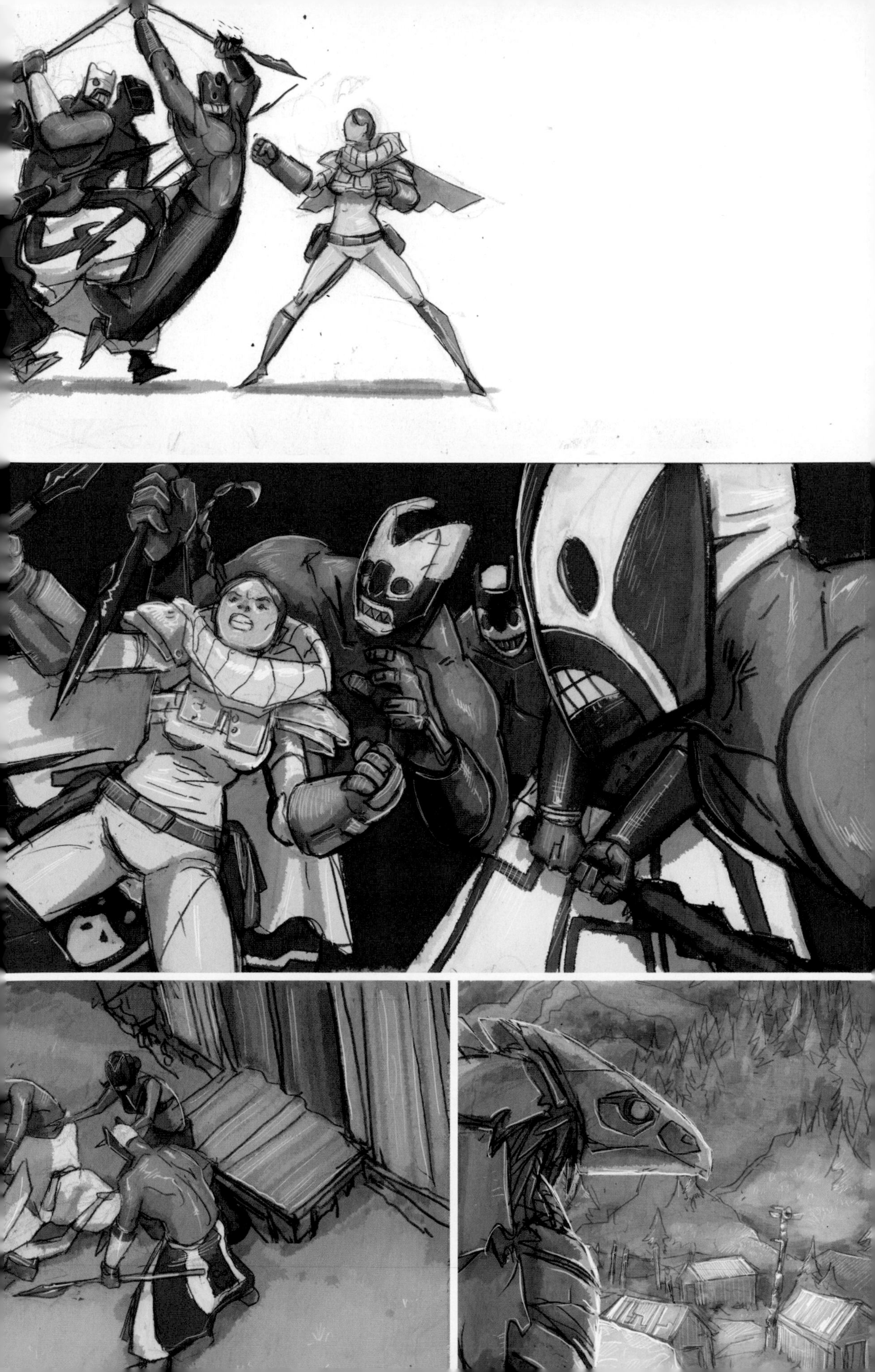

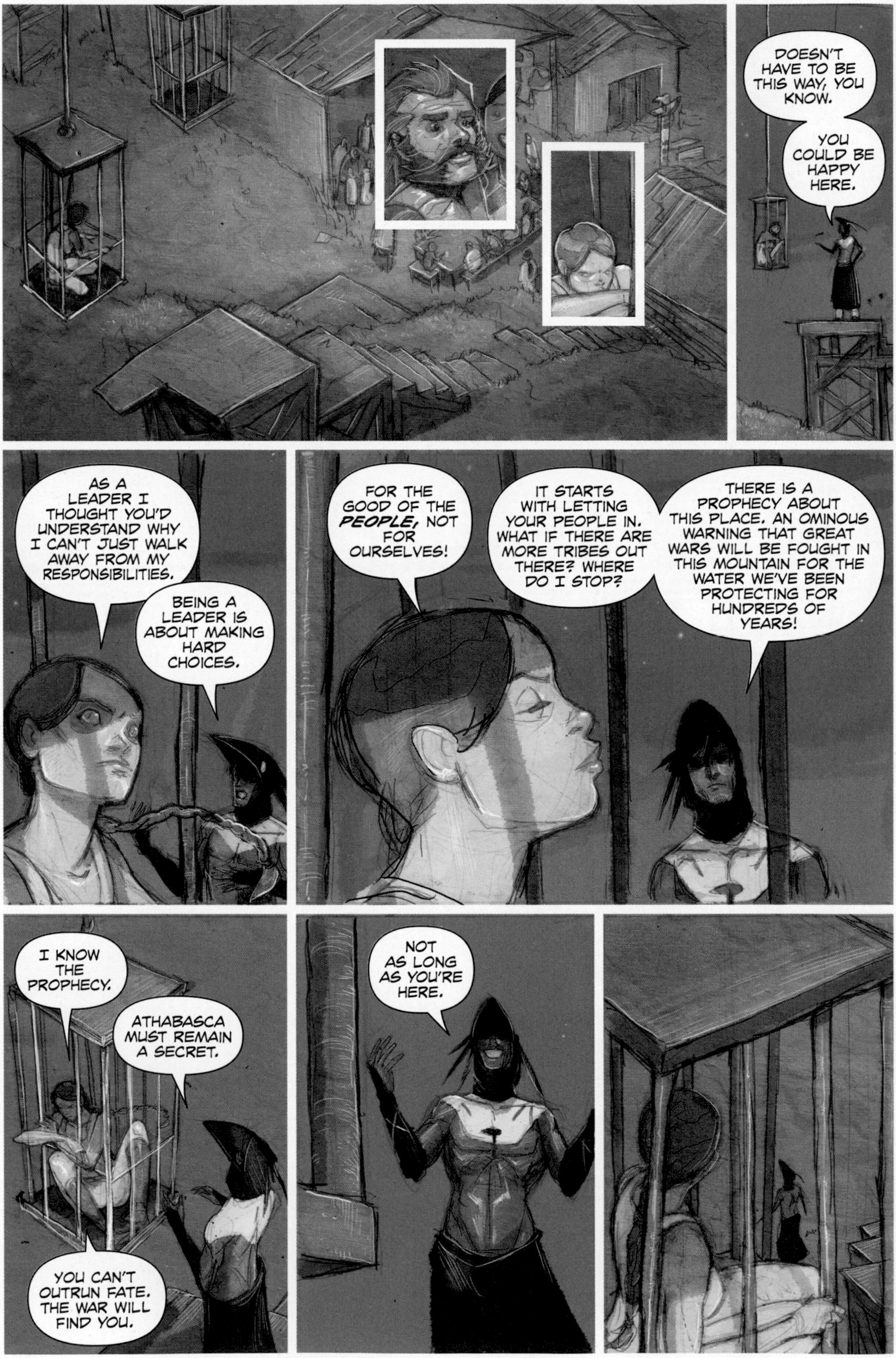
DOESN'T HAVE TO BE THIS WAY, YOU KNOW.
YOU COULD BE HAPPY HERE.
AS A LEADER I THOUGHT YOU'D UNDERSTAND WHY I CAN'T JUST WALK AWAY FROM MY RESPONSIBILITIES.
BEING A LEADER IS ABOUT MAKING HARD CHOICES.
FOR THE GOOD OF THE *PEOPLE,* NOT FOR OURSELVES!
IT STARTS WITH LETTING YOUR PEOPLE IN. WHAT IF THERE ARE MORE TRIBES OUT THERE? WHERE DO I STOP?
THERE IS A PROPHECY ABOUT THIS PLACE. AN OMINOUS WARNING THAT GREAT WARS WILL BE FOUGHT IN THIS MOUNTAIN FOR THE WATER WE'VE BEEN PROTECTING FOR HUNDREDS OF YEARS!
I KNOW THE PROPHECY.
ATHABASCA MUST REMAIN A SECRET.
YOU CAN'T OUTRUN FATE. THE WAR WILL FIND YOU.
NOT AS LONG AS YOU'RE HERE.

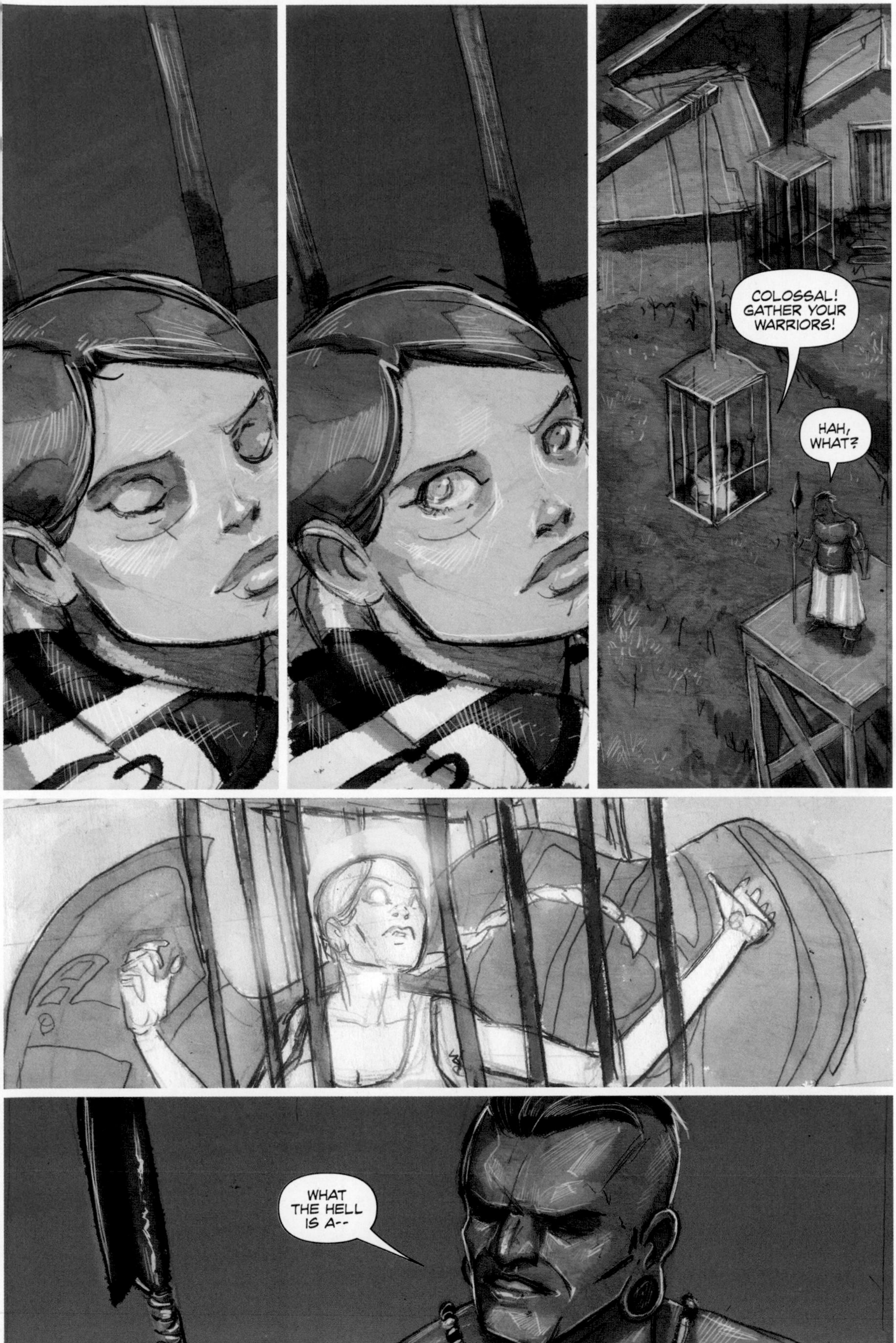
COLOSSAL! GATHER YOUR WARRIORS!
HAH, WHAT?
WHAT THE HELL IS A--

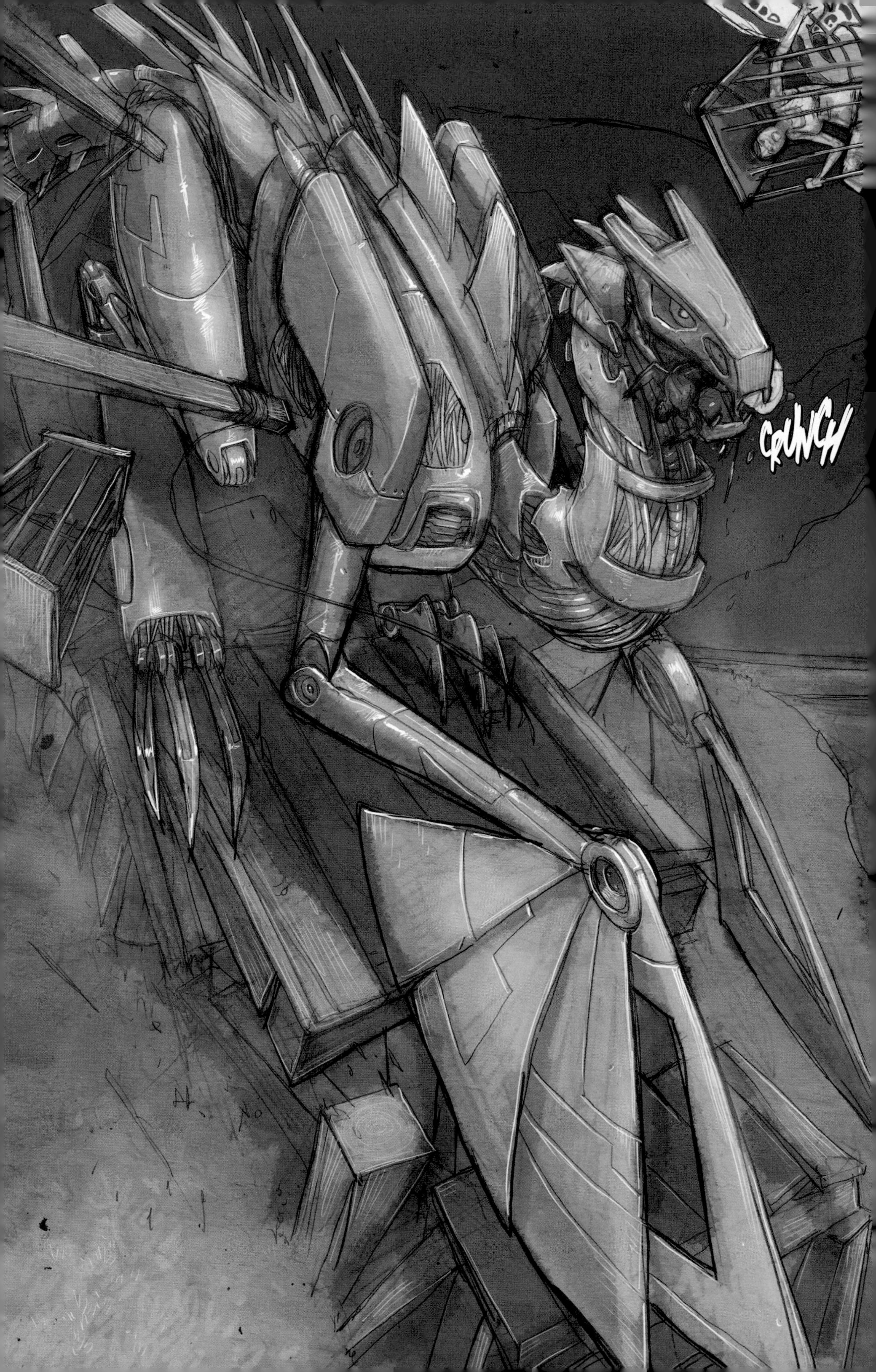
CRUNCH

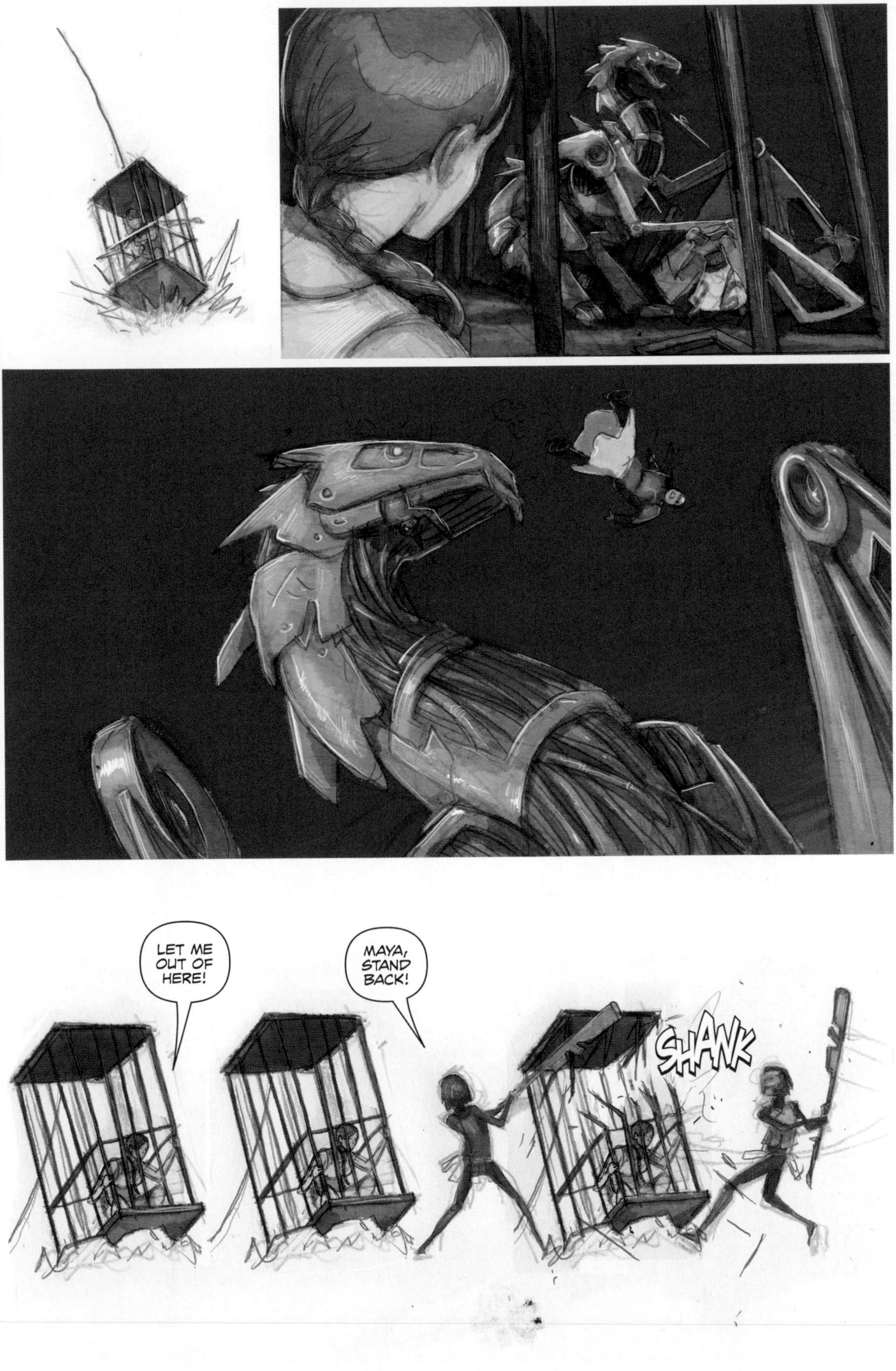
LET ME OUT OF HERE!
MAYA, STAND BACK!
SHANK

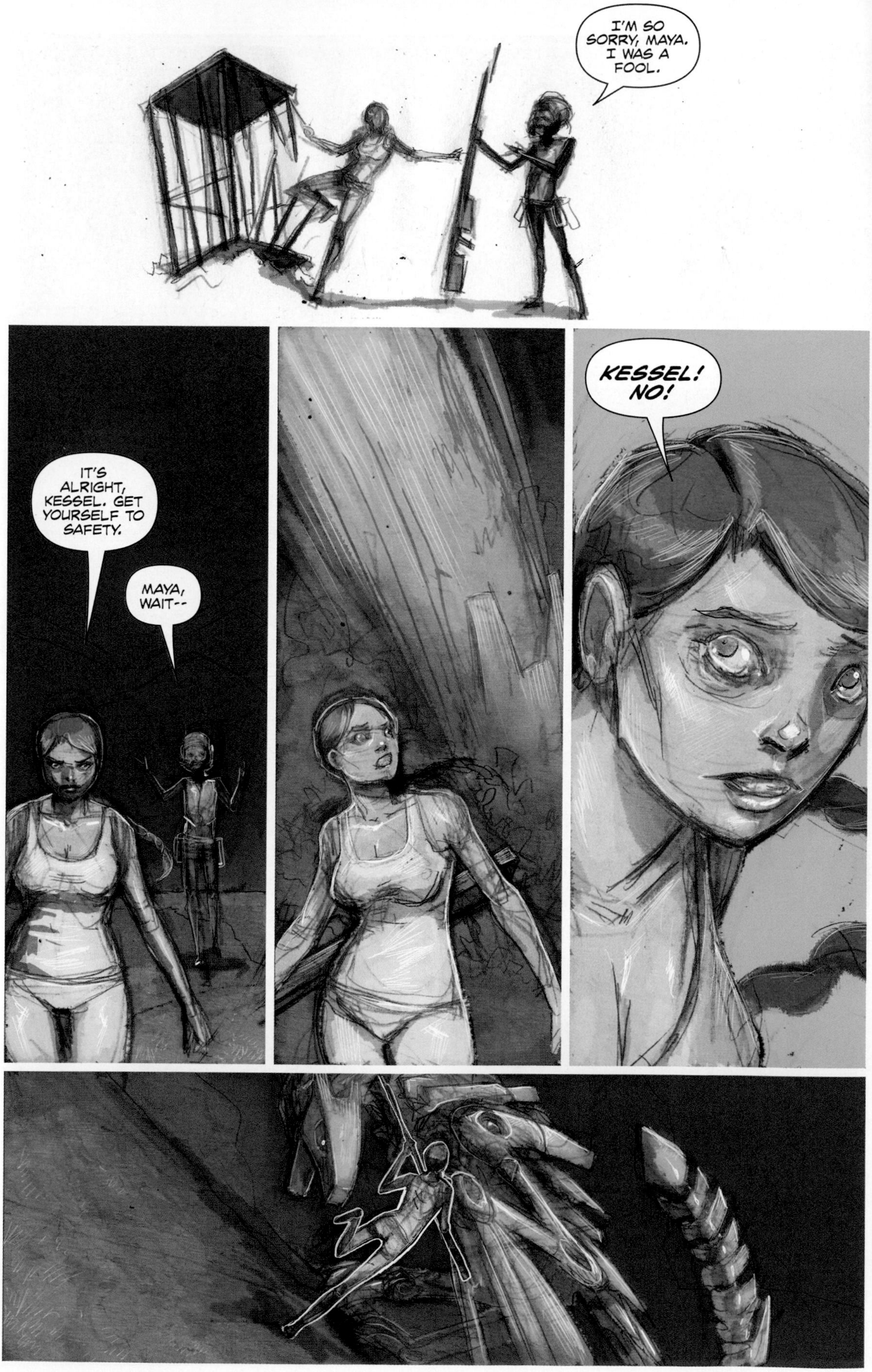
I'M SO SORRY, MAYA. I WAS A FOOL.
IT'S ALRIGHT, KESSEL. GET YOURSELF TO SAFETY.
MAYA, WAIT--
KESSEL! NO!

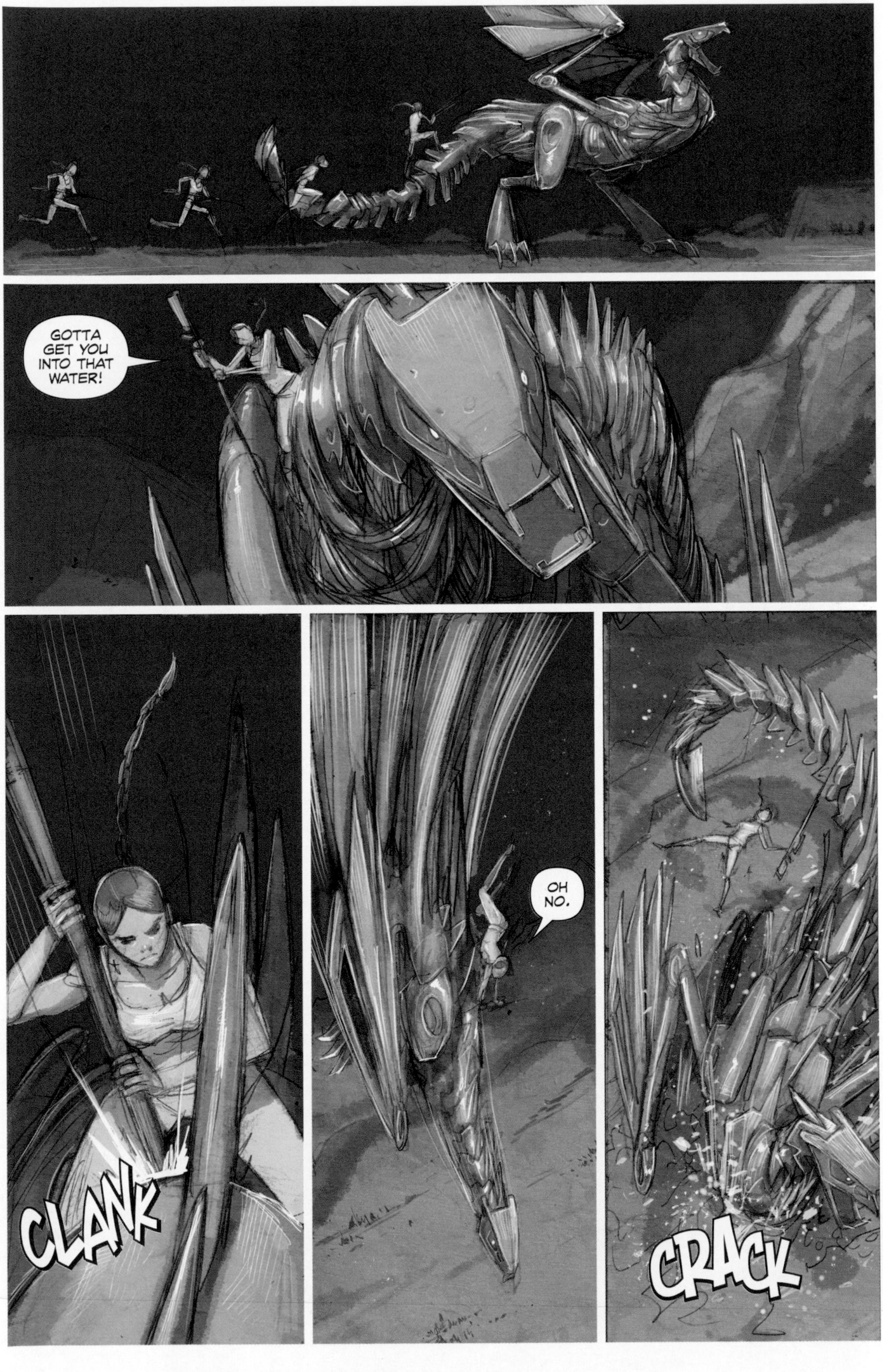
GOTTA GET YOU INTO THAT WATER!
CLANK
OH NO.
CRACK

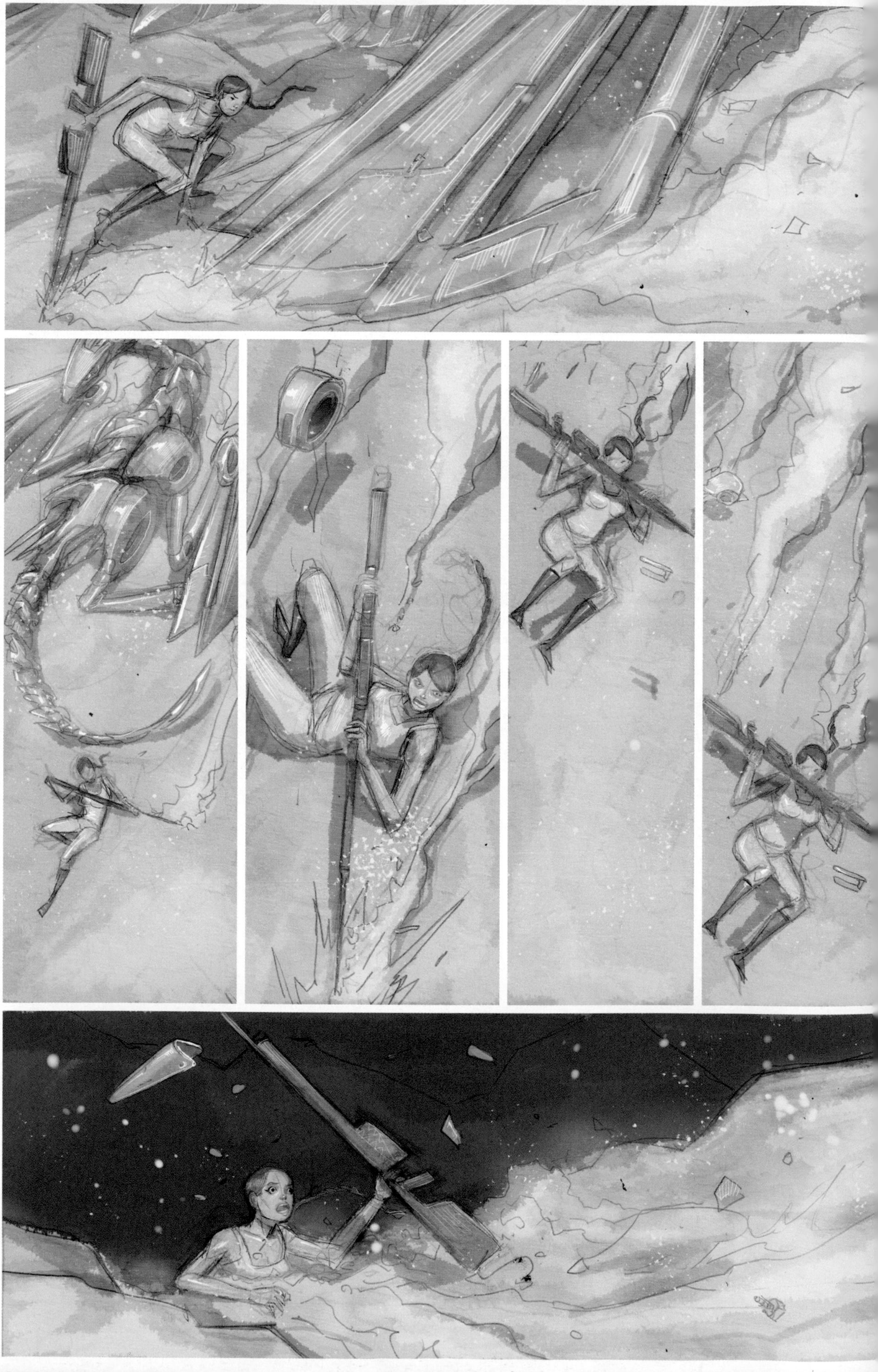

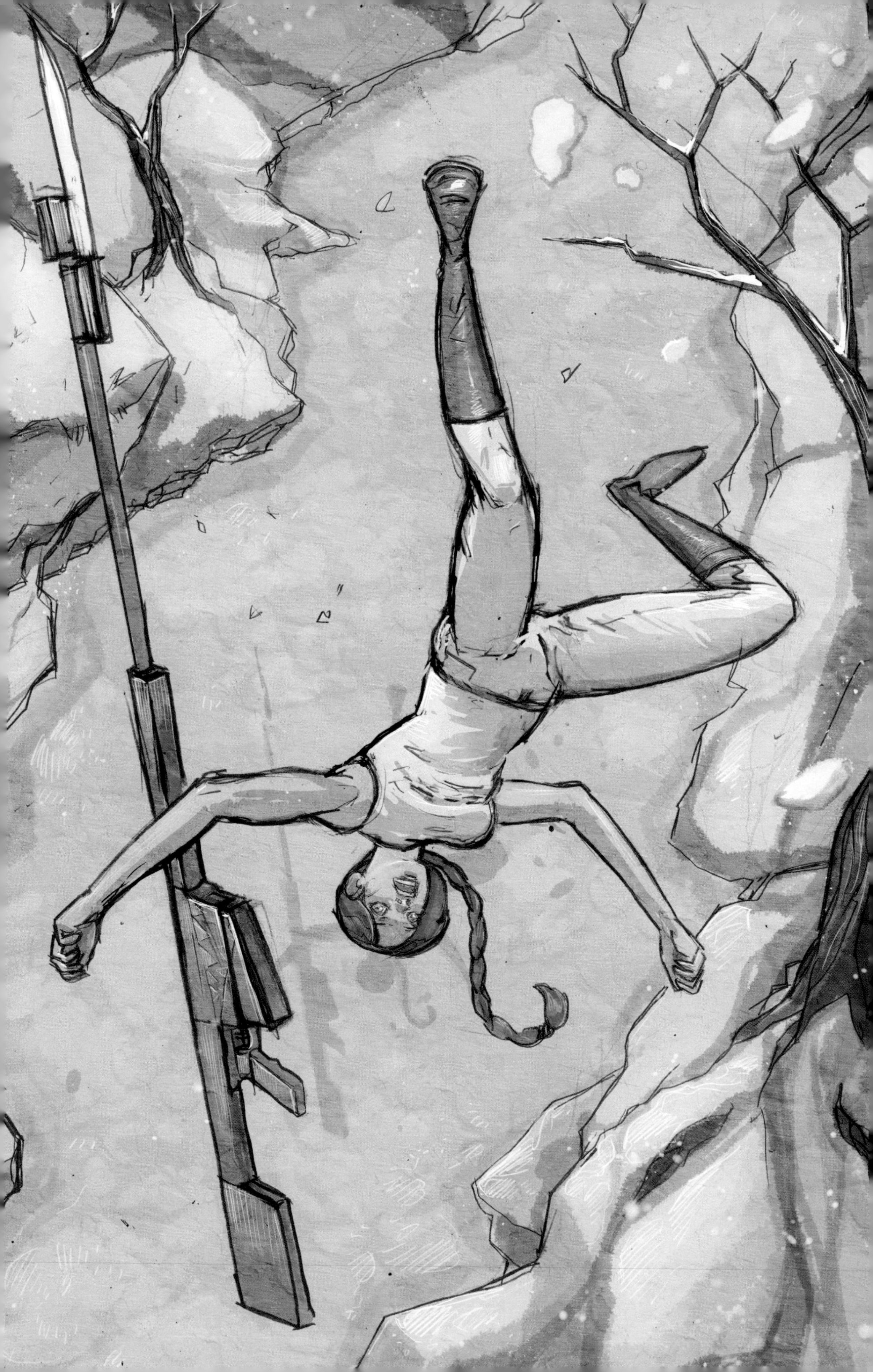

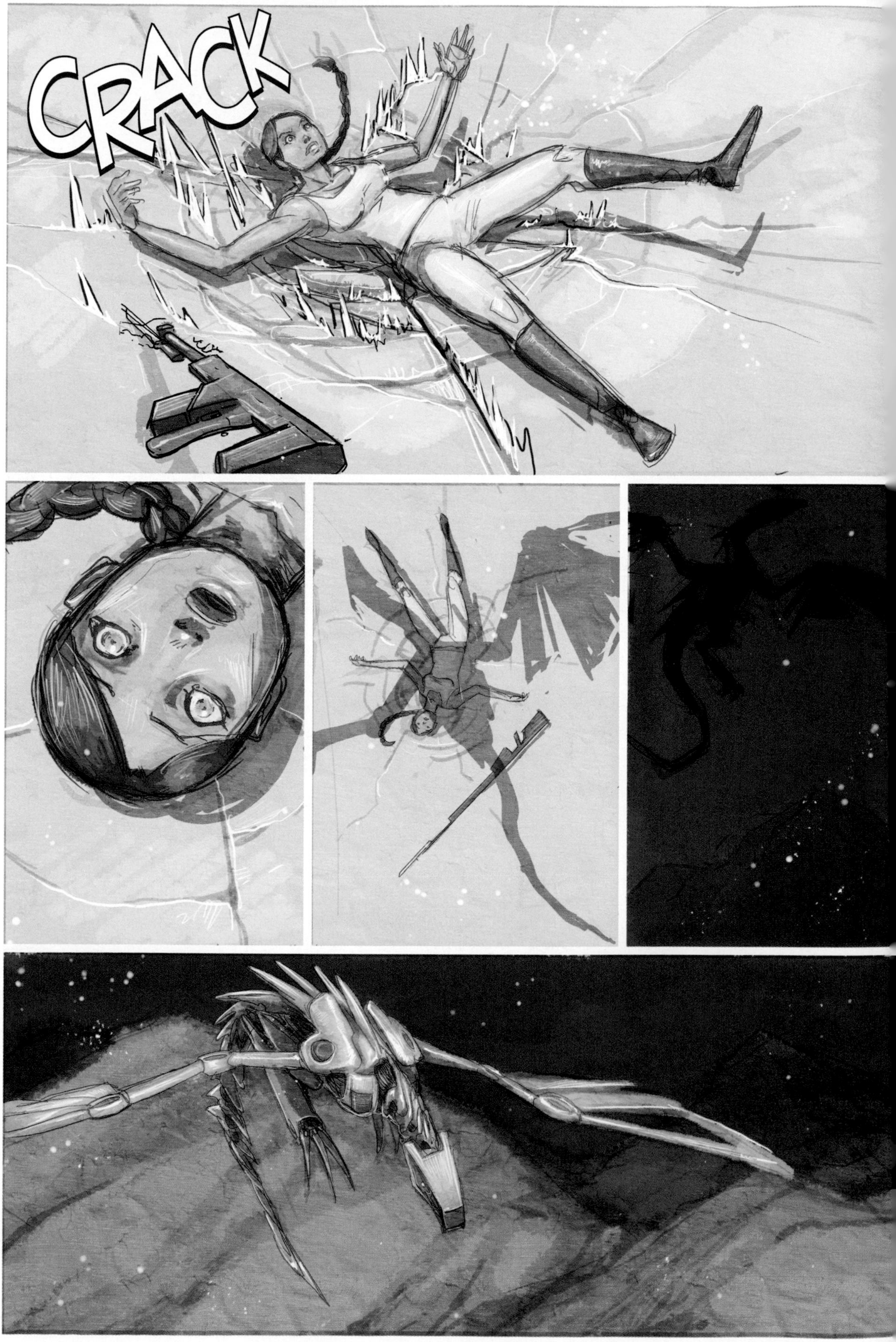
CRACK

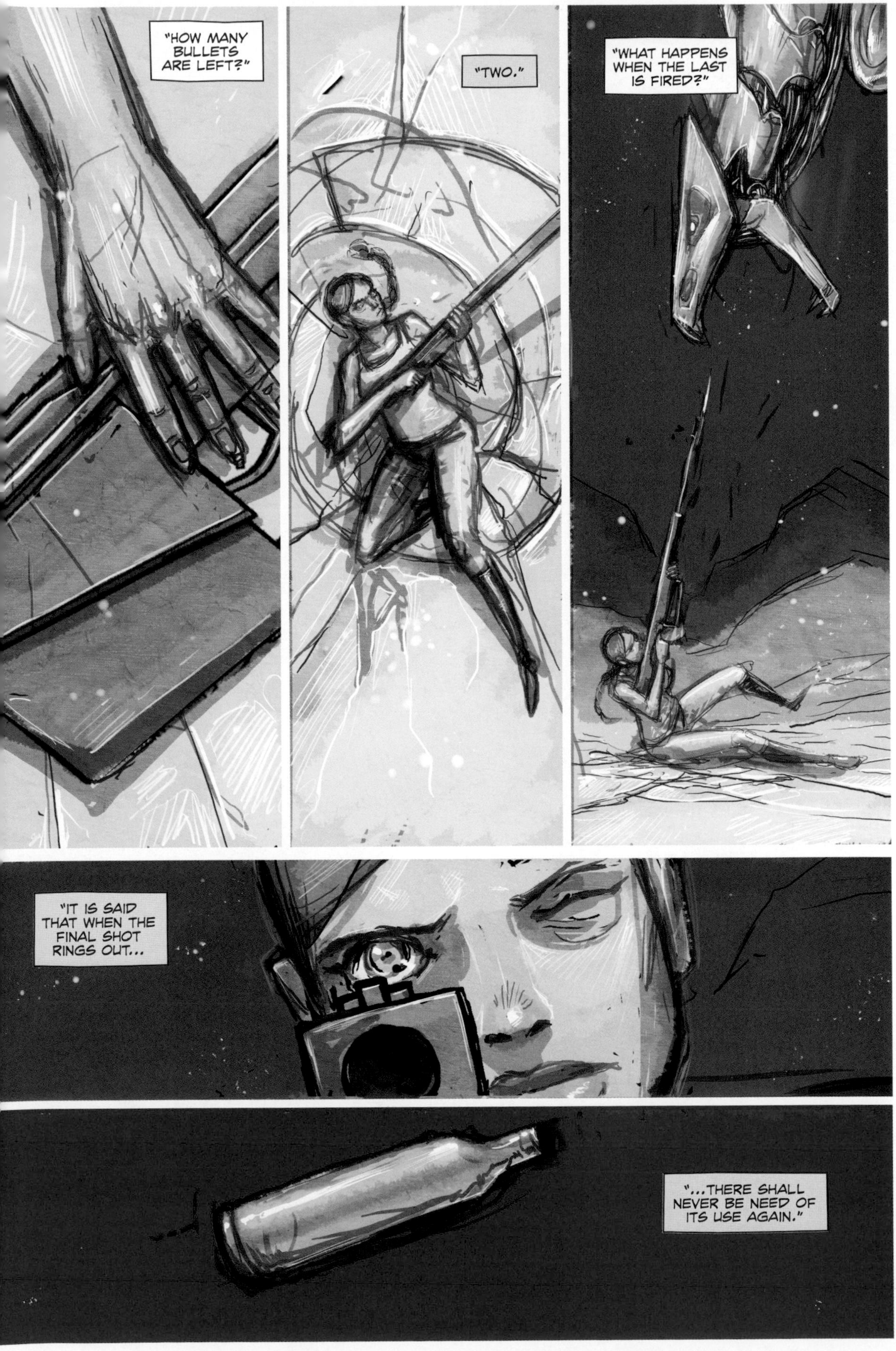
"HOW MANY BULLETS ARE LEFT?"
"TWO."
"WHAT HAPPENS WHEN THE LAST IS FIRED?"
"IT IS SAID THAT WHEN THE FINAL SHOT RINGS OUT...
"...THERE SHALL NEVER BE NEED OF ITS USE AGAIN."

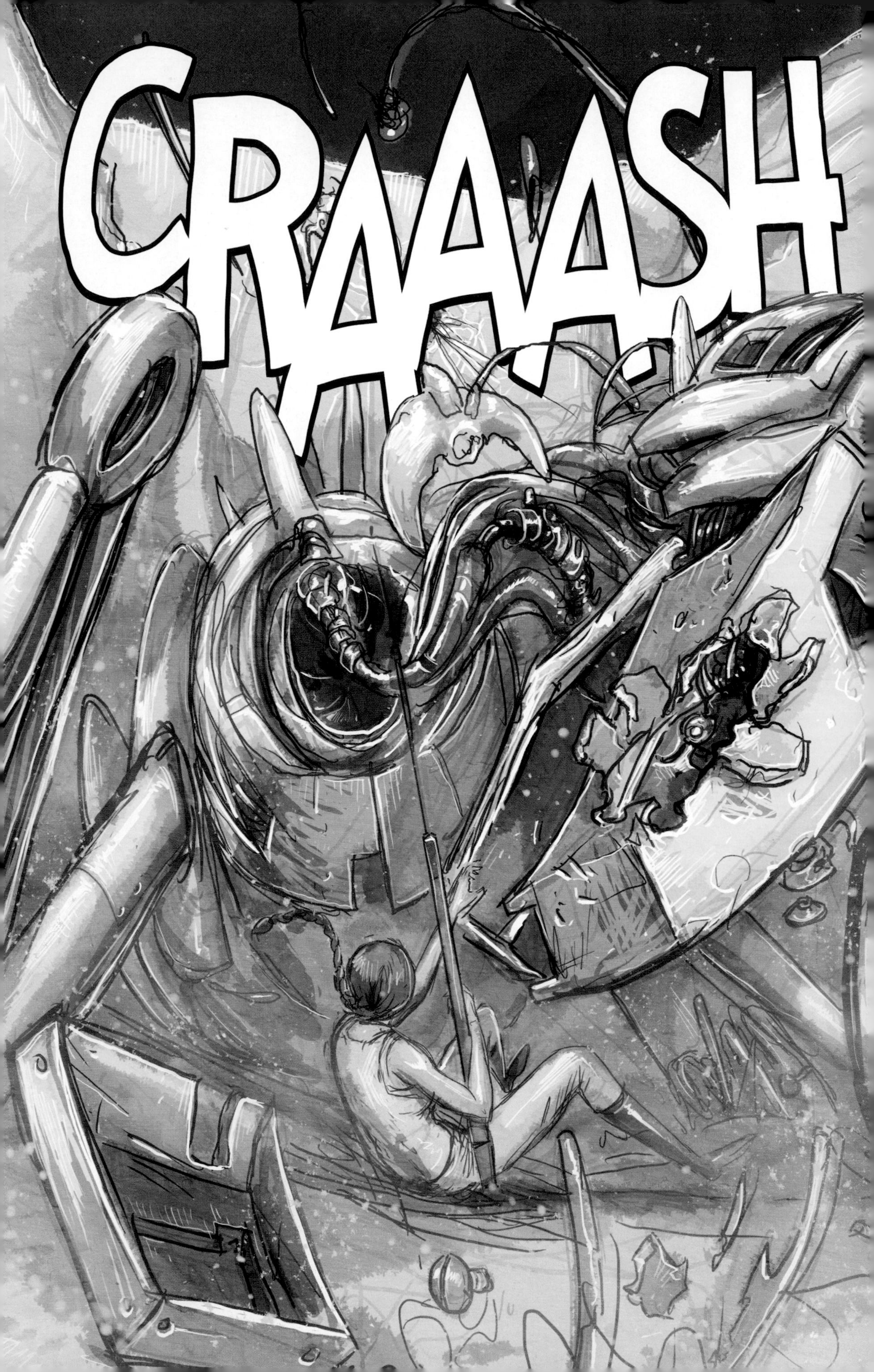
CRAAASH

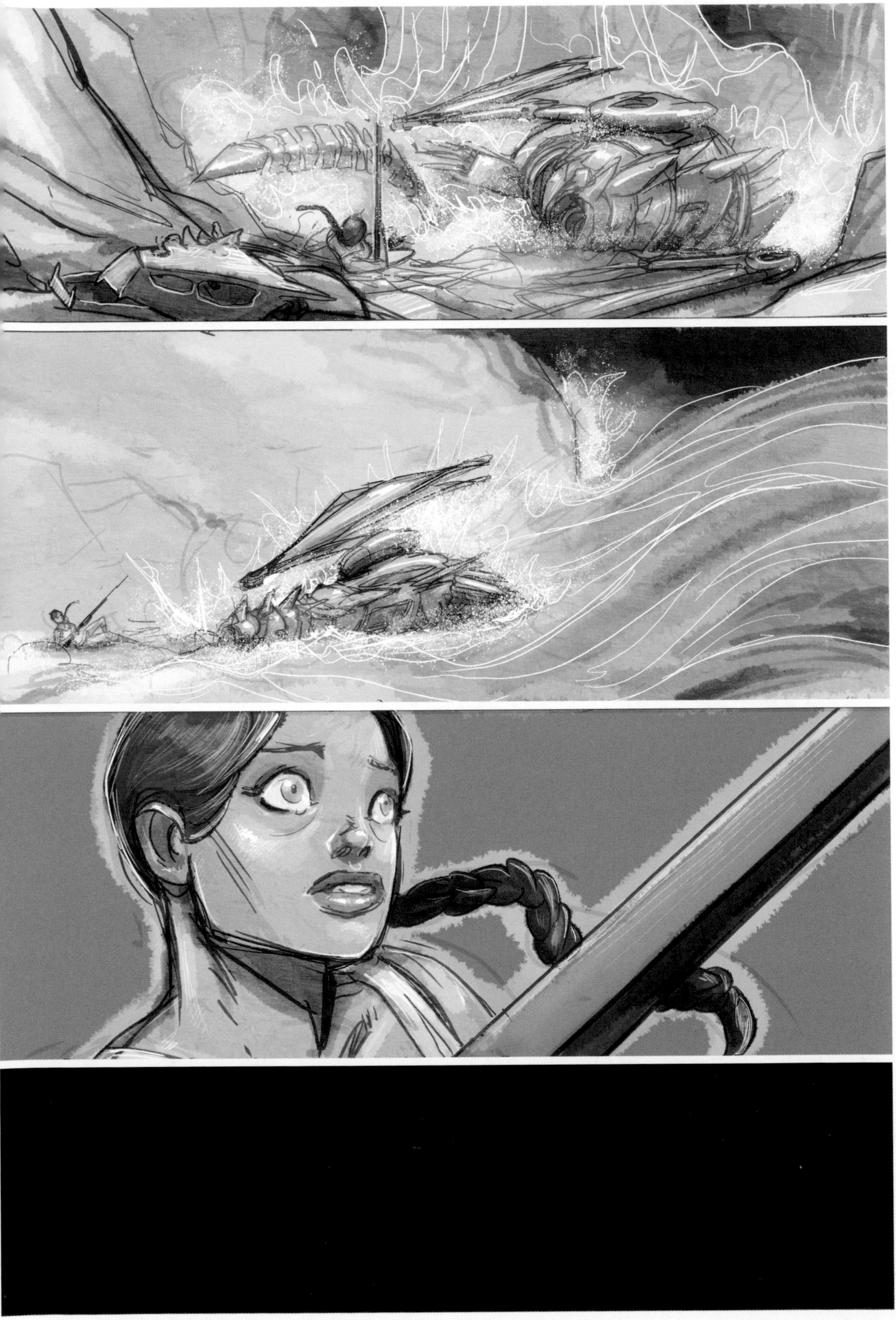

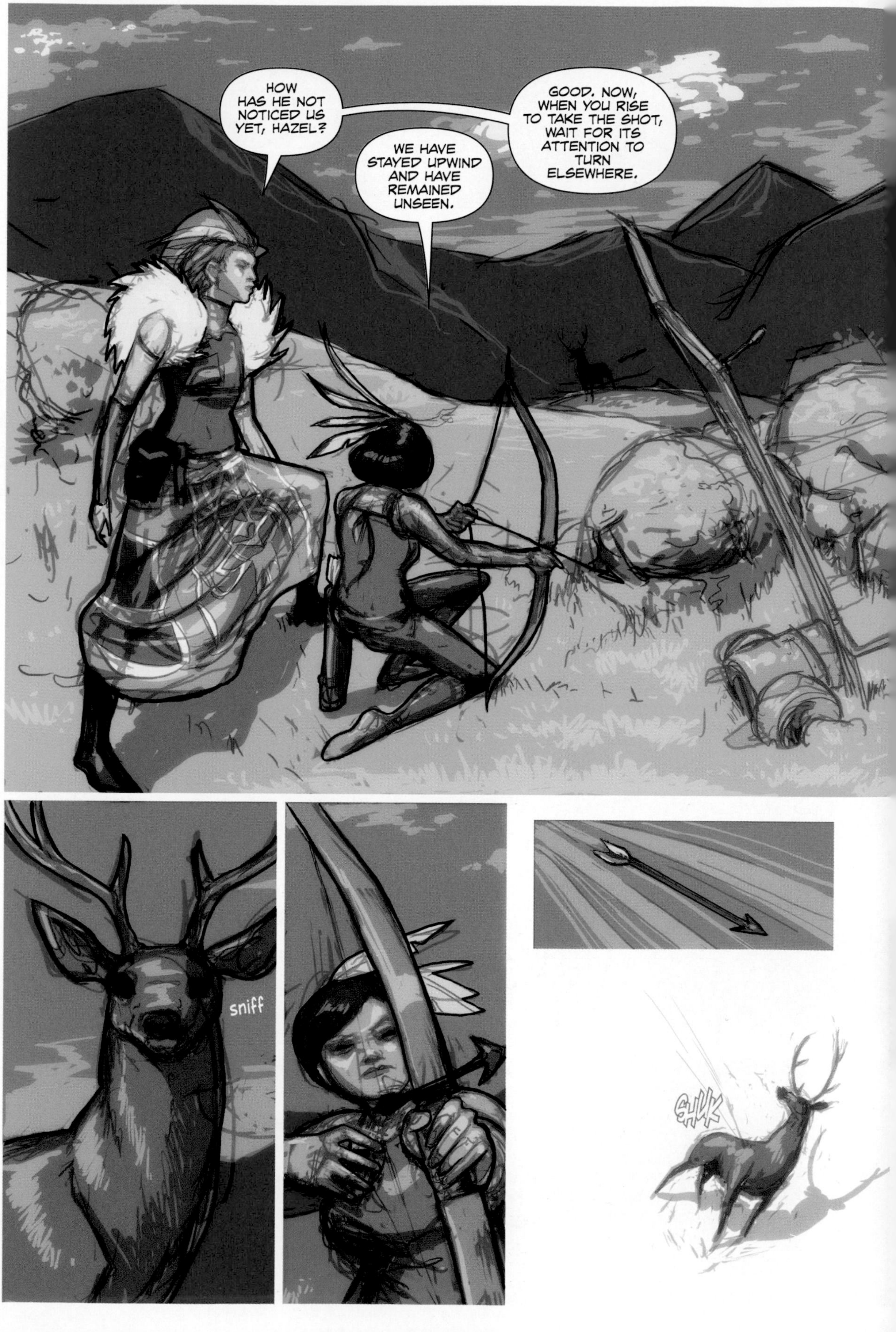
HOW HAS HE NOT NOTICED US YET, HAZEL?
WE HAVE STAYED UPWIND AND HAVE REMAINED UNSEEN.
GOOD. NOW, WHEN YOU RISE TO TAKE THE SHOT, WAIT FOR ITS ATTENTION TO TURN ELSEWHERE.
sniff
SHUK

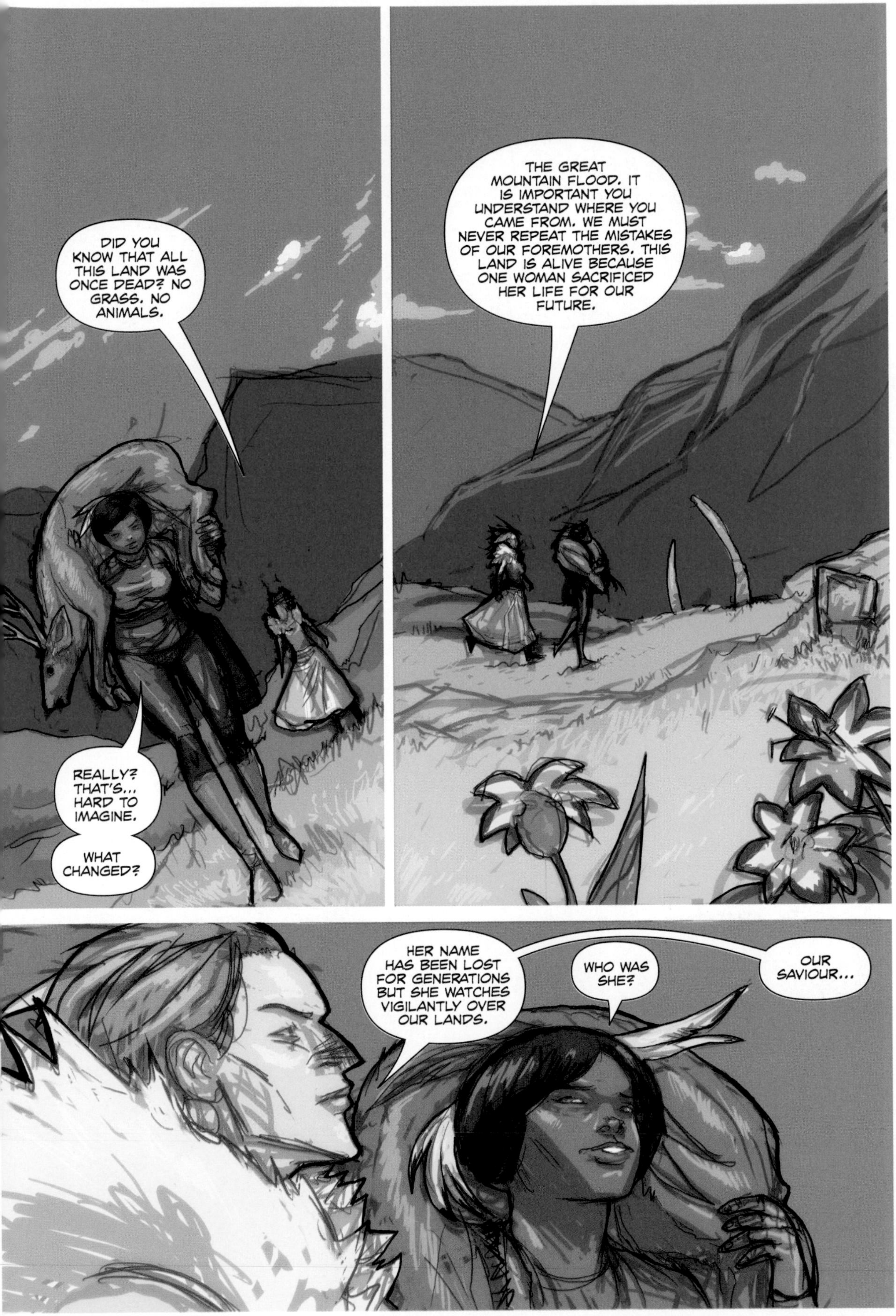
DID YOU KNOW THAT ALL THIS LAND WAS ONCE DEAD? NO GRASS. NO ANIMALS.
REALLY? THAT'S... HARD TO IMAGINE.
WHAT CHANGED?
THE GREAT MOUNTAIN FLOOD. IT IS IMPORTANT YOU UNDERSTAND WHERE YOU CAME FROM. WE MUST NEVER REPEAT THE MISTAKES OF OUR FOREMOTHERS. THIS LAND IS ALIVE BECAUSE ONE WOMAN SACRIFICED HER LIFE FOR OUR FUTURE.
WHO WAS SHE?
OUR SAVIOUR...
HER NAME HAS BEEN LOST FOR GENERATIONS BUT SHE WATCHES VIGILANTLY OVER OUR LANDS.

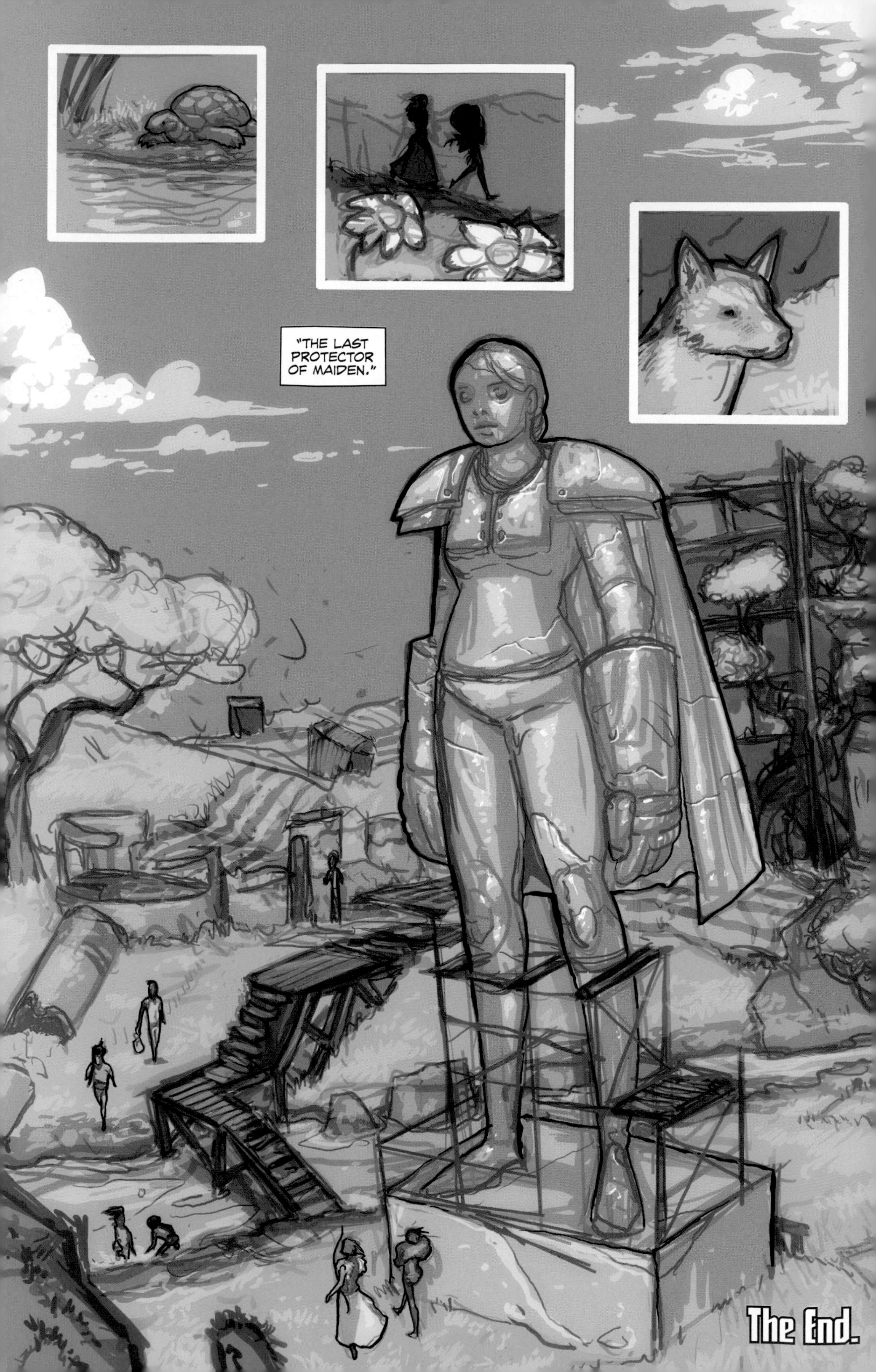
"THE LAST PROTECTOR OF MAIDEN."
The End.

EXTRAS

PAGES 108-110
Original teaser ads designed to resemble ads for Final Fantasy.

PAGE 111
Promotional poster given away at Image Expo February 24-26, 2012.

PAGE 112
One of two original color studies Riley did in preparation for the series. This one was used as the poster on preceding page, the other became the cover of this volume.

PAGES 113-118
From script to layout--a glimpse behind-the-scenes of issue #4.

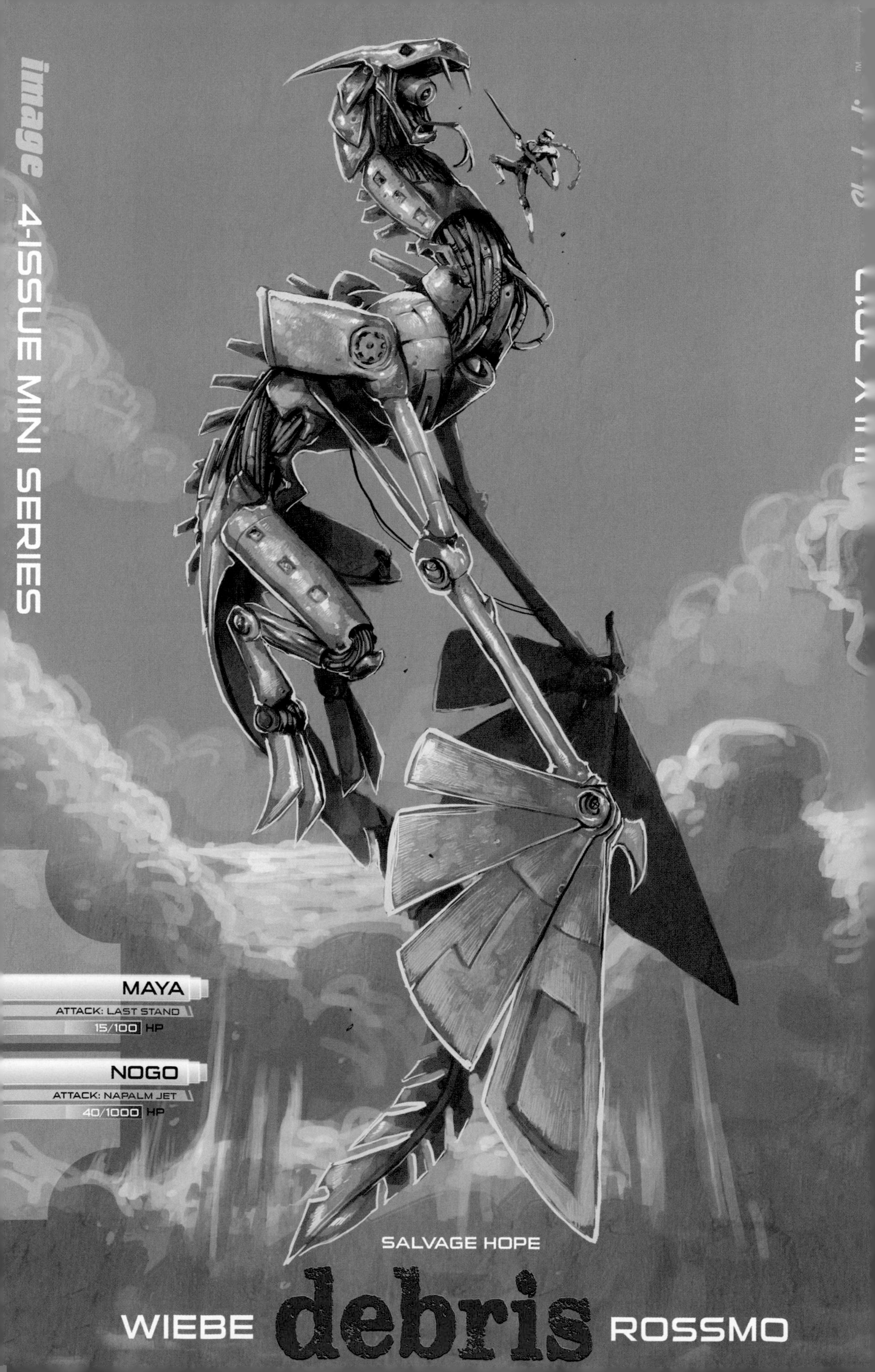
image
4-ISSUE MINI SERIES
MAYA
ATTACK: LAST STAND
15/100 HP
NOGO
ATTACK: NAPALM JET
40/1000 HP
SALVAGE HOPE
WIEBE
debris
ROSSMO

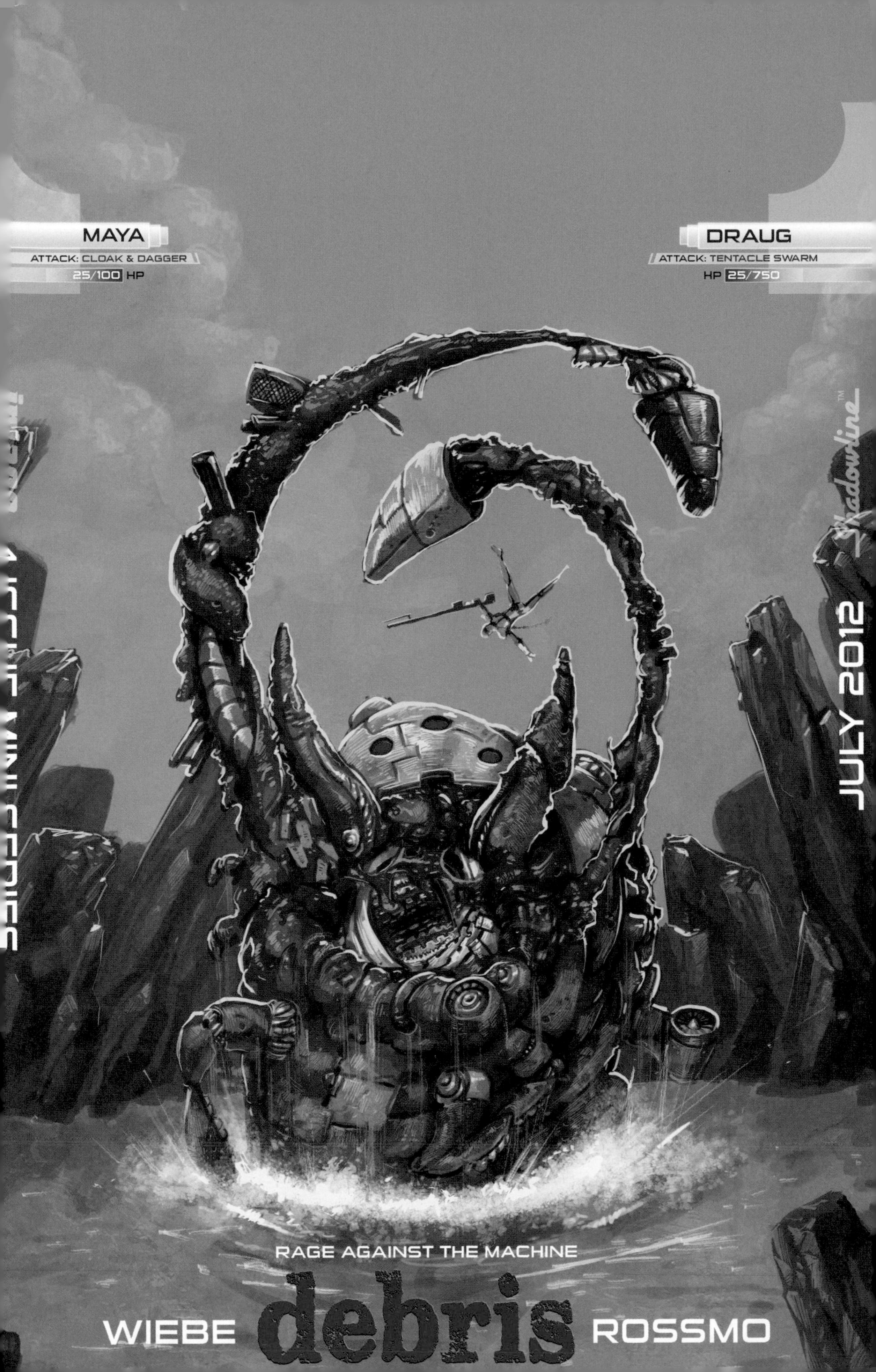
MAYA
ATTACK: CLOAK & DAGGER
25/100 HP
DRAUG
ATTACK: TENTACLE SWARM
HP 25/750
Shadowline™
JULY 2012
RAGE AGAINST THE MACHINE
WIEBE
debris
ROSSMO

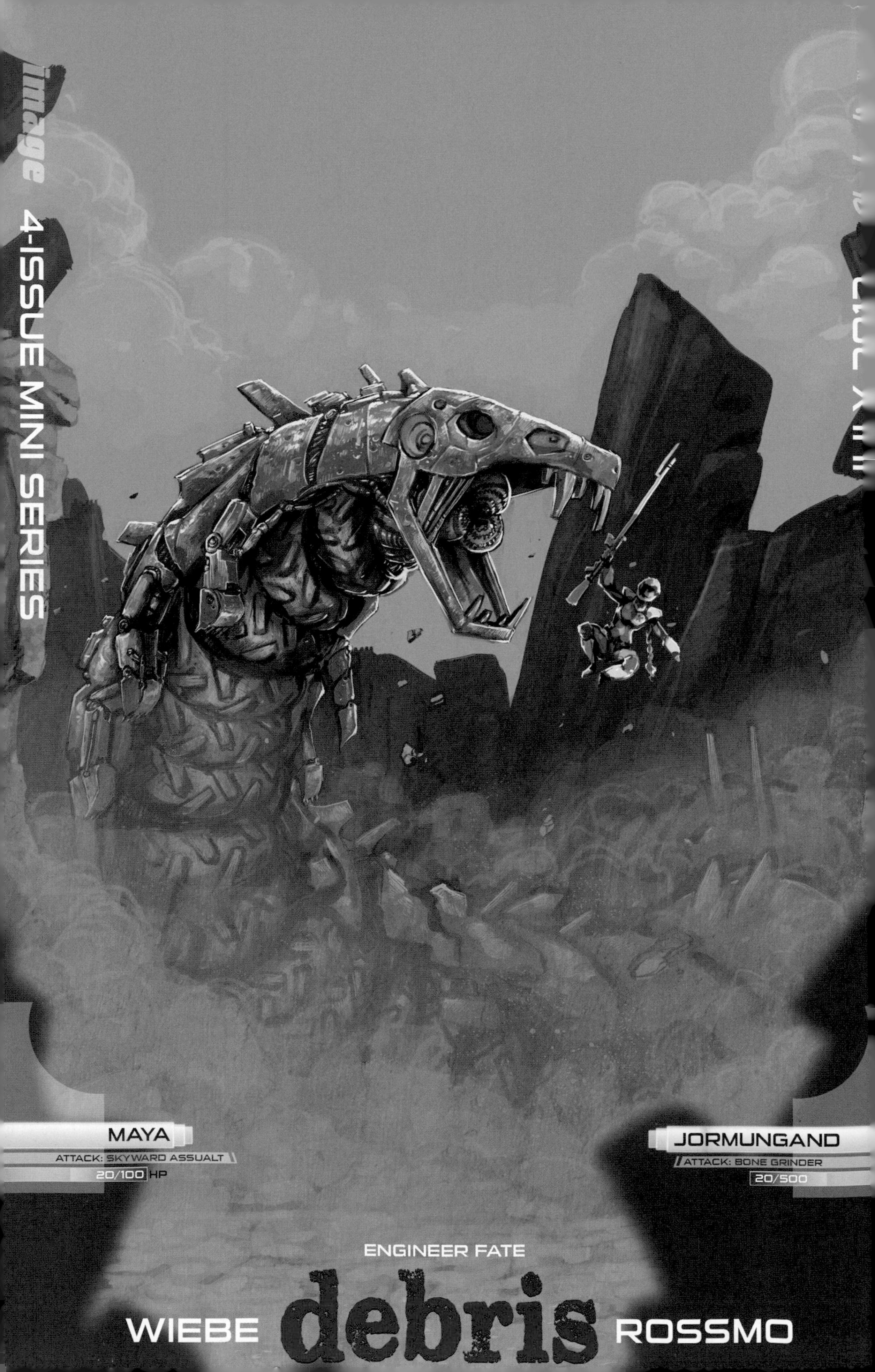
image
4-ISSUE MINI SERIES
MAYA
ATTACK: SKYWARD ASSUALT
20/100 HP
JORMUNGAND
ATTACK: BONE GRINDER
20/500
ENGINEER FATE
WIEBE
debris
ROSSMO

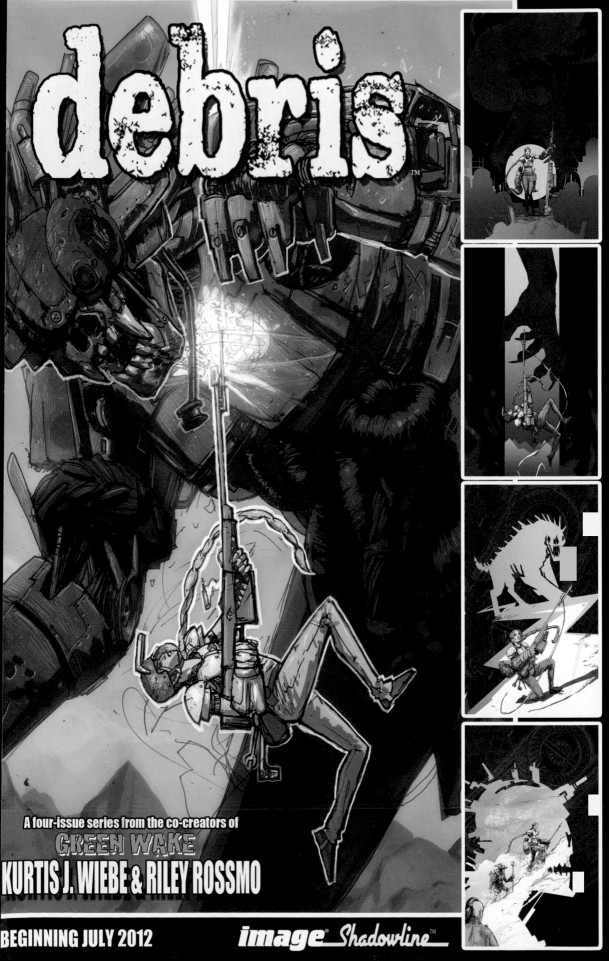

debris™

A four-issue series from the co-creators of

GREEN WAKE

KURTIS J. WIEBE & RILEY ROSSMO

BEGINNING JULY 2012

image® *Shadowline*™

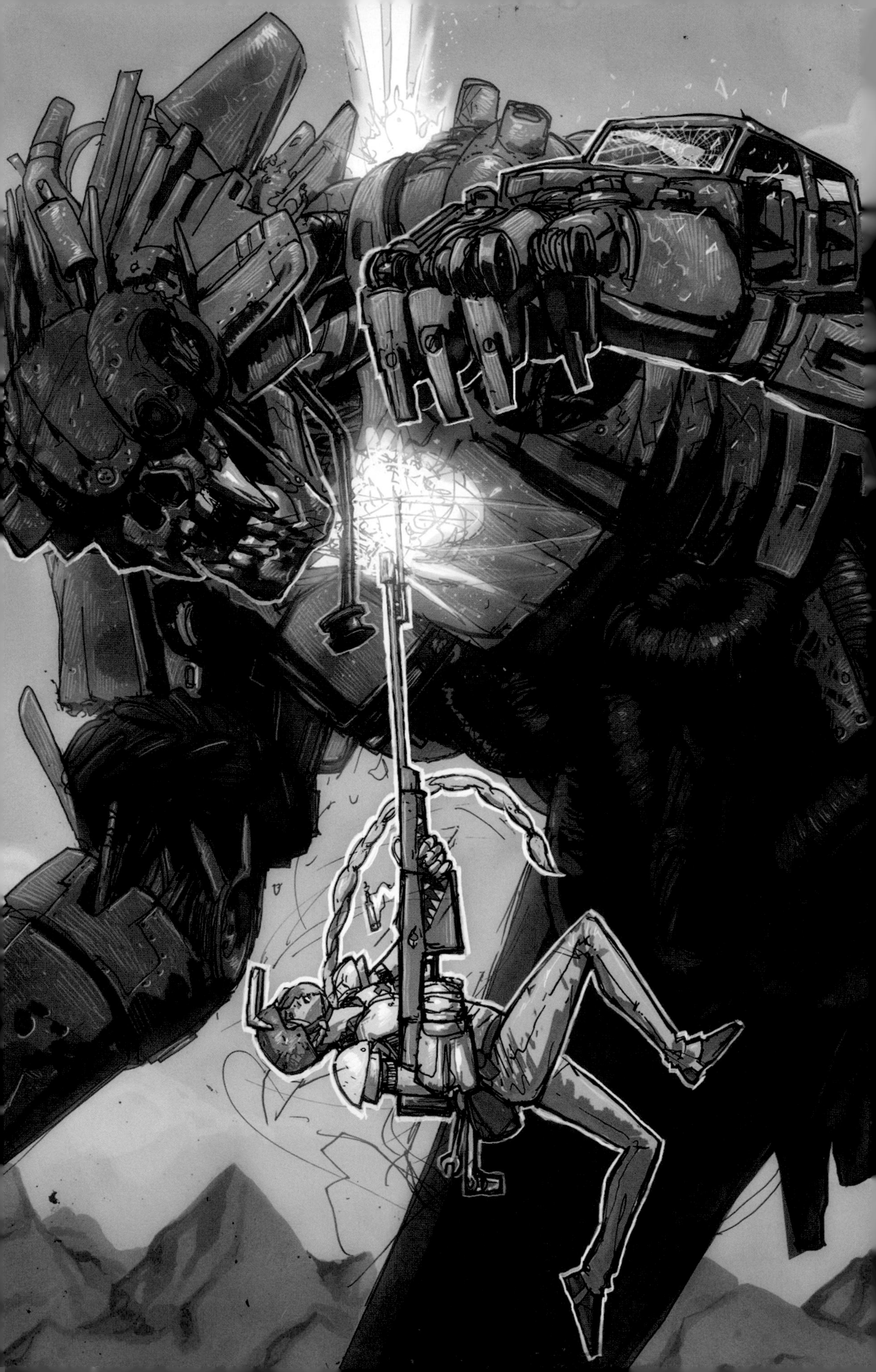

PAGE ONE (5 Panels)

Panel 1. Early evening. Maya and Kessel are being along a mountain trail, side by side with spears and blades at their backs. There is no slope here, but the path is evident. They are currently in a small valley before climbing Two of the Athabascan warriors are a little ways ahead, leading the group. Two are immediately behind Maya and Kessel, one to each of them. Kessel looks annoyed while Maya seems more intrigued than anything. The Athabascan's have stripped Maya of her weapon, but left them with the rest of the supplies they carried.

Kessel 1
So. Tell me.

Kessel 2
How is it that you manage to fight giant world destroying monsters but when confronted by four pitifully armed men you surrender?

Kessel 3
Just curious.

Panel 2. Pushed in, their faces in panel. She's turned to face him. We can see the two Athabascans behind them, prodding them on.

Maya 1
If they live in these mountains, there's a good chance they know of Athabasca. I'm hoping when we arrive at wherever it is they're taking us that we'll have an opportunity to speak.

Kessel 1
Or they *could* just eat us.

Maya 2
Or they could just eat us.

Panel 3. They have reach a plateau at the base of the ascent to the ridge that overlooks Athabasca. They will stop here for the night and begin their climb at first light. Dasher of the Athabascan's has turned to face the group.

Dasher 1
We rest here and leave at first light.

Kessel 1
Where are you taking us?

Dasher 2
Over the peak and home.

Panel 4. Maya and Kessel are sitting down on some larger stones. Kessel has his boots off and his rubbing one of his feet, he's crossed his legs. Maya is taking some blankets from Dasher, very ornately coloured Haida style, as below.

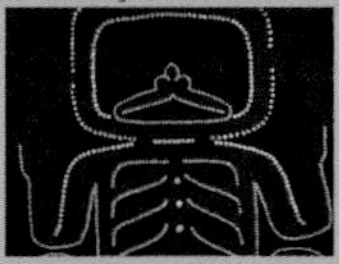

Dasher 1
It'll be cold. Share this with your friend.

Maya 1
Thank you.

Dasher 2
Sleep-

Panel 5. Shot of Dasher, he looms in the panel, we look up at him slightly. Menacing.

Dasher 1
The journey ahead will be treacherous.

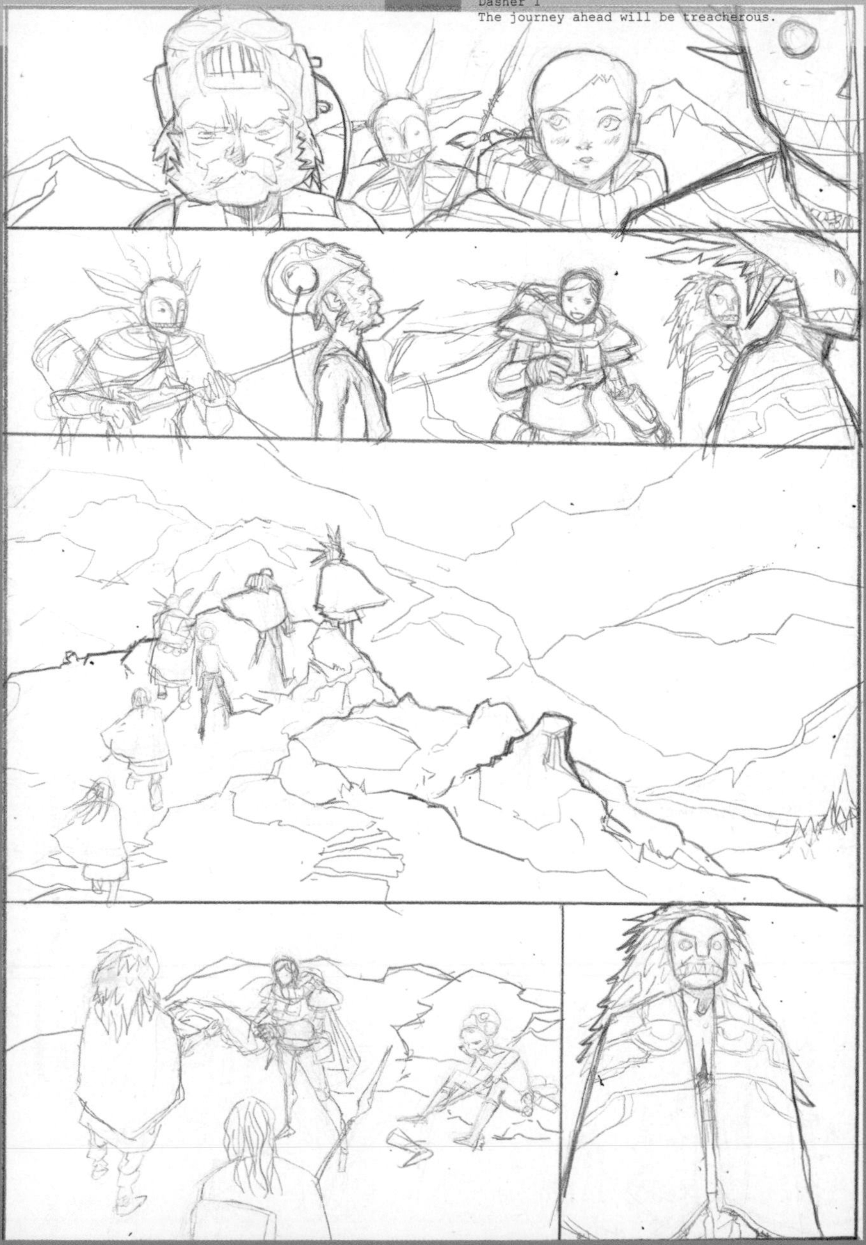

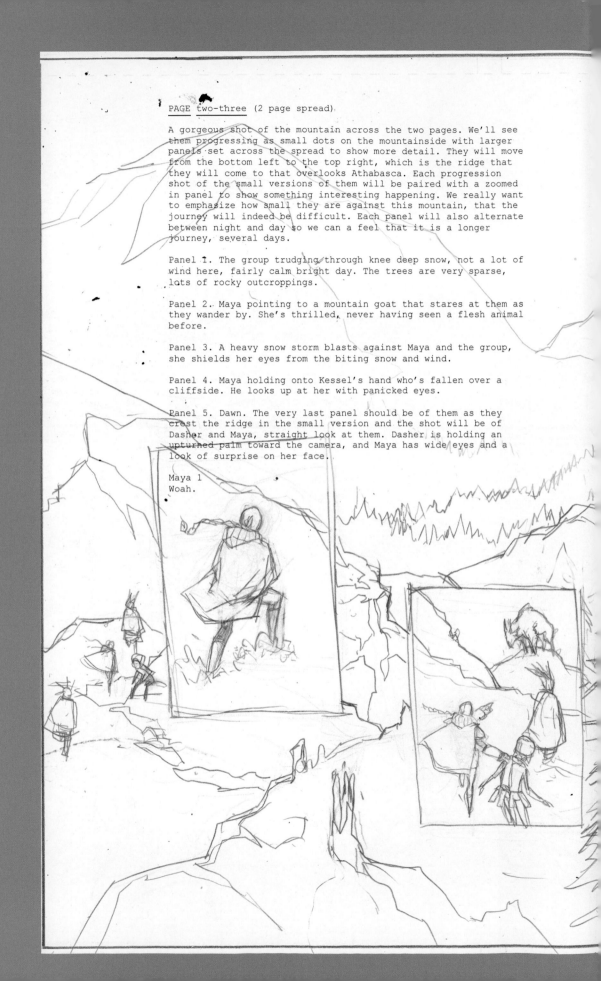

PAGE two-three (2 page spread)

A gorgeous shot of the mountain across the two pages. We'll see them progressing as small dots on the mountainside with larger panels set across the spread to show more detail. They will move from the bottom left to the top right, which is the ridge that they will come to that overlooks Athabasca. Each progression shot of the small versions of them will be paired with a zoomed in panel to show something interesting happening. We really want to emphasize how small they are against this mountain, that the journey will indeed be difficult. Each panel will also alternate between night and day so we can a feel that it is a longer journey, several days.

Panel 1. The group trudging through knee deep snow, not a lot of wind here, fairly calm bright day. The trees are very sparse, lots of rocky outcroppings.

Panel 2. Maya pointing to a mountain goat that stares at them as they wander by. She's thrilled, never having seen a flesh animal before.

Panel 3. A heavy snow storm blasts against Maya and the group, she shields her eyes from the biting snow and wind.

Panel 4. Maya holding onto Kessel's hand who's fallen over a cliffside. He looks up at her with panicked eyes.

Panel 5. Dawn. The very last panel should be of them as they crest the ridge in the small version and the shot will be of Dasher and Maya, straight look at them. Dasher is holding an upturned palm toward the camera, and Maya has wide eyes and a look of surprise on her face.

Maya 1
Woah.

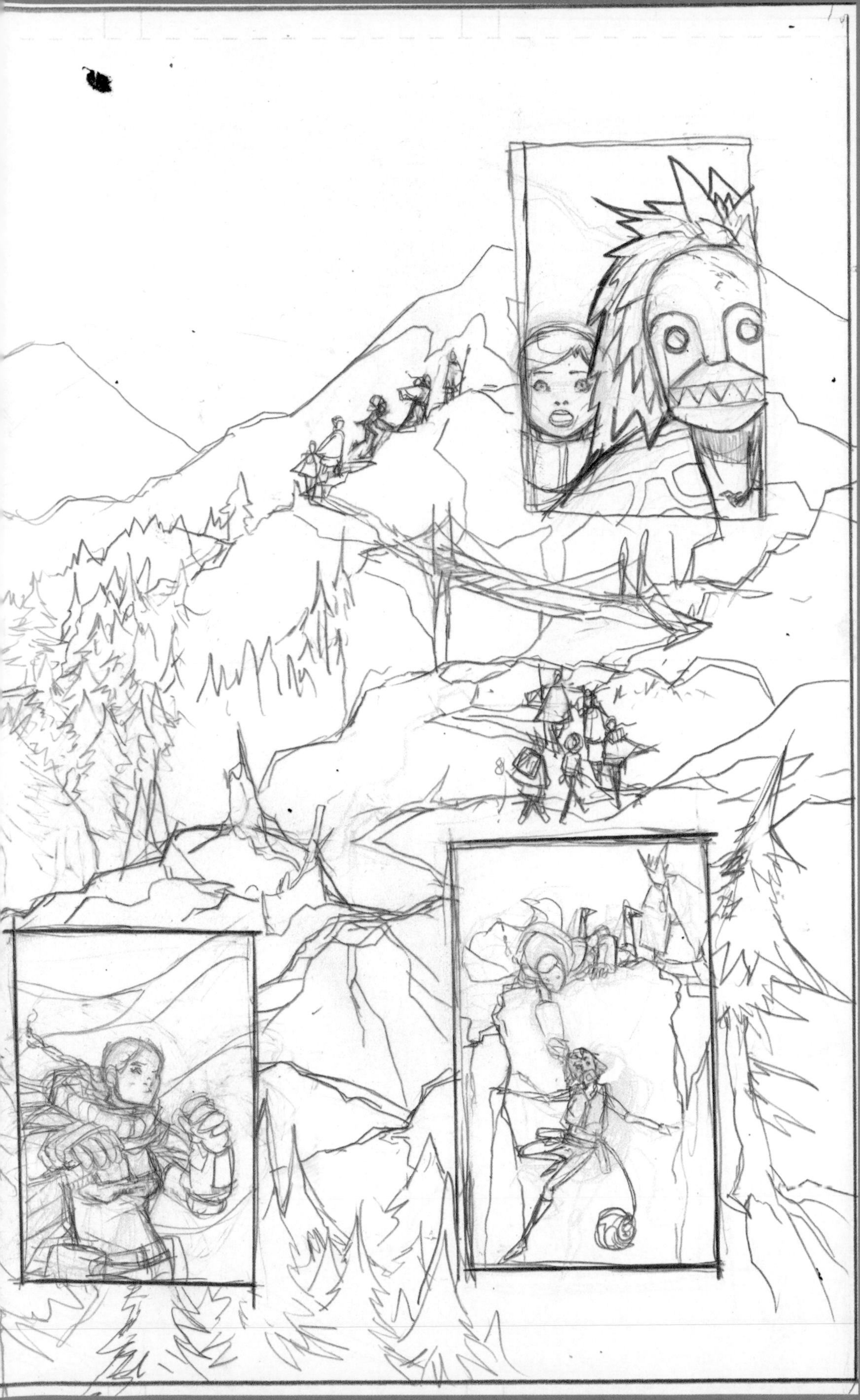

PAGE Four (1 Panel)

Panel 1. Splash. This is where we get our first look at the village. The angle should be as shown in the picture below. The town is snow covered and on the edge of a giant lake. I've decided against the dam concept and want to go with a more natural solution. The lake where Athabasca is situated isn't frozen over but at the edge of the lake, where it leads into a waterfall, it's completely frozen. Waterfall and all. One thing to note: The town shouldn't be on the water as it would destroy the town if all the water escapes. The lake should be evidently large, as well. This should be enough water to flow through the valleys and get within reach of Maiden. The valley is vast. I'm not 100% sure how we'll get this across, but this is going to be the only establishing shot as space is tight. It should also be very picturesque, with lots of evergreen trees and such. The town will be sleepy, in the early morning hours, lit by dwindling handmade tiki style torches.

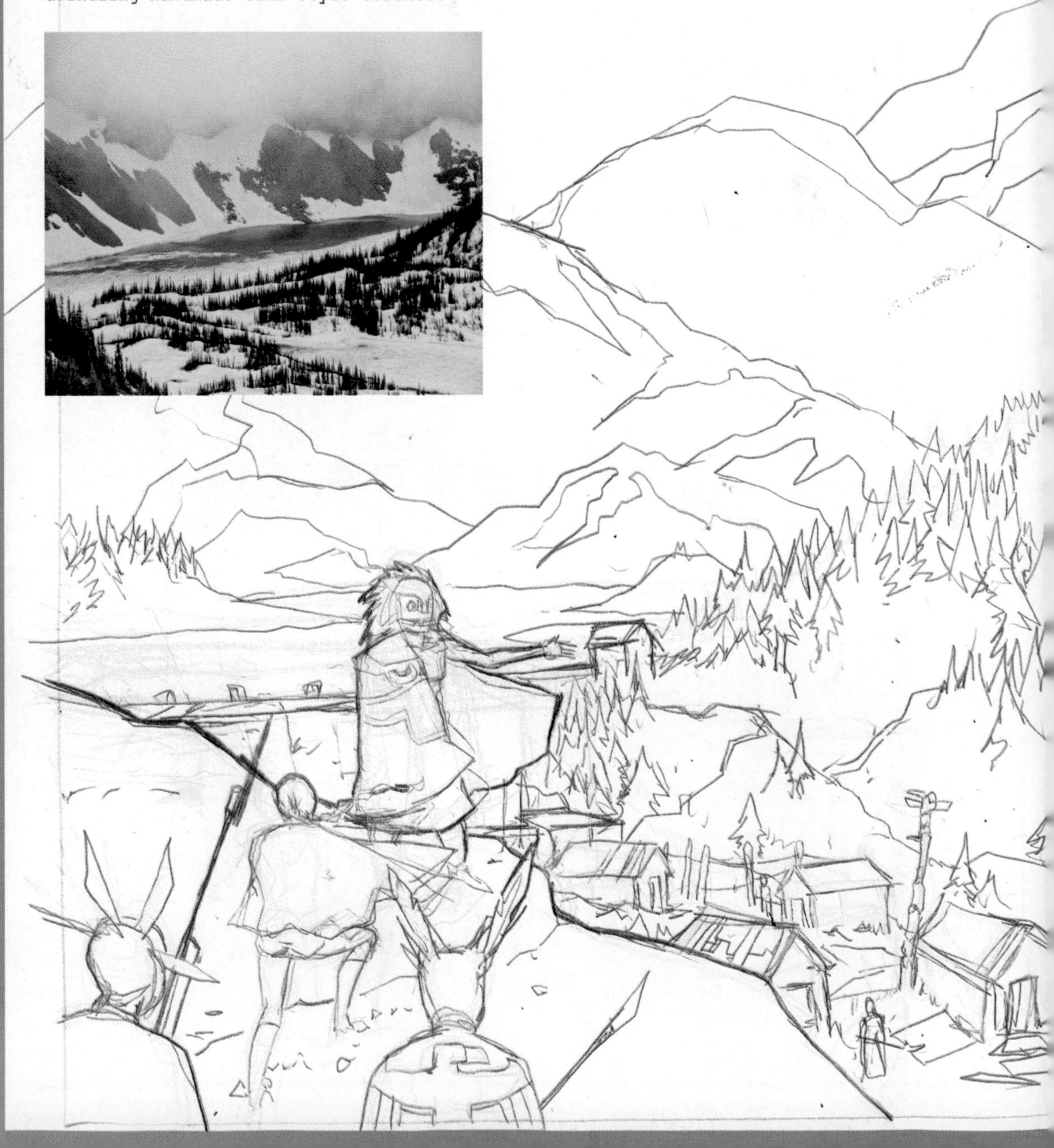

PAGE Five (5 Panels)

A walk through sequence spread over 5 panels. We're going to use
this to get a feel for Athabasca.

Panel 1. Outskirts of the town. There should be a guard tower
with a man overlooking the path that leads into town. He's armed
with an obsidian spear.

Panel 2. They walk past the docks where simple fisherman are
pushing out a boat for their early morning catch. Illustrate a
boat or two in the water already with people fishing. You can
also make this panel a bit larger to show off the ice shelf.

Panel 3. Behind shot as they walk through the winding streets.
Huts and cabins haphazardly placed with winding dirt roads.
People are standing outside their front doors, watching the new
visitors stroll through town. Outside the huts and cabins are
fish hanging over smoking fires in bunches and skins from animal
kills, including bears and wolves.

Panel 4. They walk up steps, towards the camera. Looking down
slightly. Two guards stand at the top of the steps, they are
foreground.

Panel 5. Large panel. They stand in front of the Chief's hut
which is guarded by two very large soldiers, topless with
intricate Haida tattoos of various totems. They wear masks and
capes and brandish obsidian spears with wood shafts. The journey
dasher is addressing them.

Dasher 1
Captive outsiders for presentation to Raven.

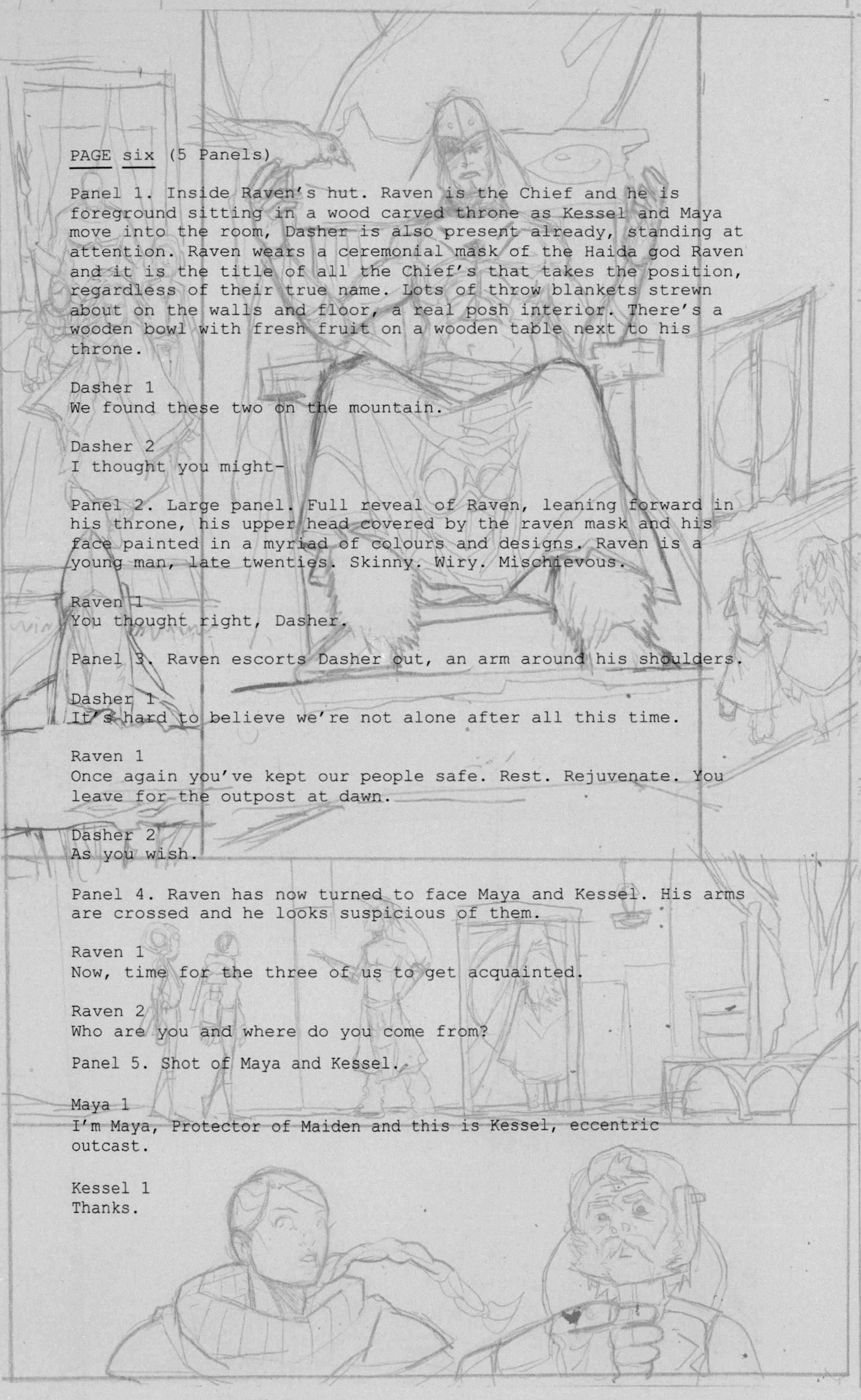

PAGE six (5 Panels)

Panel 1. Inside Raven's hut. Raven is the Chief and he is foreground sitting in a wood carved throne as Kessel and Maya move into the room, Dasher is also present already, standing at attention. Raven wears a ceremonial mask of the Haida god Raven and it is the title of all the Chief's that takes the position, regardless of their true name. Lots of throw blankets strewn about on the walls and floor, a real posh interior. There's a wooden bowl with fresh fruit on a wooden table next to his throne.

Dasher 1
We found these two on the mountain.

Dasher 2
I thought you might-

Panel 2. Large panel. Full reveal of Raven, leaning forward in his throne, his upper head covered by the raven mask and his face painted in a myriad of colours and designs. Raven is a young man, late twenties. Skinny. Wiry. Mischievous.

Raven 1
You thought right, Dasher.

Panel 3. Raven escorts Dasher out, an arm around his shoulders.

Dasher 1
It's hard to believe we're not alone after all this time.

Raven 1
Once again you've kept our people safe. Rest. Rejuvenate. You leave for the outpost at dawn.

Dasher 2
As you wish.

Panel 4. Raven has now turned to face Maya and Kessel. His arms are crossed and he looks suspicious of them.

Raven 1
Now, time for the three of us to get acquainted.

Raven 2
Who are you and where do you come from?

Panel 5. Shot of Maya and Kessel.

Maya 1
I'm Maya, Protector of Maiden and this is Kessel, eccentric outcast.

Kessel 1
Thanks.